Sally Sh——
Cambridge – September 1980

LANDSCAPE TOWARDS 2000 CONSERVATION OR DESOLATION

INTERNATIONAL FEDERATION OF LANDSCAPE
ARCHITECTS WORLD CONGRESS
LANDSCAPE INSTITUTE GOLDEN JUBILEE
CONFERENCE

CAMBRIDGE   SEPTEMBER 1979

CONGRESS UNDER THE PATRONAGE OF
HRH THE DUKE OF EDINBURGH, KG, KT

EDITOR DOUGLAS SMITH

IFLA
LI
LANDSCAPE TOWARDS 2000
CONSERVATION OR DESOLATION

Published in the United Kingdom 1979

The Landscape Institute
12 Carlton House Terrace
London SW1Y 5AH

Printed in the United Kingdom by
William Caple & Company Ltd, Leicester

ISBN 0 9506687 0 2

CONTENTS

FOREWORD

BUCKINGHAM PALACE.

The work of the International Federation of Landscape Architects and of the Landscape Institute has become progressively more important with the growth of populations and the consequent sprawl of urban and industrial development. The Landscape Institute deserves warm congratulations on its Golden Jubilee for the great efforts made by its members under very difficult conditions.

There is nothing more difficult than trying to achieve a satisfactory integration of the natural with the built environment and even where a reasonable solution has been found, the whole effect is so easily destroyed by vandalism, untidiness and neglect.

I hope the joint congress will be a great success and that all who attend it will return to their work enthused and encouraged by the experience.

1979

HRH THE DUKE OF EDINBURGH, KG, KT

Le travail de la Fédération Internationale des Architectes Paysagistes et du Landscape Institute n'a cessé de prendre de l'importance en raison de l'accroissement des populations et de l'expansion qui en a résulté au niveau du développement urbain et industriel. Le Landscape Institute mérite de chaleureuses félicitations à l'occasion de son 50ème anniversaire pour les grands efforts qui ont été entrepris par tous ses membres dans des circonstances peu propices.

Il n'y a rien de plus difficile que d'essayer de réaliser une intégration parfaite de la nature avec l'environnement habité, et même là où il a été possible de trouver une solution équitable et satisfaisante, le résultat obtenu peut être si facilement détruit par des actes de vandalisme, le désordre ou la négligence.

J'espère sincèrement que ce congrès, qui réunit les deux organisations, sera une grande réussite et que tous les participants reprendront leur travail pleins d'enthousiasme et encouragés par l'expérience qu'ils ont vécue.

ACKNOWLEDGEMENTS

I am grateful to all those who have worked on this book with me and to the Congress Secretariat Derek Lovejoy and Leona White for their valuable help. To all the authors, who have responded enthusiastically to my request for papers. I am also indebted to my colleagues for giving me the benefit of their knowledge and experience, and to the staff of my office.

The paper for the book has been provided by Wiggins Teape Group Limited, P.O. Box 88, Gateway House, Basingview, Basingstoke.

The photographs of the plans of Cambridge have been provided by Architectural Press Limited, 9 Queen Anne's Gate, London SW1.

The film *Capability Brown* by Ransomes Simms and Geoffreys Limited.

David Attenborough gave permission for the extract from the book 'Life on Earth'.

Ian Purdy for valuable information on Cambridge.

Donations have been received from:

G. Dew & Company Limited, P.O. Box 35, Oldham, Lancashire OL9 6HH.

Coblands Landscapes Limited, Eridge Road, Tunbridge Wells, Kent.

Constable Landscaping Limited, Peaslake, Guildford, Surrey.

Wellington Nurseries, Norbold Estates Limited, Brandon Crescent, Shadwell, Leeds LS17 9JH.

INTRODUCTION

Jesus College.

The 50th Anniversary of the formation of the Landscape Institute gives the profession an opportunity to review the past and look forward to the future. In 1948 the International Federation of Landscape Architects was founded at Jesus College, Cambridge. It adopted as its motif the Cock and the Rose. The Rose symbolises man's historic love for a garden. The Cock announces the dawn of a new Landscape age. The conference and congress being held simultaneously are an apt start to the second half century of the United Kingdom Institute and a challenge to the International Federation. Man has perhaps never before been in such a commanding position to effect dramatically the landscape. Science has provided tools capable of changing the surface of the earth for better or worse.

We have seen in the United Kingdom a remarkable series of television programmes, 'Life on Earth' by David Attenborough and to quote the last paragraph of the book provides a thought-provoking quotation for the conference:

'But although denying that we have a special position in the natural world might seem becomingly modest in the eye of eternity, it might also be used as an excuse for evading our responsibilities. The fact is that no species has ever had such wholesale control over everything on earth, living or dead, as we now have. That lays upon us, whether we like it or not, an awesome responsibility. In our hands now lies not only our own future, but that of all other living creatures with whom we share the earth.'

The opening session on the morning of Thursday 6th September, will enable distinguished speakers from Government and Environmental Agencies of Europe to present the International and National Environmental problems as far as their own organisations are concerned. The afternoon session on that day will be devoted to eminent speakers, practitioners and educationalists who will be asked to make constructive proposals for solutions to those problems. Friday provides both the Landscape Institute and the International Federation of Landscape Architects the opportunity to consider, in depth, ideas, new tools and methods of solving the problem.

To complete a full programme, there are four working parties on Saturday to make a major contribution to the debate – Landscape Towards 2000, Conservation or Desolation.

DOUGLAS SMITH

Le cinquantième anniversaire du Landscape Institute constitue une occasion unique pour la profession de se retourner sur son passé et de jeter un regard vers l'avenir. En 1948, la Fédération Internationale des Architectes Paysagistes a été fondée dans le Jesus College à Cambridge. Elle adopta comme emblème le coq et la rose: la rose symbolisant l'éternel amour de l'homme pour les jardins et le coq de son côté semble annoncer l'aurore d'une ère nouvelle. Le fait que la conférence et le congrès ont lieu en même temps semble être un bon point de départ pour les cinquante prochaines années de l'Institute du R.U. et une défi à la Fédération internationale. Jamais auparavant l'homme ne s'est trouvé dans cette position de maître, lui permettant de modifier le paysage de manière si décisive. La technique s'est chargée de fournir, quant à elle, les outils capables de changer la face du monde, pour le meilleur ou pour le pire.

Nous avons pu voir à la télévision anglaise une émission remarquable 'Life on Earth' présentée par David Attenborough, et si nous voulons reprendre les termes du dernier paragraphe de son livre, nous pouvons en tirer une citation digne de réflexion pour la conférence:

'Et bien que nous refusions le fait que nous occupons une place privilégiée dans le monde physique, et ceci semble raisonnablement modeste vu dans la perspective de l'éternité, nous pouvons y trouver un prétexte pour échapper à nos responsabilités. Il est certain qu'aucune autre espèce n'a jamais eu une maîtrise aussi complète de tout ce qui existe sur terre, mort ou vivant. Une terrible responsabilité nous incombe donc, que nous le voulions ou non. Non seulement notre propre avenir, mais aussi celui de toutes les autres créatures vivantes avec lesquelles nous partageons la planète repose entre nos mains.'

La session d'ouverture du jeudi matin, 6 septembre, permettra à des orateurs distingués venant d'Agences gouvernementales et de l'environnement européennes de parler des problèmes nationaux et internationaux de l'environnement dans le cadre de leur propre organisation. Les séances du jeudi après-midi seront réservées à des orateurs, des praticiens et des éducateurs éminents auxquels il sera demandé de présenter des propositions constructives menant à la résolution de ces problèmes. Le vendredi donnera au Landscape Institute et à la Fédération Internationale des Architects Paysagistes l'occasion d'étudier plus à fond les idées, les nouveaux moyens et les méthodes qui permettraient de solutionner le problème.

Pour compléter le programme, quatre groupes de travail se réuniront afin d'apporter leurs précieuses contributions au débat qui est 'Le paysage d'ici l'an 2000 – conservation ou désolation'.

DOUGLAS SMITH

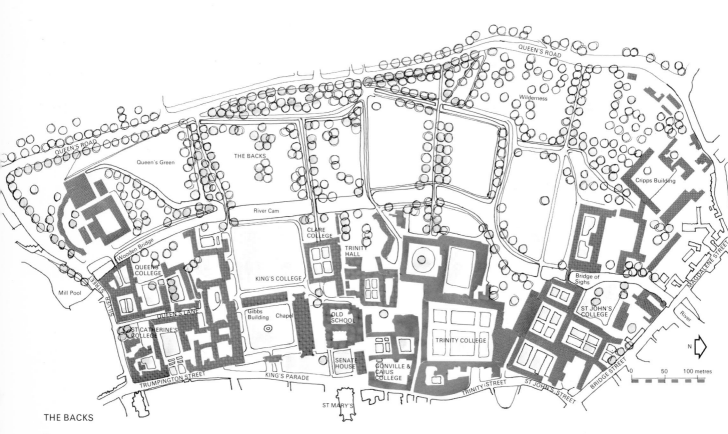

THE BACKS

CAMBRIDGE

THE CITY AND ITS LANDSCAPE

DOUGLAS SMITH

*King's College
Chapel and Gibbs Building*

The setting for the conference will provide participants with an opportunity to explore the unique visual experience that Cambridge offers. It is one of the most beautiful cities of the world, a living landscape linked by the river and a network of narrow streets and footpaths. The great variety of outdoor spaces, formed by fine old and new buildings with carefully designed landscape, provide a fascinating study for landscape architects.

Photographs and words fail to portray the true beauty of the area and these notes are intended to introduce the subject and not to provide a comprehensive guide.

The town had its origin in Roman times and the University was established in the early 13th Century, Peterhouse was founded in 1284. It is difficult to single out colleges, but one should explore the fine old buildings of Jesus College. The wealth of old and new buildings at St John's, and the fine fan vaulting of King's College Chapel with the beautiful altar piece by Rubens of the Adoration of the Magi. Clare, Trinity and St Catherine's are closely packed together with the Senate House by James Gibbs. Queens' remains the most complete example of a medieval college with an interesting series of courts and a fine modern building on the opposite side of the river.

St John's College

St John's College Cripps Building

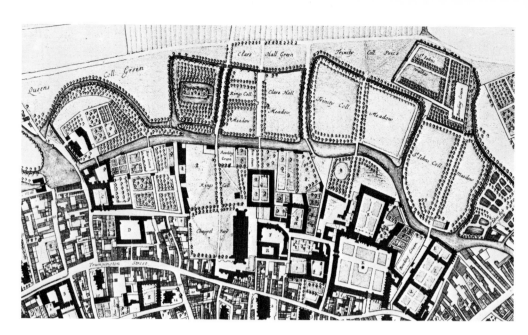

*David Loggan's plan of
Cambridge 1688*

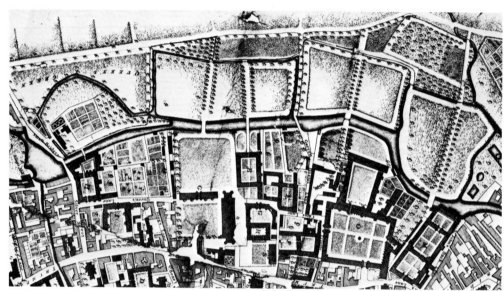

*Constance's plan 1798
illustrates the Backs
very much as today*

*(Below) The ambitious plan by
Lancelot Brown 1779 which was
never implemented*

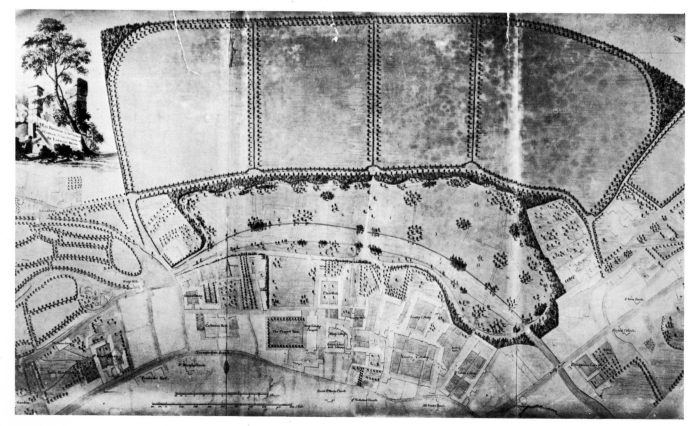

Originally, the areas of land along the river were the backs of the colleges. These were transformed in the Georgian period into a landscape park and the 'Backs' as they are known today are of unique and particular interest to landscape architects. At St John's College a detour should be made to visit the Fellows' Garden or Wilderness, designed by Lancelot Brown in 1772. The grounds of the college retain some of his work, the lawns and clumps of mature trees provide a superb setting for the old and new buildings alike.

Capability Brown lived at Fenstanton, 10 miles from Cambridge, and was a friend of Professor John Mainwaring, a renowned theologian, a Fellow of St John's College. The site for the Wilderness was the old bowling green and two adjacent rectangular plots, the design provides a lawn fringed with trees.

Much of the beauty of the 'Backs' derives from the irregular growth of the colleges and the interplay between buildings, water and landscape, the area is beautifully maintained and tended with care.

There is no linking footpath along the river, one is forced to move through the buildings and courts. The 'Backs' run from St John's College at the north to the simple wooden bridge of Queens' College near Silver Street in the south. At St John's the approach is through the buildings and courts of the college and the river is crossed by the Bridge of Sighs.

Explore the fascinating courts of Trinity College and Clare. Clare is dominated by small linked spaces and the walled garden complete with beech hedge and topiary. The enclosed space of Clare contrasts beautifully with the open landscape of King's College. The form of the Chapel thrusting upwards is complimentary to the low horizontal form of Gibbs' Senate House. Stop to admire the fine detailing of the floorscape of the first court of King's College.

Lancelot Brown saw great 'capabilities' for the 'Backs' and produced an extensive design in 1779. The concept was to transform the individual grounds of each college into a bold landscape park with a widened re-shaped river, clumps of trees set in grass, complete with meandering paths. This plan was never implemented.

George Dyer in the history of the University and Colleges of Cambridge in 1814 wrote, 'let us distinguish, too, between gardens and public walks, between a nobleman's pleasure ground, and spot to be adapted to the health and exercise of students, to academic retreats, which invite to meditation'.

St John's College
Bridge of Sighs

Wilderness or Fellows' Garden
St John's

The Backs

Queens' College
the Wooden Bridge

King's College Chapel
from the Backs

(*Top*) *Queens' College*

(*Above*) *Trinity College*
Great Court and
Nevile's Court (below).

(*Right above*)
Jesus Lock

(*Right*)
Fort St George Inn

The grounds of Jesus College a short distance away extend to the river. There is Jesus Lock, simple functional riverside architecture at its best with an iron bridge and Regency lock-keeper's house. A fine avenue of mature plane trees leads to the bridge and Victoria Avenue. The landscape dramatically changes at Mid-Summer common, an open natural grassed area and riverside walk. There is an interesting 16th Century public house, Fort St George, to be visited.

The University Botanic Garden is in Bateman Street and Charles Miller in the 18th Century was appointed the first curator of the Botanic Gardens at Cambridge. The present curator, Dr S. M. Walters, believes the gardens should play a vital rôle in the conservation of rare and threatened plant species not only in Europe but eventually throughout the world. In a paper in 1977, to support the committee of IUCN on threatened plants Dr Walters summarised the reasons why Botanic Gardens should cultivate threatened species:

1 As a minimal insurance against extinction. This is the traditional, accidental conservation rôle of Gardens.
2 For educational displays to teach students and the general public about the urgency and importance of conservation.
3 As a reserve stock to be used, instead of wild material, by scientific research workers.
4 As a reserve stock from which, eventually, a natural or semi-natural population can be re-established after extinction.

Cambridge offers a challenge, a feast of visual experiences worthy of detailed study, or casual exploration.

OPENING ADDRESS

PRESIDENT LANDSCAPE INSTITUTE

H. T. MOGGRIDGE

It is a tremendous pleasure to welcome everyone attending this World Congress of the International Federation of Landscape Architects; it is being held under the patronage of His Royal Highness the Duke of Edinburgh, KG, KT, in celebration of the Golden Jubilee of the Landscape Institute of the British Isles. We are in Cambridge because it is here that IFLA was founded about thirty years ago. I hope that it will be an occasion for all to remember.

The Landscape Institute was conceived and constituted during 1929. On 20th February 1929 Richard Sudell, acting upon an inspiration from Stanley Hart, convened a meeting at which it was agreed that a British association of garden architects was needed. We were founded by 30 to 40 people who met on 23rd May 1929 standing in the draughty marquee which is the centre of the annual flower show of the Royal Horticultural Society at Chelsea. The meeting was held in one corner, in the practical part of the tent amongst beehives, displays of research work and photographs, well away from the gaudy ranks of carefully fattened flowers where well-dressed plant-loving crowds throng. Here our farsighted founders then and there created the Institute, which it was agreed three weeks later should be professional.

Brenda Colvin, later to be our President and still active today, was present at that meeting. I point this out with special pleasure as I am now her partner, so that our practice in a special way spans the fifty years of this Institute's existence to date. Within the month Geoffrey Jellicoe was also a member; he has since, of course, been President of our Institute and founding President of IFLA. The first President, Thomas Mawson, was elected on 11th December 1929, with E. Prentice Mawson, Edward White and Richard Sudell as Vice-Presidents. Edward White's practice, already then old-established, still continues today as Milner White and Partners. The honorary solicitor was J. Murray Napier, who continued to look after us for forty-five years without charge, a gift for which we are immensely grateful.

The aims of our founders were far sighted and broad. The name finally selected was the 'Institute of Landscape Architects' in recognition of ideas from the United States, a country already having a thriving professional body of landscape architects. The first object of the constitution was 'the advancement of the ART OF LANDSCAPE ARCHITECTURE: the theory and practice of garden, landscape, and civic design; the promotion of research and education therein; and the creation and maintenance of a high standard of professional qualification'. It is notable that the wellbeing of the landscape was given more priority than the professional interests of members from the very beginning, an attitude which we still uphold.

Early issues of the Institute's Journal reveal that the membership were from the beginning aware of the wide range of their subject. Their ideals still guide us. If during the next few days the task before us all sometimes seems discouragingly formidable, we can remember what progress has been made in these offshore European islands by the courageous enterprise of our founders and their successors.

They sought proper education for students based upon technical knowledge of site engineering and horticulture, skill in draughtsmanship and report writing and appreciation of the theory and history of landscape design. Learning through visiting sites and practice in design were considered essential for 'one could hardly overstress the importance of practice'. In the last two decades we have seen six undergraduate and seven post-graduate courses (three of which are part-time) founded in this country on these basic tenets, even though we may still be seeking 'at least one place where the most perfect training possible could be provided' as was aspired to in 1931. Our founders saw their task as 'intelligently changing Nature so that it adjusts itself to our purposes'; they realised the need 'to maintain a reputation for technical ability and business efficiency' since 'talent

C'est pour moi un immense plaisir que de souhaiter la bienvenue à tous les participants de ce Congrès Mondial de la Fédération Internationale des Architectes Paysagistes, congrès qui est organisé sous le haut patronage de Son Altesse Royale le Duc d'Edimbourg, KG, KT, pour célébrer le cinquantenaire du Landscape Institute des Iles Britanniques. Nous nous trouvons à Cambridge car c'est précisément dans cette ville que l'IFLA a été fondée il y a quelque trente ans. J'espère que ce sera pour tous l'occasion de se remémorer cette conférence.

Le Landscape Institute a été fondé et constitué au cours de l'année 1929. Le 20 février 1929, Richard Sudell, sur l'instigation de Stanley Hart, convoqua une réunion au cours de laquelle on convint de la nécessité d'une association britannique d'architectes paysagistes. En fait, l'association fut fondée par 30 ou 40 personnes qui se rassemblèrent le 23 mai 1929 sous le chapiteau qui constitue le point central des floralies annuelles présentées par la Royal Horticultural Society à Chelsea. La réunion se déroula dans un coin de la tente, le 'coin pratique' où l'on trouvait des ruches, des panneaux consacrés aux travaux de recherche et des photos, bien loin des rangées bigarrées de fleurs soignées avec amour, où se pressait une foule de personnes bien habillées, venues pour admirer les fleurs. C'est là que nos fondateurs prévoyants créèrent l'Institute, qui, trois semaines plus tard, devait, de l'avis de tous, être un Institut professionnel.

Brenda Colvin, qui devait plus tard devenir présidente et qui mène encore aujourd'hui une vie active, assistait à cette réunion. C'est avec un plaisir particulier que je souligne ce fait puisque je suis son associé, ainsi le cabinet que nous tenons couvre d'une certaine façon les cinquante ans que compte l'Institute aujourd'hui. En l'espace d'un mois, Geoffrey Jellicoe devint également l'un des nôtres; depuis lors, il a bien entendu été président de l'Institute et il fut aussi le président fondateur de l'IFLA. Le premier président, Thomas Mawson, fut élu le 11 décembre 1929, MM. Prentice Mawson, Edward White et Richard Sudell étant vice-présidents. Le cabinet d'Edward White, qui avait déjà acquis une solide réputation à l'époque, existe encore de nos jours sous le nom de Milner White and Partners. L'avoué honoraire, J. Murray Napier, se fit un devoir de veiller à nos affaires pendant quarante-cinq ans, et ce sans demander de rémunérations; c'est un travail pour lequel nous lui sommes extrêmement reconnaissants.

Les membres fondateurs établirent des objectifs à long terme et de grande envergure. Le titre finalement choisi fut 'Institute of Landscape Architects', en reconnaissance des idées reçues des Etats-Unis, pays qui avait déjà un corps professionnel très actif d'architectes paysagistes. L'objet premier de la constitution consistait à 'faire progresser l'ART DE L'ARCHITECTURE DU PAYSAGE: théorie et pratique de la conception des jardins, des paysages et de l'environnement; la promotion de la recherche et l'éducation qui y est relative; la création et le maintien de niveaux élevés en matière de qualifications professionnelles'. Il faut remarquer que l'importance accordée à l'harmonie du paysage prédomina sur les intérêts professionnels des membres dès le départ, une attitude qui est toujours de rigueur.

Les premiers numéros du bulletin de l'Institute soulignent le fait que, dès le départ, les membres étaient conscients de l'ampleur et de l'étendue du sujet. Mais leurs idéaux nous guident toujours. Si dans les jours qui viennent, les tâches qui nous attendent nous semblent quelquefois trop grandes, il serait bon de se rappeler les progrès qui ont été réalisés dans ces îles du continent européen grâce au courage de nos membres fondateurs et de leurs successeurs.

En effet, ils cherchèrent l'éducation adéquate pour leurs étudiants, éducation qui reposait sur les connaissances techniques de l'horticulture et de l'aménagement du site, la compétence dans le dessin et la rédaction des rapports, ainsi que l'appréciation de la théorie et l'histoire du dessin de paysages. L'apprentissage qui was useless without knowledge', and 'interferences with Nature and the creation of new objects of natural beauty are difficult and highly specialised tasks'. Members of our Institute are now called upon to advise on the development of many large scale projects. Several of our members hold responsible jobs in government and local government. The landscape profession plays some part in national affairs in both the United Kingdom and Eire, both of which countries are served successfully by our same Institute. Our founders were also aware 'that the application of principles of landscape architecture ... was essential to the proper building of towns'. Landscape architects have played a valuable part in the making of our New Towns, but have not been called upon to assist with the adaptation of ageing cities. Some European countries excel in such work; we in this country have a particular task ahead if our cities are to be rejuvenated as is now urgent. Above all our founders supported the definition by Charles Eliot, President Emeritus of Harvard University, that 'Landscape Architecture is primarily a fine art, and as such its most important function is to create and preserve beauty in the surroundings of human habitations and in the natural scenery of the country'.

At this Congress we are particularly privileged that HRH the Duke of Edinburgh, KG, KT, who has done so much in this country to encourage interest in both design and in the countryside is Patron of our Congress. In this way, he reminds us that a growing number of statesmen throughout the world are coming to attach importance to the landscape. Indeed I believe that we stand now at a moment of great opportunity, when the basic ideas for which both IFLA and the Landscape Institute stand are becoming widely accepted. Because fewer technologists are being required to work with sophisticated machinery and computers, those occupations based upon maintenance of the world's fabric and the inherent artistic bent in human beings is becoming more valued. At the same time the Landscape Institute has come to feel the need for scientific and management skills to unite with the arts to achieve the best results, and so we have recently widened our scope to welcome fellow professionals from new but allied disciplines. For the first time, in this our 50th year, our list of associates includes landscape scientists and landscape managers alongside landscape architects.

We should gain confidence that we can maintain our ideals and learn the technical skills to achieve our aims, by remembering those forty founders who collected in the marquee on 23rd May 1929. We now have 1,650 members, a fortyfold increase, supported by an excellent permanent staff to help us from our headquarters in Nash House. I therefore want to start the Congress with a thank-you from all our present membership to our founders and their successors. May their work be continued internationally, multiplying in every country of the world in the next half century.

consistait à visiter des sites et à pratiquer le dessin, était essentiel car 'on ne saurait insister suffisamment sur l'importance de la pratique'. Au cours des vingt dernières années, nous avons assisté à la mise sur pied de six cours pour étudiants et de sept cours postscolaires (dont trois à temps partiel), qui reposent sur ces principes de base, et ce bien que nous soyons toujours à la recherche 'de l'endroit idéal où l'on pourrait dispenser la meilleure formation possible', auquel on avait aspiré en 1931. Les fondateurs pensaient que leur tâche consistait à 'changer la Nature de façon intelligente, afin qu'elle s'adapte à nos besoins'; ils se rendirent également compte de la nécessité de 'maintenir une réputation en matière de capacités techniques et d'efficacité dans les affaires' puisque 'le talent n'est rien sans la connaissance', et que 'les ingérences dans la Nature ainsi que la création d'objets nouveaux possédant une beauté naturelle sont des tâches difficiles et hautement spécialisées'. Il est souvent fait appel aux membres de l'Institut pour des conseils portant sur la mise au point de projets à grande échelle. Un certain nombre de nos membres occupent des postes de responsabilité au sein du Gouvernement ou sur le plan local. La profession d'architecte paysagiste occupe une certaine place dans les affaires nationales à la fois au Royaume-Uni et en république d'Irlande, pays qui sont gérés de façon satisfaisante par le même Institut. Nos fondateurs étaient aussi conscients du fait que 'l'application des principes de l'architecture du paysage ... était essentielle à la construction adéquate des villes'. C'est ainsi que les architectes paysagistes ont joué un rôle précieux dans la construction de nos villes nouvelles, par contre on n'a pas fait appel à leur aide dans le domaine de l'adaptation des villes plus anciennes. Quelques pays européens sont devenus des maîtres dans cet art; nous nous trouvons devant une tâche bien spécifique si nos villes doivent être rajeunies, comme cela semble s'imposer. Nos fondateurs s'appuyèrent avant tout sur la définition que donna Charles Eliot, président émérite de l'Université de Harvard, selon laquelle: 'L'architecture du paysage fait partie des beaux-arts, et en tant que telle, sa fonction la plus importante réside dans la création et la conservation de la beauté dans l'environnement de l'habitat humain et dans les sites naturels de la campagne'.

Nous avons le rare privilège de voir Son Altesse Royale le Duc d'Edimbourg, KG, KT, patronner notre Congrès; il n'a d'ailleurs pas épargné ses efforts dans ce pays pour encourager l'intérêt que l'on porte à la fois à l'étude et aux paysages. Sa présence nous rappelle qu'un nombre croissant de chefs d'Etat, de par le monde, commencent à attacher une importance certaine au paysage. Et je suis intimement persuadé que nous vivons un grand moment de l'histoire, car les principes de base que n'ont cessé de défendre l'IFLA et le Landscape Institute, sont maintenant couramment acceptés. Puisque l'on a besoin de moins de technologues pour travailler sur des appareils et des ordinateurs perfectionnés, ce sont les professions s'inspirant de la structure même du monde et les talents artistiques inhérents à chaque être humain qui prennent de plus en plus de valeur. En même temps, le Landscape Institute a ressenti le besoin d'allier l'art aux compétences scientifiques et de gestion afin d'atteindre les meilleurs résultats possibles. C'est la raison pour laquelle nous avons ouvert les portes à des collègues venant de disciplines nouvelles, mais connexes. Pour la première fois en cinquante ans, notre liste de membres associés comprend des directeurs et des experts en paysages aux côtés des architectes paysagistes.

Nous devrions nous assurer de pouvoir maintenir nos idéaux et apprendre les compétences techniques nécessaires à la réalisation de nos objectifs, en nous souvenant des quarante membres fondateurs qui se rassemblèrent sous un chapiteau le 23 mai 1929. Nous comptons à l'heure qu'il est 1650 membres, quarante fois le nombre initial, plus une excellente équipe de personnel permanent, pour nous assister au siège social de Nash House. Je souhaiterais donc commencer ce Congrès en remerciant, au nom de tous les membres ici présents, nos fondateurs et ceux qui ont suivi leurs traces. Souhaitons que leur travail se poursuive sur le plan international, et se multiplie dans chaque pays du monde au cours des cinquante prochaines années.

OPENING ADDRESS

PRESIDENT INTERNATIONAL FEDERATION OF LANDSCAPE ARCHITECTS

DR WERKMEISTER

It is an honour for the members of our Federation to be here in Cambridge, at the historic Jesus College, where the International Federation of Landscape Architects was founded 31 years ago. And it is our pleasure to be present at the Golden Jubilee of the Institute of Landscape Architects. The United Kingdom has a great tradition in gardens, parks and landscapes. There are famous schools and universities which educated generations of qualified landscape architects for the benefit of this country as well as for the world. IFLA got many impulses from its first President, Prof Jellicoe, and other Foundation members and officers of the Federation. IFLA appreciates all those contributions for the development of landscape architecture very sincerely.

The present situation in the world is marked by harassed, endangered or at least exhausted ecological resources. Mankind, till now accustomed to a steady growing of the GNP becomes more and more aware of the fact that furthermore every growth will be limited. The wise treatment of those resources by all responsible authorities and disciplines of planners is worldwide the great duty of man.

The landscape architect has to play and will play a growing important rôle. Not to embellish *fait accompli* but to co-ordinate planning of all kinds and on all levels from the very beginning – that's what should be a rule in future. High qualification of the landscape architects is needed, therefore IFLA's Education Committee is working intensively in order to register worldwide all universities and schools, offering full or partial courses, and to advise, with the help of IFLA's Co-ordinator for International Educational Programmes, the young profession. IFLA has established some international committees which are covering a broad field of urgent activities. IFLA keeps close contacts to international organisations, for instance, UNESCO, IUCN, UNEP, UIA, ICOMOS, etc.

In the three regions of IFLA, namely Far East, Central and Western, there are carried out seminars and symposiums for professional discussions and qualified promotion of landscape architects. At least our congresses are meeting places for many colleagues and non-professionals, giving views and aspects on the mutual situation of the profession.

'Landscape towards 2000', the general theme of this XVIIth World Congress of IFLA, will join many landscape architects, planners, ecologists and neighbouring disciplines in order to know their ideas, reflections and concerns about the present situation in the world. Their lectures and discussions might encourage us to keep up with the solutions of the environmental problems. It will be stated again, that IFLA has to take over a kind of brotherhood for all those colleagues in developing countries, who need advice and help.

I am sure the Congress will be a successful one. Thanks to all who have worked hard to prepare this Meeting.

C'est un honneur pour les membres de notre Fédération que d'être réunis ici à Cambridge, dans cet édifice historique qu'est le Jesus College, et où fut fondée, il y a 31 ans, la Fédération Internationale des Architectes Paysagistes. Et nous sommes particulièrement heureux d'assister au cinquantenaire de l'Institute of Landscape Architects. Le Royaume-Uni possède une grande tradition dans le domaine de jardins, parcs et paysages. Célèbres sont les écoles et les universités dans lesquelles ont été formées des générations d'architectes paysagistes qualifiés, et ce pour le bénéfice de ce pays aussi bien que pour celui du monde entier. L'IFLA a bénéficié de tout l'élan que lui ont donné son premier président, Monsieur Jellicoe, ainsi que les autres membres fondateurs et responsables de la Fédération. L'IFLA apprécie très sincèrement toutes les contributions apportées au développement de l'architecture du paysage.

La situation actuelle dans le monde est caractérisée par des ressources écologiques qui sont dans un état alarmant, menacées, ou du moins épuisées. L'humanité, jusqu'à présent habituée à une augmentation régulière du PNB prend de plus en plus conscience du fait que, désormais, chaque croissance sera limitée. L'utilisation rationnelle de ces ressources par les autorités responsables et la discipline des planificateurs est, dans le monde entier, l'un des grands devoirs de l'homme.

L'architecte paysagiste doit jouer, et jouera, un rôle de plus en plus important. Non pas pour 'décorer des faits accomplis', mais pour coordonner tous les types de planification, et à tous les niveaux, depuis leur stade de départ – voilà ce qui devrait désormais être la règle. Les architectes paysagistes doivent être hautement qualifiés; aussi, le comité à l'éducation de l'IFLA s'emploie activement à produire la liste de toutes les écoles et universités dans le monde qui proposent des cours à temps partiel et à temps complet et pour conseiller la jeune école grâce au concours du coordonnateur de l'IFLA pour les programmes d'enseignement internationaux. L'IFLA a établi des comités internationaux qui couvrent un vaste champ d'activités pressantes et elle est en relation très étroite avec les organisations internationales, telles l'UNESCO, l'IUCN, l'UNEP, l'UIA, l'ICOMOS, etc.

Dans les trois régions du globe où l'IFLA est présente, notamment en Extrême-Orient, et dans les regions centrale et occidentale, des séminaires et des symposiums sont organisés pour des discussions professionnelles et la promotion d'architectes paysagistes. Du moins, nos congrès sont des lieux de rencontre pour nombre de nos collègues et des non-professionnels, échangeant leurs points de vue et leurs idées sur la situation de la profession.

'Le paysage d'ici l'an 2000', le thème général de ce XVIIème Congrès Mondial de l'IFLA rassemblera de nombreux architectes paysagistes, responsables de projets, écologistes et personnes appartenant à des disciplines similaires afin de confronter leurs idées, réflexions et inquiétudes quant à la situation mondiale actuelle. Leurs conférences et discussions peuvent nous encourager à nous tenir au courant des solutions proposées aux problèmes de l'environnement. On rappellera une fois encore, que l'IFLA doit faire preuve d'un peu de fraternité pour tous ses collègues des pays en voie de développement qui ont besoin d'aide et conseil.

Je suis persuadé que le congrès sera une réussite, et j'aimerais remercier tous ceux qui ont travaillé avec ardeur à la préparation de cette rencontre.

A DISCOURSE

GEOFFREY JELLICOE CBE

It is a great honour for me to address this joint conference that celebrates the fiftieth anniversary of the British Institute and the thirty-first of the International Federation. I remember well the foundation of each body; of those present at the first, it is a delight to know that Miss Brenda Colvin is still active. Of the second, I am happy to see here today so many of those who were present on that dramatic night in Jesus College when IFLA was founded. It is, too, a specially happy thought that the foundation Honorary Secretary elected on that occasion was later the first landscape designer to receive what in England constitutes knighthood – Dame Sylvia Crowe. In welcoming the foundation members who are with us today, let us not forget those who are absent and those – like Gustav Ammann – who are no longer with us, whose lives, like ours, were dedicated to the betterment of the world about us.

And what of the hopes and aspirations formed in that small office of Richard Sudell's in Gower Street in 1929, and of that mysterious corner room somewhere in Jesus College in 1948? Have they been fulfilled? And if the answer is yes – and it is – why should this be so in a world that seems more than ever bent on self-destruction?

Last summer some of you may have received a remarkable book, *Choose Life*, a dialogue on world affairs between a western philosopher, the late Arnold Toynbee, and the Buddhist philosopher Daisaku Ikeda. From this we can detect that beneath the chaotic outer reality of things there is an underlying inner reality common to all, towards which humanity is groping. The universal inner reality is creative and has, indeed, created our profession. However much we are individuals, we are also part of this universal creative process and I doubt if the individual alone, however skilful, can reach fulfilment without being so; it is why we are assembled here in Cambridge from all parts of the world.

I think there is little doubt that landscape design is on the threshold of becoming the most comprehensive of the arts. It can never be the most pure, for the abstract quality that creates music, poetry, painting and sculpture is too compromised by the realities of life. But it has one quality possessed by no other art that is not ephemeral – certainly not architecture – which relates it uniquely to the way of thought of the modern world: the sense of constant change. Classical architecture was intended to be a rock standing for ever in a stream that has neither beginning nor end. Now the rock is being eroded and the occupants have taken to the water; but instead of being drowned, have found themselves passing towards new and undreamed of landscapes. This concept of movement has been crystallised by the American philosopher John Dewey with an analysis of art that is revolutionary. He proclaimed that art was not merely the finished object, but the whole experience of creation. He believed that art was a unity of time and space, an experience that should have a beginning and a consummation. Probably the painter who most clearly expressed this philosophy was his fellow American Jackson Pollock, but our own art of landscape seems to do so even more explicitly. All of us know that our art is not only in constant motion for many years, from planting to maturity, but that this movement is itself only an incident between what happened before and what will happen afterwards. The practical application of Dewey to landscape, therefore, is that every moment of transition, and not merely the final result, is an experience and a work of art. This is being recognised in our schools of landscape.

In reviewing the vast sweep of this Congress, the tremendous achievements of its members since the war, and its potential future, I think there is one aspect that does not come easily to practitioners involved in day-to-day anxieties but is to my mind outstandingly the most important for all who are concerned with the created environment. I mean the recognition and study of what the archaeologist Jacquetta Hawkes has described as the strange furnishings of the subconscious mind. Today, the repression of instinct is the cause of quite unnecessary unhappiness. I believe it is a prime purpose of our profession to release these instincts, and that only by probing into the different layers of the mind can we acquire the knowledge to do so.

There seem to be four recognisable phases of the subconscious: that of the sub-tropical forester, when our physiology was perfected; the hunter; the settler; and today the voyager (as he can truthfully be described). In what way, to quote Siegfried Giedion, are these phases *The Eternal Present?* To answer this we must begin with the first and deepest, and work upwards.

In 1877 a professor of mental and moral philosophy, Grant Allen, published an analysis of aesthetics called *Physiological Aesthetics*. Today this little classic is virtually forgotten, but if a copy can be found, I commend it to all. The aesthetic conclusions were geared to the emotions of the day and to us now seem horribly sentimental, but the scientific method is unanswerable. It explains the hostility of modern man to what he feels is a soul-less machine-made environment, and is a basic guide to landscape. From this primitive treasure house my own first choice is the power of stereoscopic vision to create *feeling* as well as sight in environment, how we can and should design for it, and how a *felt* foreground will connect our psyche to middle and far distance.

But of course the perceptions are only a technical part in the long manufacture of the emotions in that marvellous green and restless habitat. In a period described as the golden age of the mammals, we were vegetarian, peace-loving and monarchs. No wonder the irrational parts of us hanker for that carefree if cruel existence, which created our basic sense of beauty and subconsciously inspires most private gardens today.

Then, as *Homo erectus*, ambitious and adaptable, man leaves the protection of the forests for the dangerous life of carnivore and hunter in the open savannah – the only animal to have within him the dual personality of peace-lover and aggressor. Society changes from the individual to the collective, for hunting calls for organised team-work. Man now spreads over the globe, adapting himself to climate and geography and thus creating diversity of species. In Europe he endures the incredible hardship of ice age and mountain terrors – a challenge that called forth the first works of art as an expression of inner reality and probably implanted in technocratic man an occasional urge to return to, and experience, the sublime in landscape. He so venerates the specialist power of his monster prey that he hopes the spirit will pass into him when he eats the flesh.

Ten thousand years or so later the hunter society in the west had already been superseded by the settler but seems, in essence, to have re-appeared in China. The abstract evidence of this is to be found in a generic similarity in painting, the factual in the early hunting parks. China is a genial land and once the monsters had been domesticated and lost their mystique, veneration passed from them to the natural environment as a whole. So the aggressive hunter emerged into the peace-loving agriculturalist. Taoists believed that all man's works should be gentle and submissive to the earth-mother, a very different concept from that of the western settler, who saw himself as master of all and centre of the universe. Today the west takes a more modest view and, as usual, the first evidence of this is seen in the arts rather than the sciences.

Through such an artist as Henry Moore we can trace a new philosophy of humility towards the landscape, groping back towards our very beginnings. Moore sees men and rocks as one landscape and one creation, just as the Chinese saw rock and man as one in a single stone, where hollowed forms and penetrations were prized. There is still some doubt whether it was Henry Moore or Barbara Hepworth who first conceived the idea of piercing the human figure with a hole. Personally, I think it was simultaneous, and by doing so they by-passed classicism and linked modern Europe to ancient China and so to the caves of pre-history.

The third phase, the western settler, was concerned with the beauty of mathematical proportion, and environment was solely the province of the architect.

Phase four began when Galileo and others broke out of the secure classical box that had taken ten thousand years to come to maturity. The search for the infinite beyond the finite had begun. The effect upon landscape design was revolutionary. Although Vignola in the Villa Lante had already shown that the garden could be greater than the house, the search meant a totally different conception of space. Landscape was freed from architecture and opened up perspectives of imaginative space and ideas denied to its ancient parent. For me, the two symbols of this liberation are Bernini's Piazza of St Peter's, which created the sense of infinity beyond its columns and is still the greatest collective urban space in the world; and the contemporary Villa Gamberaia near Florence, which for the first time in history set out to record in space the contrasting facets of the individual mind.

The liberation became absolute in the English eighteenth century park, where the voyager in imaginary space travelled backwards in time: through William Kent he participated in the classics; through Brown, the hunting savannah; and through Uvedale Price and others the primitive forests. In the nineteenth century the voyager went round and round in a whirlpool, but re-appeared in France through painters groping, like Monet, towards the revolutionary art of movement and experience described by Dewey in his philosophy. In landscape, Le Corbusier proclaimed, like a clap of thunder, a new vision of human habitation: a city of termite towers poised above a romantic landscape flowing below like a Dewey river. This heroic concept now fills us with alarm and even horror, but it did decisively re-affirm the landscape of the future as being independent of architecture. Despite his protestations, Le Corbusier was preoccupied more with the beauty of the machine than with humanity, and with the universal and international rather than the particular.

Le Corbusier pulled us up with a jerk. We have seen in recent years that the human cannot live on geometry alone – and mostly bad geometry at that; nor, of course, can he live solely on his rich heritage of biology, for this would be to discard the divine gift of intellect. This is why I believe that our new profession is essential to the future of civilisation in any part of the world, for it is the only one that can unite these two aspects. It can explore the meaning and purpose of life and express its findings on a scale never before conceived; and in doing so, it can lift the spirit from the body, like the dream of the Chinese philosopher of old.

Let me end with a quotation from *The Eternal Present*, written by Professor Giedion seventeen years ago:

'So soon as inner and outer reality agree, a corresponding development occurs in the psyche of man. Our period demands a type of man who can restore the presently lost equilibrium between inner and outer reality. This equilibrium, never static but, like reality itself, involved in continuous change, is like a tight-rope dancer who, by small adjustments, keeps a continuous balance between his being and empty space.

The human organism requires equipoise between its organic environment and its artificial surroundings. Separated from earth and growth, it will never obtain the equilibrium necessary for life.

It is time we became human again and let the human scale rule over all our ventures. The man in equipoise we need is new only when seen contrasted with our distorted period. He revives age-old demands which must be fulfilled in the terms of our own times if our civilisation is not to collapse.'

INTERNATIONAL UNION FOR THE CONSERVATION OF NATURE

PROPOSED TRANSFORMATIONS TO THE CONTEXT OF ENVIRONMENTAL DISCOURSE: BEYOND THE TWENTY-NINTH DAY.[1]

PROFESSOR PETER JACOBS[2]

Introduction

The parable is told of the conscientious farmer who has provided a new, automatically controlled and rot-proof feeding container for his chickens. The chickens are bred and cared for in the most sanitary and modern manner such that their food consumption doubles each day. The new container is designed to alert the farmer when it is half empty such that he can order new feed. The consciencious farmer checks his container almost daily but observes that very little food is consumed. Then, on the twenty-ninth day, the alarm sounds and he realises that the container is, indeed, half empty. Given the rate of consumption he realises, too late, that he has only one day left in which to secure new feed.

The parable of the twenty-ninth day is, in fact, the dilemma of the conservation movement. How can we foresee the twenty-ninth day across a wide array of disappearing species of animal and vegetable life such that we might nurture and extend, beyond our own life time, the natural and cultural heritage of the planet Earth? The parable carries with it a subtle message particularly germain to the dilemma of the conservationist. Even had the farmer observed the feeding container more closely than he did, he would not have noticed any appreciable loss of feed until the twenty-ninth day. Far too many of the resources on the planet Earth are approaching the twenty-ninth day, many have long since passed this limit and have disappeared, forever reducing the genetic pool of life on Earth.

The World Conservation Strategy

Within three weeks following this joint congress, the International Union for the Conservation of Nature and Natural Resources will launch the 'World Conservation Strategy'. The aim of the World Conservation Strategy[3] is to achieve the following conservation objectives:

The maintenance of vital ecological processes.

The preservation of genetic diversity.

The maintenance of exploited ecosystems and population of plants and animals at sustainable levels.

The strategy is designed to co-ordinate world wide efforts necessary to avoid the farmer's dilemma, and the farmer is everyman.

The advent of the World Conservation Strategy is not an isolated evidence of concern. In a recent report from the Science Council of Canada, the principles of a 'conserver society' were postulated.[4]

These include, but are not limited to, stressing diversity and flexibility as mechanisms that would promote the decentralisation of responsibility as well as achieving optimal performance from local resources. The Conserver Society would recognise the total costs of development to others, ourselves, and to future populations. It would cultivate a respect for the regenerative capacity of the biosphere. The Science Council report observes that ... 'The ecological balances in the biosphere are the culmination of millions of years of evolution. They represent a highly ordered state or a state of low entropy, even though the nature of the order is not always obvious to us. With increasing knowledge of ecology comes increasing respect for the subtle feedbacks and interdependences, the checks and balances – and potential instabilities – of the living systems of the Earth. If a living species is rendered extinct, or a finely adjusted ecological system destroyed, it is irreplaceable'.[5]

Against the positive principles and observations cited above, a recent report from Brazil is expressive of the odds against which the conservation movement operates.

'Brazil abounds with vigorous and articulate conservation groups, but they are powerless in the presence of one crushing fact: the desperate need of the country's many poor. In January, O Journal do Brasil published figures showing that in Rio de Janeiro alone, 918,000 people were living in 'absolute poverty' and of the city's total population, nine millions, 27 per cent lived in 'relative poverty'. These are the statistics that blunt conservationist scruples. There is a constant pressure to develop more sources of food, joined to an irrepressible belief that sooner or later a way will be found to turn the relatively unproductive five million square kilometres of the Amazon Basin into a bottomless larder'.[6]

For these reasons and many others the aims and objectives of conservation are far from being achieved. As a consequence, vital ecological processes are increasingly disrupted, genetic diversity destroyed, and otherwise renewable living resources dissipated. The World Conservation Strategy contains disturbing evidence of our romance with 'the twenty-nine day limit'. A brief summary of the current state of the biosphere is ample cause for sombre reflection.[7]

The Disruption of Ecological Processes

Huge quantities of fertile soil are stripped each year from the highlands of Asia, Latin America and Africa; for example: 240 million cubic metres a year from Nepal; 426 million tons a year from Columbia; more than a thousand million tons a year from Ethiopia.

At current rates the world will lose about one-third of its cropland between now and the end of the century. In the USA alone, 10,000 km² of arable land are usurped each year by industry and urbanisation.

Forty per cent of the world's tropical forests – genetically (with coral reefs) the richest environments on the planet – have been destroyed already. The rest are being felled and burned at the rate of 30 hectares a minute. The magnitude of this loss – quite without precedent in evolution – can be surmised from the fact that as many as half of the world's land species live only in tropical rain forests.

Some 43 per cent of the Earth's land surface is already desert or semi-desert. A further 19 per cent (30 million km²) is threatened with desertification. The world's drylands are being degraded at a rate of 58,250 km² a year.

Many coastal wetlands and shallows – the support systems of two-thirds of the world's fisheries – are either degraded already or are being destroyed by dredging, dumping, pollution or shore 'improvement'. Almost 75 per cent of the estuaries of the USA are degraded, 23 per cent severely so.

The Destruction of Genetic Diversity

Species and varieties of plants and animals are being destroyed faster than they are being discovered. More than a thousand vertebrate species and sub-species and an estimated 25,000 plant species are threatened with extinction. These figures do not take account of the inevitable losses of small vertebrate species – let alone of invertebrates – whose habitats are being eliminated in their entirety.

The genetic base of much modern food production is dangerously narrow. Only four varieties of wheat produce 75 per cent of the crop grown on the Canadian prairies; and more than half the prairie wheatlands are devoted to a single variety (Neepawa). If one variety of a crop succumbs to a new strain of disease or to an unexpected period of excessive cold, heat, rain or drought, then most (and in some cases, all) of that crop could easily be destroyed.

The Dissipation of Renewable Resources.

Past and present depletion and overexploitation of fish stocks have resulted in an annual loss of potential catch of about seven million tons (some 10 per cent of the current annual world catch). An additional seven million tons of fish are killed accidentally and discarded every year. At least 25 per cent of the world's most valuable fisheries are seriously depleted.

Similarly, forest resources are being overexploited. Some 1,500 million people in developing countries depend on wood for fuel and their annual consumption of wood is estimated to be 1,300 million cubic metres – 90 per cent of developing countries' total wood use. Already the effect of such intense demand has been to denude parts of Asia and Africa of trees so that rural people are forced to burn as fuel, 400 million tons of dung and crop residues, which could otherwise be used to improve soil structure and fertility.

The World Conservation Strategy postulates that the main causes of the problems concerning ecological processes, genetic diversity, and the sustainable exploitation of living resources are ecologically unsound development and poverty. These in turn are influenced by several factors, principally overpopulation, excessive consumption of resources, inequities among and within nations, and ecological ignorance.

The strategy argues that ecologically sound, sustainable development offers the only prospect of conserving the world's ecosystems and species, on which human survival and wellbeing depend. Therefore, the task of conservation is not to resist development but to guide it.

Aspects of the Conservation Guidance System

We are increasingly aware that current plans affect our future. We have begun to understand that cause and ultimate effect can span years and even decades and that the planning process must be increasingly sensitive to the very first signs of environmental degradation if we are to avoid the twenty-nine day horizon. The environmental planning process has begun to address design problems on an unprecedented scale that will impact on increasingly large numbers of people. Many projects that would have been conceived and implemented by a very limited group only a short time ago are now held up to public scrutiny, frequently through the environmental assessment process. These two characteristics, the recognition of the sensitivity and frequently counter-intuitive aspect of cause and effect through time; and the sensitivity of the human condition, sometimes referred to as the quality of life, must be incorporated within the conservation guidance system if it is to be effective.

Recently, a gas pipeline project was proposed to deliver gas from the Arctic Ocean to Southern Canada and the United States. The pipeline would follow the MacKenzie valley across the northern permafrost, where four races of people speaking seven different languages live. An inquiry process was established, led by Justice T. R. Berger, who stated that the issues confronting the MacKenzie valley pipeline inquiry were, in fact, profound, '. . . going beyond the ideological conflicts that have occupied the world for so long, conflicts over who was going to run the industrial machine, and who was going to get the benefits. Now we are being asked, how much energy does it take to run the industrial machine, where does the energy come from, where is the machine going, and what happens to the people who live in the path of the machine?'[8]

Development projects of a scale and potential impact similar to the MacKenzie valley pipeline proposal are no longer the exception but rather an emerging development norm. If the enquiry was successful from a conservation viewpoint, Justice Berger recommended against implementing the project, the process raises significant issues that will require important transformations to the current context of environmental discourse. These transformations include the nature of our laws, and in particular those laws that deal with the protection of nature. The nature of our perception of time, an irreplaceable and irreversible human resource, and the nature of our institutional structures including institutions devoted to conservation.

Proposed Transformations to the Context of Environmental Discourse

Notwithstanding the integration of the environmental assessment process within the legislative and legal framework of a growing number of nation-states and international development agencies, nature and natural processes are still discussed in the third person singular. In a fascinating article, Christopher D. Stone proposes that '. . . we give legal rights to forests, oceans, rivers and other so-called 'natural objects' in the environment – indeed, to the natural environment as a whole'.[9]

He argues that historically, legal rights have been extended from the privileged few to increasingly large segments of the human population including all races, the maimed and handicapped, the illiterate, and indirectly to the lower animals. The extension of these rights to nature, *per se*, is an essential element in the transformation of the current conservation context.

The issue of the legal standing of natural objects is clearly illustrated in the opinion and dissenting opinion of the United States Supreme Court in the case of Sierra Club v Morton.

In delivering the opinion of the Court, Mr Justice Stewart argued that:

'Aesthetic and environmental well-being, like economic well-being, are important ingredients of the quality of life in our society, and the fact that particular environmental interests are shared by the many rather than the few does not make them less deserving of legal protection through the judicial process. But the 'injury in fact' test requires more than an injury to a cognisable interest. It requires that the party seeking review be himself among the injured'.[10]

Mr Justice Douglas, in his dissenting opinion, suggested that:

'The critical question of 'standing' would be simplified and also put neatly in focus if we fashioned a federal rule that allowed environmental issues to be litigated before federal agencies or federal courts in the name of the inanimate object about to be despoiled, defaced, or invaded by roads and bulldozers and where injury is the subject of public outrage. Contemporary public concern for protecting nature's ecological equilibrium should lead to the conferral of standing upon environmental objects to sue for their own preservation'.

'With all respect, the problem is to make certain that the inanimate objects, which are the very core of America's beauty, have spokesmen before they are destroyed'.[11]

If transformations of our legal structures are essential in guiding development, so too are transformations in the very manner in which the human condition is formulated and perceived. If historically, we have tended to focus on the spatial and material parameters of the conservation crisis, attention must now be brought to bear on the temporal aspects of environmental discourse. Mention has been made of the time lags that occur between cause and effect relative to our interventions in the complex web of the biosphere, but time also has a human non-linear dimension. Ignacy Sachs[12] observes that . . . 'Time is our basic existential category. Two consequences follow immediately from this trivial observation. On the one hand, wasting the irreversible flow of unique human lives is certainly the worst form of wastefulness. On the other, looking into the ways in which a society makes use of its time provides a convenient entry point into the subject of lifestyles, cultural patterns, broad consumption structures and societal goals, or, in other words, into the core of meaningful planning'.[13]

Our current context is fraught with problems that arise from a poorly distributed workload where many are overworked, others unemployed, and all are subject to workloads that are unevenly distributed over our life spans. Further, much of our working time is devoted to activities of marginal social utility and much of this time is devoted to earning an income rather than realising our collective human potential. A critical aspect of the proposed conservation guidance system must focus on the planning of our time for 'the satisfaction of genuine societal needs in conditions favourable to the realisation of each human self'.

The third critical transformation that I propose we consider, deals with the nature and structure of our institutions, including the wide array of conservation institutions. The basic premise underlying the mandate and operating procedures of the vast majority of our institutional frameworks is one of continuity and of stability. Yet, the luxury of these assumptions is contrary to the evidence of our daily experience where the basic tenants of the state, the economy, religion, science and the arts is subject to constant revision.

Donald Schon proposes that institutions must learn to learn. They must be transformed into learning systems capable of transforming themselves to respond to the creative aspects of situation that are inherently open ended. The alternatives to institutional transformation include three basic forms of behaviour: a desire to return to the Golden Age, some mythical point in the past where present problems are assumed to have been absent; revolution, a rejection of the past that operates against existing institutions but not always towards clearly articulated alternative goals; and escapism, an active or passive attempt to avoid the present condition, to 'opt out'.

Dr Schon suggests that the transformation of our institutions to systems capable of learning to learn will demand the invention of new professions. 'New bodies of projective models are required, or the revitalization of old ones by their translation across professional and disciplinary lines. The learning agent must be willing and able to make the leaps required in existential knowledge. These are the leaps from informational overload to the first formulation of the problem, from an absence of theory to convergence on a design for public action, and from the experience of one situation to its use as a projective model in the next instance. These are leaps, because they cannot be justified except by what happens after they are made. They are conditions, not consequences, of knowledge'.[14]

These transformations to the current context of environmental discourse have been proposed as performance criteria, against which the conservation/development guidance system must be designed. It is suggested that nature have standing in law, that the use of human time be rationalised with respect to personal and societal goals, and that our institutions learn to learn. There are undoubtedly other transformations that must occur if we are to master the limits inherent to the twenty-ninth day.

The Design Task Ahead

The joint congress of the International Federation of Landscape Architects and the Landscape Institute provides an opportunity to address one final aspect of the integrate network of environmental planning, an aspect that is most easily visualised in spatial terms although the issue is not fundamentally physical. I refer to the enormous energy and commitment that has been invested in the securing of conservation areas throughout the world that are subject to special protective status in law. These critical areas represent at most four per cent of the Earth's terrestrial surface, and less than one per cent of the Earth's marine areas. Clearly, the conservation movement cannot achieve the basic aims of the World Conservation Strategy in these areas alone.

The conceptual polarity between green spaces, nature preserves, and grey places, the urban realm, must be buried. Conservation must extend beyond the borders of our ecological reserves, our national parks and wilderness areas, to embrace the totality of human settlement. Conservation can no longer be perceived as a constraint against development but rather an integral part of the development process itself. The conservation ethic must not only guide the development process, it can and should lead such a process.

On behalf of the International Union for the Conservation of Nature and Natural Resources[15], I invite you to join with us in the design of the Conservation/Development Guidance System that lies ahead. We must learn to design more with less, and I can think of no better group of individuals than those colleagues assembled here to spearhead our design efforts towards the twenty-first century and away from the twenty-ninth day.

References

[1] A recent publication by Lester R. Bown, deals at length with the dilemma of the twenty-ninth day and with a holistic approach to development. The book, *The Twenty-Ninth Day*, is published by W. W. Norton & Co, and is an excellent follow-up on such books as 'The Limits of Growth'.

[2] The author is currently Chairman, Commission on Environmental Planning, IUCN; President, Canadian Society of Landscape Architects; Vice-doyen, Faculté de l'Aménagement, Université de Montréal.

[3] International Union for the Conservation of Nature and Natural Resources; *World Conservation Strategy*; 26 September 1979; 1110 Morges, Switzerland.

[4] Science Council of Canada; *Canada as a Conserver Society: Resource Uncertainties and the need for new Technologies;* Report No 27, September 1977; Minister of State for Science and Technology; Ottawa, Ontario.

[5] *Ibid*, page 37.

[6] Lewis, Norman; 'The Rape of the Amazon Forest'; in *The Montreal Star;* May 7, 1979, p A13.

[7] The World Conservation Strategy, Section 1.4, pages 1-6.

[8] Berger, Thomas R., 'The MacKenzie Valley Pipeline Inquiry', *Queen's Quarterly*, Vol 83, No 1, Spring 1976, reprint p 12.

[9] Stone, C. D.; 'Should Trees Have Standing? Toward legal rights for Natural Objects'; 45 S. California Law Review, 450; 1972.

[10] Sierra Club, v Morton; United States Supreme Court Decision, April 19, 1972.

[11] *Ibid.*

[12] Sachs, Ignacy; 'Crisis of Maldevelopment in the North: A Way Out': *IFDA Dossier 2*; Fondation Internationale pour un autre développement, Nyon, Suisse.

[13] *Ibid*, p 6.

[14] Schon, Donald A; Beyond the Stable State; W. W. Norton & Company, Inc, New York, p 235.

[15] The International Union for Conservation of Nature and Natural Resources, consists of a General Assembly, a Secretariat in Morges, Switzerland, and six commissions. These commissions include:

Commission on Environmental Planning: The Commission on Environmental Planning is that organ of IUCN which serves to gather, systematically review, and disseminate information on the status, techniques and application on environmental planning throughout the world; and to advise on the most appropriate application of environmental planning techniques to conservation.

Commission on Ecology: The Commission on Ecology is that organ of IUCN which serves to co-ordinate ecological research work for the conservation of nature being done in different parts of the world, and promote co-operation between scientists of different countries engaged in their work.

Commission on Education: The Commission on Education is that organ of IUCN which serves to maintain an overview of the status of environmental awareness and education in the various regions of the world, and to identify regions and localities where lack of awareness may be a factor limiting public acceptance and effectiveness of conservation programmes. It also serves to co-operate with and support governmental, intergovernmental and non-governmental organisations interested in, or responsible for, activities aimed at increasing environmental awareness through information and education. It also helps to foster professional training in relevant environmental fields.

Survival Services Commission: The Survival Service Commission is that organ of IUCN that serves as a primary source of the scientific and technical information required for the conservation of endangered and vulnerable species of fauna and flora, and recommends and promotes measures for their preservation. Its object is to do all in its power to prevent the extinction of species, sub-species and discrete populations of fauna and flora, thereby maintaining genetic diversity.

Commission on National Parks and Protected Areas: The Commission on National Parks and Protected Areas is that organ of the IUCN that serves as a source of the scientific and technical information required for the planning, establishment, and management of a network of protected areas of conservation significance throughout the world and recommends and promotes measures to extend, maintain and monitor the network.

Commission on Environmental Policy, Law and Administration: The Commission on Environmental Policy, Law and Administration is that organ of IUCN which serves as a source of technical opinion and guidance on the strategic policies and legal and institutional arrangements required to ensure that mechanisms for the conservation of the environment, together with the related measures, legislation and procedures, are compatible with the best available environmental management techniques.

MAN AND HIS ENVIRONMENT – OUTLINE OF THE ACTION TAKEN BY UNESCO

W. TOCHTERMANN

The spectacular and almost universal development of technology, coupled with the never-ending growth of urban development, has had the evident consequence of profoundly changing the traditional ways of life, firstly in the industrialised countries and then increasingly in the developing countries. The effect of these changes has been to isolate whole sectors of the population from the intimate contact which they had hitherto enjoyed with the natural environment. This could be described as a divorce between man and nature, brought on by a victorious technology but leading gradually to a growing weakness in a civilisation which neglects the very bases on which it could develop. Paradoxically, this movement away from natural living principles took place at the very moment when the population explosion, accompanied by the desire to obtain better living conditions, caused an unprecedented drain on the resources, undoubtedly considerable but nevertheless limited, offered to us by nature.

Unawareness of the systems and natural mechanisms enabling life to be maintained on the earth, neglect of the unwanted effects of technology, particularly pollution, inefficient management of the soil, forests and water resources, unrestricted consumption of fossil fuels, unbridled urban development, whittling down of rural areas, destruction of the framework of life, the breakdown of traditional cultures, all these are the most clearly and most frequently seen adverse manifestations of the transformation of the relations between man and his environment. Although this change is not recent – and more specifically, although the concern aroused by it has made its presence felt in UNESCO's programmes ever since the birth of that organisation – it is none the less true that the access of collective awareness of what we have agreed to call problems of the environment, and also the international action resulting from it, constitute a new phenomenon from the point of view of its size and its consequences: the UNESCO Conference on the rational use and conservation of the resources of the biosphere in 1968, and the United Nations Conference on the environment in 1972 constitute the characteristic stages of this access of awareness on the part of governments.

In this perspective, what is often called the 'environmental crisis' refers primarily to the deterioration of physical and biological environments in the face of the violent acceleration of man's ascendancy over the planet, and particularly in face of the unrestricted exploitation of its natural resources.

But it should be noted additionally that this 'environmental crisis' has made its appearance at the very moment when the demand for a new international economic order is being pressed home, and when the traditional forms of development and the methods of giving technical assistance to the countries which need it are being contested. Thus we speak of a 'crisis of civilisation' which we are attempting to remedy by making an improvement – still tentative and groping – in the 'quality of life'. In this context, in which man finds himself once again face to face with himself, the search for a state of equilibrium and harmony between man and his environment must be considered as an additional dimension of the search for a future which will be fairer, better adapted and more firmly bound up with the human species.

The interest taken by UNESCO in the problems of the environment goes back, in effect, to the first years of its existence. Thus, as far back as 1948, the Organisation sponsored the creation of the International Union for the Conservation of Nature and its Resources.

Twenty years later, in September 1968, UNESCO summoned together in Paris, with the co-operation of the United Nations Organisation, the United Nations Food and Agriculture Organisation, and the World Health Organisation, an intergovernmental conference of experts on the scientific bases of the rational use and conservation of the resources of the biosphere. It was the first time that an approach at intergovernmental level had been made to this question taken as a whole, and this conference led to the launching, in 1970, of the interdisciplinary programme of research into man and the biosphere (MAB), which today constitutes one of the essential elements of the activities of UNESCO in the field of the environment.

Numerous other activities have developed during recent years in the various sectors of the programme, and it is possible today to distinguish seven main themes in the vast field represented by the environment:

1. Knowledge of the earth's crust and its resources.
2. The biosphere: the surrounding environment of man within his grasp.
3. The distribution of water.
4. Man and the sea.
5. Man in the town.
6. Safeguarding man's past and the permanence of nature.
7. The art of living: an education to be given.

Knowledge of the Earth's Crust and its Resources

Mineral and fossil fuels are the essential materials of the industrial era. Fuels provide heat and energy; metals and non-metallic elements provide the raw materials of machines, buildings, transport networks, communication systems, etc.

However, mineral raw materials and fossil fuels are not renewable. In certain cases, reserves have already been seriously run down, and the growing needs of agriculture, industry and private individuals in a period of rapid population expansion will exert heavy pressure on the capacity of the globe to satisfy them.

The processes at work in the Earth's crust, which are responsible for the observed distribution of mineral resources, are also the source of natural hazards, such as earthquakes and volcanic eruptions, which every year cause heavy losses in human lives and considerable material damage. A better knowledge of the processes at work in the Earth's crust will enable us to understand these phenomena better and to improve the means of protecting us against them: firstly, by marking out the danger zones more precisely and obtaining a better estimate of the threats posed to human lives and property; secondly, by setting up alarm and warning systems; thirdly, by supplying architects and engineers with the information they need to design and construct earthquake-proof buildings and public works.

All the problems mentioned above are closely linked to the training of geologists, geophysicists and geochemists, not only in the business of making up geological maps and mineral survey charts, but also training them in seismological and other geophysical methods of research into natural hazards.

Co-operation regarding the fundamental aspects of Earth sciences go back well into the past. An essential step forward in international action was achieved with the launching in 1957 of the International Geophysical Year, a great common research effort in which 30,000 scientists and technicians from some 70 countries took part. During the Geophysical Year, the entire planet Earth, from its central core to its magnetosphere, became the subject of intensive examination.

Ever since UNESCO was created, the main objectives of its programme on the earth sciences have been to promote international co-operation and to provide aid to member States to enable them to strengthen their scientific potential in this field.

UNESCO has given its support to two major international research programmes, the project on the upper mantle (1963–71) and the geodynamics project (1973–79), launched by the International Council of Scientific Unions. These projects produced scientific results which made it possible for the first time to draw up a complete table showing the continuous evolution of the earth's crust during the course of geological time.

In co-operation with the World Geological Map Commission, the preparation and publication of an important series of geological maps and small scale maps for the Earth sciences were undertaken.

While these activities are continuing, a major geological programme, given the name of the International Geological Correlation Programme (PICG) was launched in 1973. The essential aim of this programme is to obtain a better knowledge of the phenomena whose origin is to be found in the Earth's crust, which need to be observed and evaluated through international co-operation and which have a direct influence on the origin and distribution of mineral and fuel resources.

UNESCO has been engaged since 1961 in studying natural hazards, particularly earthquakes and volcanic eruptions, and also in studying means of protection against these hazards. After a number of preparatory missions had been sent to the main earthquake zones throughout the world, a first intergovernmental meeting on seismology and paraseismic engineering was held at UNESCO in 1964. This meeting established the bases of the programme which UNESCO has carried out during the last 14 years, with substantial support from the United Nations Development Programme. Amongst the results obtained should be noted the creation of the international seismological centre at Edinburgh (United Kingdom) in 1970; the creation of the Seismological Regional Centre for South America in 1966, the creation, with the support of UNIDP and the Japanese government, of the International Seismology and Paraseismic Engineering Institute in Tokyo, where 200 seismologists and specialists in paraseismic engineering from about 40 developing countries have since received advanced training.

The Biosphere; the Surrounding Environment of Man within his Grasp

The fine layer of earth, water and air found around the periphery of our planet, in which all life is confined and man has evolved, embraces a number of complex self-sufficient units called ecosystems, within which a certain equilibrium is maintained due to the interactions between the populations of animals, plants and other organisms and the chemical and physical elements of which their habitat is made up.

Technical progress has enabled man to transform his immediate environment in a general way so as to make it more favourable for him; only by altering the ecosystems more and more profoundly and making them more and more 'artificial' has he obtained the highly efficient performances of modern agriculture without which it would be impossible to feed the present population of the globe.

The key question is as follows: up to what point can man succeed in manipulating the environment? With world population doubling within the next thirty years, and economic activity increasing at least threefold, the overall impact of man on his environment could soon become overwhelming.

Limits of resources, but also limits of knowledge. A considerable store of scientific and practical knowledge has been accumulated during the course of the centuries on the soil, animals, plants and the use of biological resources, and some remarkable successes have been chalked up in the fields of use of soils, agricultural production and forest management, particularly in the temperate zones. However, contrary to widely held belief, the long term effects of certain very important innovations such as the massive use of pesticides and fertilisers or the introduction of new varieties of crops are not at all well known, even in those privileged zones where a high and sustained level of efficiency is maintained.

This inadequate knowledge is still more marked when it comes to the tropical and sub-tropical ecosystems. It is therefore necessary to acquire a basic knowledge of the structure, functioning and productivity of the ecosystems, and also necessary to work out reliable methods of exploiting them continuously.

In short, the equilibrium between population, environment and natural resources constitutes the key problem on the subject of which new information must be assembled in every region of the world.

At international level, the sharing out of the sectors of activity amongst the majority of the organisations of the United Nations reflects the structures which have been developed and which still persist in most of the national administrations.

FAO and UNESCO, recognised as being converging points with regard respectively to the management of the Earth's resources and research into the ecosystems, have made arrangements to ensure that their programmes in these fields mutually complement and strengthen each other.

The meeting of the United Nations Conference on the environment at Stockholm in June 1972 gave an added spur to the efforts being made in this field, and contributed towards calling the attention of governments and the public to the urgent need for action. The United Nations Programme for the Environment (PNIE), created as a result of this conference, provides the machinery for co-ordinating and supporting international activities in this field.

Faced with the changing needs of a developing world, UNESCO has a special mission, perhaps unique of its kind, to fulfil in the field of the environment and its resources. This mission stems from the traditional role of the Organisation with respect to the scientific, cultural and educational aspects of the environment, and the result is that this general mandate predisposes it to a non-sectorial approach to the fundamental problems of development.

Within the framework of these activities, UNESCO summoned together, in 1968, a major international conference of experts responsible for the task of defining a scientific basis for the rational use and conservation of the resources of the biosphere.

The Conference recommended that a common research programme should be drawn up to cover this field, which was officially launched by the general Conference in 1970 in the form of a Programme on Man and the Biosphere (MAB). This programme offers a solid interdisciplinary basis at intergovernmental level for improving our knowledge of the Earth's biological resources and the relations between human activities and the ecosystems of the Earth.

The Distribution of Water

The development of human societies and cities amongst which they are spread has always been conditional upon the availability of the supplies of water essential for their existence. Despite all its technological changes, the modern world has not changed this immutable law. Quite the contrary, the problem of water has gained new dimensions in our times, due not only to population increases but even more to the rapidly increasing needs of agriculture and the phenomenon of urban development.

Fluctuations in water levels imply not only restrictions in the use of water; their two extremes – floods and droughts – often manifest themselves as natural disasters bringing serious consequences for society. Floods are a frequent phenomenon which affect most regions of the world.

With causes and hydrological characteristics very different from those of floods, less spectacular but much more insidious and persistent, droughts bring about effects which are perhaps even more catastrophic, since they are closely allied to endemic famine throughout the world and may in addition endanger the prosperity of an entire region for many years (for example, the Sahara).

The problems of water resources have engaged the attention of UNESCO from its beginnings; a research programme on the arid zone was launched in 1950, in which hydrology was given an important place.

The interest shown by governments in the management of water resources and the growing awareness of the scientific problems implied by it led to the general Conference of UNESCO deciding, during its thirteenth session, to introduce the International Hydrological Decade (1965–74). The programme of the Decade (DHI) represented a remarkable example of international co-operation contributing to an understanding of the processes and phenomena occurring in the hydrosphere, and the theoretical and practical training of hydrologists occupied a place of primary importance in it.

UNESCO's action in the field of water resources is today undertaken in three main directions: the promotion of scientific and technical research, education and practical training in the disciplines concerned, the study of the problems posed by rational management of water resources, and the strengthening of the infrastructures of training, study and research in the member States.

Man and the Sea

Expressions such as 'inner space' or 'the last untouched spaces' are used to describe the oceans, invoking their immense volume and expanse, the vast resources they conceal and the importance of the rich source of information on the entire planet which they represent. The ocean masses cover approximately 70 per cent of the globe, and yet, apart from the principal navigation routes, they remained almost totally unexplored until the middle of the twentieth century.

The sea exerts a direct action on man, due to its influence on the weather and climate and also due to the natural disasters it causes. It also exerts a profound influence over the society of men. Man exploits the sea in many different ways; for him it is a reservoir of natural resources, a source of pleasure and amusement, a trade highway, etc.

One of the major problems which the nations will have to solve, therefore, consists in establishing a rational equilibrium between this multiplicity of uses they make of the sea, so as to ensure that the environment will not be degraded. Unfortunately, the nations at present in a position to face up to the problems posed by the marine environment are few and far between. It is up to UNESCO to find a way to put its member States in a position to gain the basic knowledge they need in order to exploit the resources of the sea in a rational and balanced manner, so that this exploitation will contribute towards the long term survival of humanity and towards improving the quality of life. The creation in 1960 of the Intergovernmental Oceanographic Commission (COI) under the auspices of UNESCO showed that only a concerted effort at international level would make it possible to obtain a knowledge of the ocean, and it has stimulated international oceanographic research.

Man in the Town

The relationships which man maintains or establishes with the environment in which he lives are nowadays generally described as conflicting relationships. It is an undoubted fact that the built-up environment, the environment of town and villages, undergoes such violent changes that, in many countries, the public authorities declare themselves powerless to control its development. The news that the population will double by the end of the century, the progress of industrialisation, and the almost universal trend towards urban development have added to these worries.

Already now, in the industrialised countries, the population is mostly urban. Some censuses undertaken before 1970 showed percentages of urban population as being in the region of 70 per cent or even close to 80 per cent.

In the developing countries, urbanisation is continuing at an accelerated rate, and is concentrated in a few large towns, the population of which is increasing out of all bounds. In view of its growth rate, it is hardly surprising that such an expansion cannot be accompanied by a corresponding development in infrastructures. Hence the appearance and proliferation of 'shanty towns', where unintegrated populations are crowded together in unhealthy improvised shelters, without water, drains, gas, electricity, and with no defence against fire or flood hazards.

Genuine planning, the planning of a territory and urban development which cares for the quality of life, will consider human settlements as extremely complex systems which can only be dealt with in a scientific spirit by a great deal of patient research. Only a synthesis of such areas of research can take account of the whole range of ecological, economic, social, anthropological and psychological interactions involved. This means that such planning will be progressively less absolute and less authoritarian: too many of the decisions which affect the rural or urban environment are still taken in ignorance, or even in contempt, of the needs and aspirations of the societies concerned. It is well known that poor communications between men lead to illogical relationships between man and the environment.

The United Nations Conference on the Environment (Stockholm, 1972) underlined the complexity of the problems of urban development by comparing them with the problems of energy and by linking the development of the human settlements considered as ecosystems to the equilibrium of the biological environment.

Subsequently, the United Nations Conference on Human Settlement which was held in Vancouver in 1976 aroused a new concept of awareness of the phenomenon of urban development and the dangers threatening the habitat in the developed and developing countries. Faced with this burgeoning of activities, UNESCO should not have any difficulty in defining its field of competence. Even though no overall programme existed, up to the financial year 1975–76, dealing with 'Man and his environment', various undertakings had a hand, at least to some extent, in dealing with the problems covered by this expression: they were concerned with research into social sciences, the teaching of architecture and the protection of our natural and cultural heritage.

Investigations have been made into our perception of the environment (amongst children and adults) and also into the share taken by the population in the decisions which affect the environment. Work has been undertaken on the systems of indicators of the quality of the environment. Studies have been made concerning the social and cultural consequences of tourism. Exercises in programming have been worked out, aimed at those responsible for the environment. Other studies contribute towards our knowledge of traditional architecture and of the problems posed by adapting it to the needs of modern life. Finally, a school of architecture founded by UNESCO is in operation, and is beginning to affirm its regional vocation in West Africa. Regional meetings on the training of architects and town planners are being organised regularly. An important programme dealing with the training of managers of human settlement, currently in progress, is being given PNUE assistance.

Safeguarding Man's Past and the Permanence of Nature

Action to encourage the preservation and proper appreciation of the value of our cultural and natural heritage should, as a matter of principle, be based on two main requirements.

In the first place, by safeguarding or fostering the appreciation of the works, monuments, archeological or natural sites which form part of the heritage of a given people or region, we are not merely obeying a normal reflex urging us to fight against destruction or decay, or an ancestral concern to shield the most remarkable witnesses to the past from the outrages of time or vandalism.

Within this perspective, it would be impossible to underline too strongly the fact that the notion of cultural heritage, understood as an all-embracing concept, does not cover only the visible and material heritage – monuments in particular – in which a country or region can take pride, but extends also to the word-of-mouth tradition, the musical, ethnic, folklore heritage, etc, even as far as the laws, morals and customs which are deeply ingrained in the nature of an ethnic or national temperament.

As part of the detailed undertakings in connection with a monument or site, the action of preserving or enhancing the cultural and natural heritage tends nowadays to widen its horizon. Protection is given not only to a monument, but to an entire historic district. We no longer protect a particular species of animal, we wish to preserve in its entirety the whole of the ecosystem in which this species is to be found.

Referring only to the recent past, international action has been undertaken through the use of an increasingly comprehensive array of international legal instruments and standards. After the Hague Conventions of 1899 and 1907 and the Washington Pact of 1935, other standards have been adopted, notably the Convention establishing the measures to be taken to prohibit and prevent the illicit import, export and transfer of ownership of cultural property (1970) and the Convention on the protection of the Earth's heritage and our cultural and natural heritage (1972). Various recommendations addressed to member States on particular aspects of the preservation of natural heritage have been adopted.

Since the launching in 1960 of the first international campaign aimed at safeguarding the monuments of Nubia, which has now attained its final objective – the preservation of the temples on the Island of Philae – the activities of the Organisation, which had at first been on a fairly modest scale, have never ceased to grow larger. It is relevant to mention here the measures taken for the preservation of Venice, the restoration and enhancement of the site of Mohenjo-Daro (Pakistan) and Borobudur (Indonesia); the restoration and improvement of the monuments of the Cuzco-Puno region (Peru); the preparation of guideline schemes for Fez (Morocco) and for the preservation of the cultural and natural heritage of the Katmandu valley; the preservation and enhancement of the monuments of Ethiopia.

The protection and enhancement of the cultural heritage throughout the world will be encouraged by improving methods and perfecting new techniques of conservation, the establishment of national systems of stocktaking, increasing the number of museums and conservation laboratories and reinforcing the resources and means available for training specialists in conservation.

The Art of Living: An Education to be Given

In respect of many environmental problems, it can be said that, taken as a whole, the world today is only in the first stage of the search for solutions. Certainly, some brand new, and ecologically sound theories have been perfected, and also some strict regulations, to assist in solving some of the more urgent problems. On the other hand, the question of attitudes, values and human behaviour still remains. Amongst other beliefs held and attitudes adopted by modern man, the failure to perceive the state and degradation of the environment is the root cause of behaviour which is reflected in pollution, waste of energy and the destruction of nature. As far as the Earth is concerned, and the mechanisms which maintain life, there is no universal ethic in existence capable of guiding the attitudes and behaviour of individuals and societies in a direction compatible with the place and the critical role assigned to humanity in the realm of the biosphere.

In a general way, there are no teaching programmes currently available aimed at ensuring that education on the environment will be systematically assured from the earliest age either within or outside the framework of the traditional school system. 'The environment' could not be considered to be a subject on the same footing, for example, as mathematics, biology or languages. Emphasis should be placed on the interdisciplinary character of education on the environment, which implies that it should form an integral part of each of the subjects taught in school.

The United Nations Conference on the Environment, held in Stockholm in 1972, clearly expressed this concern for education on the environment to be made general, and recommended the establishment of 'an international interdisciplinary educational programme, for teaching either in or out of school, on the environment, covering every grade of teaching and aimed at everyone, young people or adults, aimed at giving them an awareness of the simple action they could take, within the limits of their capabilities, to control and protect their environment'.

The most recent UNESCO initiative on the subject is therefore the programme for general education on the environment, which was launched as a result of the recommendation of the United Nations Conference on the Environment, and given its final details in collaboration with PNUE. The aim of the new programme is to mobilise all the resources which the Secretariat has available at its disposal in this field, to establish collaboration with the other institutions of the United Nations and the competent international bodies, and also to work out overall guidelines for carrying out a common international programme aimed at promoting education on the environment.

NATIONAL AND INTERNATIONAL STRATEGIES FOR THE NATURAL ENVIRONMENT

R E BOOTE

The word 'strategy' is used so widely that its true meaning has been obscured. Originally it was a military term but has become part of the vocabulary of the multi-national industries, commerce and government, where it is liberally used in relation to economic and land-use planning. I define a strategy as a means of utilising resources in ways which are most favourable to the achievements of specified goals.

Having defined the meaning of a strategy we must now consider why strategies for the natural environment are particularly relevant now, and what dangers we face if we do not have them. Before the industrial revolution both our population and use of resources were comparatively low and no strategy was required to sustain the needs of the people. However, in the twentieth century the expectations of the developed countries have risen dramatically and the people in the Third World will inevitably demand a similar standard of living to the Americans, Europeans and Japanese. The pressure upon our biosphere – for energy, food, land and minerals – is increasing and will continue to do so as the population of the developing countries escalates along with the material expectations of the industrialised nations.

Technology has developed at an alarming rate – between 1859 and 1979 we have seen engineering masterpieces such as Brunel's 'Great Eastern' totally eclipsed by the development of the microprocessor. As technology becomes more sophisticated, the erosion of finite resources accelerates with demand. The need for a strategy is self-evident – we must achieve a balance between growth and conserving both our resources and the natural environment, which is so often disturbed by exploitation. The management of resources should integrate the key environmental, economic and social considerations and produce a satisfactory equilibrium between man's conflicting demands.

The exact form which a strategy takes – documents, plans, computerised records and systems, charts, and any combinations of these methods of data collection – is of second order importance. What is vital, and must permeate all strategies, are the main goals to be sought.

A strategy can only be worthwhile if it leads to results which are more valuable than those which are likely to be achieved without it. I will start by describing certain strategies with which I am acquainted and from them deduce some of the ingredients needed to develop strategies for the natural environment.

Some Strategies

The strategies I have chosen to outline briefly are:

A World Conservation Strategy[1] prepared by the International Union for Conservation of Nature and Natural Resources (IUCN) (backed by United Nations Environment Programme (UNEP) and World Wildlife Fund (WWF));

The Nature Conservancy Council's strategy[2] for its work in Great Britain;

The Scottish Development Department National Planning Guidelines[3];

The South-East England Strategy[4];

Agriculture and Countryside in the UK; and

International Legislation and Resolutions.

World Conservation Strategy of IUCN[1]

This will shortly be published worldwide and is of direct relevance to the Landscape Architect. It has become an urgent need because of the remorseless diminution of the basic resource of land throughout the world, the degradation of habitats, and the loss of wildlife, which are so vital to our own survival as well as to the quality of our lives.

The aim of the WCS is to identify those species and ecosystems which require urgent measures for their conservation; to define

effective preventative or remedial action (by governments, inter-governmental bodies and non-governmental bodies); and to propose priorities for action.

The theme of the Strategy is that conservation is the key to sustained development; a subsequent version will concentrate on the interconnection with other major influences such as poverty, economic growth, population, the consumption of energy and raw materials, inappropriate technologies and the satisfaction of basic human needs.

The three main functions of the Strategy are: to provide UNEP, WWF and other interested organisations with a global appraisal and plan for the protection, maintenance and rational use of the planet's wildlife; to enable IUCN to decide its programme of action; and to advise WWF on the most effective ways of utilising funds.

The broad approach of the WCS will enable more specific programmes to be derived from it, consisting of high priority projects, and facilitate the allocation of resources to them to ensure optimal use. The WCS is an ongoing document, to be reviewed every three years at the General Assembly of the IUCN.

IUCN will be consulting very widely within the United Nations (UN) 'family' and with many other international and national bodies to ensure that it is properly advised. The impetus for other bodies to develop strategies in relation to the world's major environmental issues will be further reinforced by the implementation of the WCS. And for those national and local bodies with responsibility for resource conservation and other environmental activities, the WCS will be a spur to the development of their own strategies. It is, therefore, timely to examine one such national strategy, that of the body responsible for nature conservation in Great Britain.

Nature Conservancy Council

The NCC has been evolving a strategy to foster nature conservation – its statutory aim since its foundation in 1973[5] – based on site and species safeguard and advice on nature conservation, both of which depend upon scientific and professional knowledge and on using the full support of the voluntary movement.[2] These activities are integrated at the GB, country and regional levels of the organisation; they reflect the involvement of the NCC and its predecessors since 1949 in the planning and management of land and water – both rural and urban.

Britain is a small, densely populated island on which the demands for land are very high. Inevitably sites of high value to nature conservation have to compete with commercially orientated land uses such as forestry, agriculture and housing. In 'A Nature Conservation Review',[6] the NCC has identified 735 sites of National Nature Reserve status which should have a primacy of use for nature conservation, but these only occupy 950,000 hectares, about 4% of the land surface of Great Britain. It is, therefore, important that the conservation of important wildlife habitats should be regarded as a land use in its own right, and that those wishing to alter any of these areas must justify the need to do so as well as the choice of location for their activities.

But nature conservation cannot be fostered just by establishing nature reserves or designating Sites of Special Scientific Interest over which there is some consultation. It has to permeate the whole environment. Some of the factors which the NCC has therefore to take into account in conserving natural habitats and species of flora and fauna include, for example, food and timber production; maintaining water supplies; providing minerals; enhancing and maintaining landscape; providing leisure facilities; public health requirements; and enhancing the living environment. Nature conservation must be integrated into other land uses if wildlife is to flourish in areas which are not formally protected. It is for this reason that the NCC advises other bodies at various levels, such as planning, decision making and operations, and seeks to persuade them of the need to integrate nature conservation measures into other land uses. An integrated land-use strategy is, we believe, an essential element in all countries. And a lead in this direction has been given by Scotland.

National Planning Guidelines for Scotland

The genesis for the National Planning Guidelines (NPG)[3] can be found in the 1972 Report[7] of the Select Committee on Scottish Affairs – 'Land Resource Use in Scotland'. This recommended a structure plan for Scotland to strike a balance between too specific and rigid guidelines on the one hand, and, on the other, an insufficiency of them so that there are excessive claims and insufficient information for developers. The Committee's view was that in the past there had been unsufficient guidelines.

The first NPG was published by the Scottish Development Department (SDD) in 1974, called 'Coastal Planning Guidelines'. In 1977, three more were published, dealing with large industrial sites and rural conservation; petrochemical developments; and the working of aggregates. More recently an NPG has been published on the location of major shopping developments. These guidelines are supported by SDD circulars, and land-use summary sheets dealing with a wide range of particular factors (eleven at the time of writing). The third sheet to appear was on nature conservation, illustrating its importance in land-use planning.

The guidelines deal first with general principles and then give specific guidance on selected topics. In general they relate to developments involving Scottish issues on which planning authorities, other agencies and developers might feel the need for guidance. The gradual integration of these guidelines into the planning 'bloodstream' in Scotland has led the Secretary of State to require planning authorities to notify him *only* about those applications for planning permission likely to raise nationally important issues. One example in relation to the natural environment is that any proposal which would affect the status of a site in Scotland included in 'A Nature Conservation Review'[6] should be referred for consideration to the Secretary of State.

Of particular relevance to landscape architects is the NPG for 'Large Industrial Sites and Rural Conservation'. It shows how a balance can be struck between conserving good agricultural land and safeguarding nature conservation interests while promoting major industrial investment. The NPG is strengthened by the identification of particular rural resources such as agricultural land, nature conservation sites, forestry areas, national park direction areas and so on. Most importantly, the NPG refers to those areas illustrated on the map as having special characteristics which implies *a general presumption in favour of them*. These NPGs are helping to give more precision to objectives and offer a number of benefits of general significance which are dealt with later.

Strategic Plan for the South East

The South East of England, which includes London, is perhaps one of the most complex areas for strategic planning in the world. It is the largest of the English regions, and the diversity and resilience of its economy provide a substantial part of the strength of the nation. Despite a number of significant problems – population and migration, employment, transport infrastructure, housing, land and development – it retains strength, flexibility, vitality and, of considerable importance, continuing potential for growth. The 'natural environment' of the South East is largely man-made but through the weight of public opinion has retained many natural components, eg deciduous woodland, demonstrating its value to a large urban population wishing to enjoy rural surroundings.

The South East was the subject of a strategic development plan produced in 1970.[4] This was reviewed in 1976 and again by the Government and the regional and local authorities concerned in 1978.[8] It is now the intention to re-examine and revise this strategy when necessary in the light of regular monitoring by the Government and the Regional Planning and Economic Planning Bodies for the area.

The 1978 review takes account of the Government's current view of the trends and issues affecting the region's development and the problems and opportunities they are likely to create. For example, it is expected that there will continue to be development pressures from a rising population, although these will not be evenly distributed across the region; that the economy will continue to develop from the established range of activities and skills within the region, and will continue to benefit from its geographical advantages; and that, apart from the decline of some of the Upper London Docks, there are few

sectors of the regional economy where decline is likely to have a profound structural effect. Transport systems will remain critical (air, sea and land), with substantial increases in traffic of all kinds expected during the next 15 years. While the region's other services are adequate, there will be a need to maintain continuous improvement in their quality.

This strategy has elements similar to those found in the Scottish National Planning Guidelines, eg guidance on trends and relative priorities. The strategy relating to land provides for a slow change in the existing pattern of use, with enough land suitable for development to meet foreseeable demand. It sees a need for restraint to protect such elements as mineral deposits, natural environments and water supplies. No specific time scale is set to the strategy and its policies are not inflexible.

It is obvious from the SPG and SE England strategy that they must operate within the framework of national economic policies.

Agriculture and Countryside

I have briefly discussed the industrial revolution and its implications for the increasing use of our natural resources. However, it is arguable that the agricultural revolution had an even greater effect; it transformed civilisations which were previously nomadic, using hunting and gathering as their means of obtaining food, into more structured, stable societies which remained in one village, had an excess of food which could be stored and had time to follow other pursuits. The present primitive state of nomadic tribes is an illustration of how important the agricultural revolution was to future development. The agricultural system is still basic to modern society and, in spite of the growth of industry, it remains the most significant of man's utilisation and interference with natural forces. Where man has failed to understand these forces, and sought short term gains without nurturing the soil, disasters such as the massive erosion in the American Dust Bowl have been the result. Against this background it is ironic that only a handful of countries have anything resembling a strategic approach to agriculture.

The UK has come near to a strategy for its agriculture. The latest attempt was earlier this year in the form of a White Paper 'Farming and the Nation'.[9] This document reviews medium-term prospects for the agricultural industry and defines where the national interest lies. It sets out the Government's approach to policy to provide a firm basis for farmers' own decisions.

'Farming and the Nation' reviews the demand for food in the UK; production from home agriculture in relation to consumption; the UK approach to the Common Agricultural Policy, and the currency arrangement known as the 'green pound'; and reviews the three major factors of production: viz labour, land and capital. The Government concludes that a sustained increase in agricultural net product is in the national interest and can be achieved without undue impact on the environment. Its policies will pay due regard to rural land uses during this expansion. The White Paper sets out no precise targets and is a statement of intent rather than a specific strategy.

Nevertheless, informed opinion recognises that much more is required. In Britain, the Centre for Agricultural Strategy (established in 1975 at the University of Reading) is attempting to define these requirements. The Country Landowners' Association is pressing for a major inquiry into rural land use to provide a coherent national strategy for the place of the countryside in future social and economic development. The Government's Countryside Review Committee has published a main Report[10] and Topic Papers on key subjects.[11] These have formed the basis for informed discussion by numerous official and voluntary bodies leading to the elements of a strategy for the countryside. In fact, a response from the Association of District Councils (representing 333 Councils in England and Wales) is a paper entitled 'Rural Recovery: Strategy for Survival', in which the Association emphasises that the problems of town and country are inseparable and 'must be viewed in the context of the Government's overall *national economic* and *social strategy* . . .'.

International Legislation and Resolutions

The increasing number of conventions is a reflection of the interest in discussing and formulating international strategies. These go under a variety of names; some are legally binding and others more by way of exhortation, but basically they are a response to the recognition that many problems which face states can only be solved by joining forces with other states – agreeing on objectives and specifying ways to achieve these, both the action that needs to be taken by each state separately to a common goal and those measures which can only be taken by acting in harmony.

Conventions are, in effect, strategies for particular sectors of human interest and represent the emergent efforts of the forces tending to create a world strategy of government. Some, such as those for control of the movement of oil and its pollution, have wide repercussions in economic, social and environmental affairs, with their success or failure having locally frequent impacts and publicity. Others such as the Ramsar Convention[12] are concerned with global problems having an essential natural unity – in this case to ensure that wetlands are conserved, particularly because so many of our migratory birds depend on them. Another important world convention is the Washington Convention[13] which recognises the need to avoid extinction of species, and specifies rules to regulate trade that puts species in danger of extinction.

There are also conventions at what is known internationally as the Regional Level – such as Europe. As well as formulating conventions such as the Conservation of European Wildlife and Natural Habitats (which is expected to be signed shortly), the Council of Europe has also used another method – Resolutions in its Committee of Ministers that specify agreed goals and encourage member states to take the necessary action to achieve that end. Several of these resolutions have relevance to the protection of the landscape even though they are drafted principally with wildlife in mind. Whether legally binding like conventions, or merely stating desirable goals, all these international instruments are truly strategic in their effect.

In addition to the growing number of conventions there are conferences, seminars and working parties all over the world which seek to devise means of formulating strategies.

(In fact, one International Conference on the Environment takes place this month – September 1979 – in Belgium, with UNESCO and IUCN support, to examine 'Methods and Strategy for Integrated Development'.)

Appraisal

The common features which emerge from the summary examples of actual operational strategies are that they seek to relate activities at levels below their own (world, regional, local) with wider objectives. It is necessary to have a coherent strategy not only on a broad basis but at all levels of government, industry and elsewhere, ideally harmonising action in every sector. Strategies also enable issues to be identified and their implications understood more clearly.

An effective strategy requires a *comprehensive approach* and inter-related environmental issues should be assessed in a *unified manner* rather than in isolation. The use of resources and quality of the environment should be optimised by *defining priorities* clearly and implementing them through efficient integrated planning and management. Obviously, the processes of *consultation* are much more meaningful if in the formulation and development of strategies they result in *participation and collaborative action*, in contrast to some of the relatively mechanical processes set up in recent years.

IUCN's World Conservation Strategy[1] obviously relates these requirements to the management of the world's natural living resources on which our survival and quality of life ultimately depend. It prescribes priorities for action at all levels and has been prepared through collaboration with experts throughout the world. It is intended to be developed through continuous consultation with international bodies and governments.

The NCC's strategy for nature conservation certainly reflects these principles but while the NCC can conserve some areas itself, it can only ensure the proper safeguard of adequate key habitats and species through the work of other bodies and with public support. Thus its primary thesis – of infusing nature conservation policies and practices into the operations of those organisations whose functions affect the flora and fauna of these Isles – is of outstanding strategic importance. It is indeed a very pervasive thesis and will, in time, have far-reaching effects on attitudes and activities relating to the natural environment.

The SDD National Planning Guidelines seek to reconcile potentially conflicting land uses in the national interest. They are increasingly comprehensive in range and certainly exert a unifying influence on the approaches of local authorities and developers to the planning and management of land. They identify priorities for certain levels of responsibility and are the subject of continuing consultation. The Guidelines have a pervasive ethos of resource conservation and optimal use.

The SE England strategy for development lacks adequate attention to the availability of natural resources. In its concern to meet short-term demands, it shows the characteristics of much political activity and gives insufficient thought to conserving valuable resources for future generations. But the strategy is becoming comprehensive, it is

relating many interests, and it is the basis of much on-going consultation as its various features become ripe for action.

The policies put forward in 'Farming and the Nation'[9] are not backed up by a strategy for reconciling the needs of food production with potentially conflicting goals, such as those involved in the increasing conflict throughout Europe between land drainage for agriculture and the conservation of our diminishing, biologically-vital wetlands. In this country the moves to harmonise nature conservation and water management are exemplified in the Conservation and Land Drainage Guidelines to be issued by the Water Space Amenity Commission and the work of the County Farming and Wildlife Advisory Groups. However, national and EEC priorities remain to be defined and substantial financial incentives are given for drainage for single-purpose aims which often conflict with other national policies.

International conventions for wildlife conservation bring benefits as they are more effectively implemented. However, they are often ignored by those nations or individuals who feel a strong economic or social pressure to continue with activities which have been proscribed by the convention (eg whaling, flushing of oil tanker ballast).

All strategies have potential shortcomings. A strategy can become an end in itself, rather than a means to achieving a desired goal; it can become a substitute for real action. And strategies could become monolithic and inflexible if the dynamic of our physical environment is not fully recognised – that changes are constantly taking place and that, to be effective, any strategy should be sensitive to these changes. Strategies for the natural environment and its resources need to take account of the diversity of many countries with differing geography, attitudes to conservation and political backgrounds; for this reason they need to be flexible. They should also complement each other, not be inhibitory, and give a dimension above and beyond the sum of their individual parts.

Authorities

Quite clearly the implementation of a strategy involves the existence of appropriate strategic authorities. The Centre for Agricultural Strategy referred to earlier, the centres and 'think-tanks' so typical of military, industrial and economic bodies, intellectual power-houses in universities, and organisations such as the Regional Councils for Sport and Recreation in England responsible for the development of regional recreational strategies, do not meet the pre-requisites of a strategic authority. Its responsibility is to determine aims and policies and take key decisions, in particular over the broad allocation of resources.

One example of this type of authority is the Bundesbank of West Germany which, probably more than any other body, has demonstrated a capacity successfully to devise and maintain an international financial strategy. The European Economic Communities are also emerging as strategic bodies. Their directives and regulations provide frames of reference for national policies and international relationships, not only in Europe but throughout the world.

IUCN would never pretend to be an authority in these ways – the power to implement its strategy will flow from the decisions of its governmental and non-governmental members which subscribe to its aims. But it will have much moral persuasion through its survey and monitoring work and the alertness of its members, both gaining increasing significance as our natural resource base crumbles. Similarly, the success of the NCC's strategy depends largely on the decisions of others in central and local government and the landowning and farming community. Inevitably this is a feature of most strategies for specific sectors of the natural environment including Conventions and those measures for agriculture. In contrast the general strategy for south-east England has the advantage of including all the key levels of government in those responsible for its preparation. It *could* be very significant to the future of the natural environment in the South East, as well as having the potential – not yet realised – of being an exemplar. The SDD National Planning Guidelines may prove to be of international importance. If the ideas in these documents continue to be developed, coupled with the powers of the Secretary of State to enforce them as a strategic authority, they could become a model for later strategies.

The full potential of any strategy can only be realised if it is well co-ordinated and administered, making the most effective use of modern systems of communication, collation, retrieval and the dissemination of knowledge. Despite the marvellous techniques now available, our performance is very imperfect in these respects. In addition, it is essential for strategic authorities to avoid the inertias of bureaucracy, whether in government, industry or voluntary bodies. To counteract these problems an authority should relate its guidelines to realistic assessments about the efforts and inputs available and maintain continuous processes of consultation and monitoring of performances.

The deficiencies in the various strategies should not, however, obscure their value and importance. Their successes and failures may hold particular lessons for pursuing future strategies – some of which are already being realised for the natural environment.

Having said all this in favour of the concept, and of those successful strategies to which I can personally testify, we must be quite ruthless about the criteria for success. Do they help towards *better* decisions and *better* results? Are they referred to positively by decision makers to aid them in their work? Is their influence continuous?

Strategies and the Landscape Architect

What then are the particular values of strategies to the landscape architect?

The landscape architect seeks to create a better environment and to integrate the planning management and use of resources to this end. He, more than most, knows the importance of the principles of comprehensiveness, unity and quality. He knows how easily environmental schemes can be wrecked or spoiled if they are out of economic or social context. He knows, too, the problem of dealing with a wide range of disparate bodies whose communication is often non-existent. Thus, for the member of the Landscape Institute and of IFLA, the question is not whether there should be strategies, but his rôle in formulating and implementing them.

The landscape architect has to comprehend the whole range of social, economic and physical factors which make up the total backcloth to life in the community. He should know not only the requirements of his own profession, but also appreciate the contribution to planning and management by other professions and be capable of creating a synthesis of related concepts and data. He needs to interpret assessments of the ability of land and water to sustain, without detriment, the uses to which they are put. Obviously in recent years he has had to take into account the knowledge emerging from the rapid spread of ecology and other environmental sciences as well as the views of many protest groups concerned with the misuse of natural resources.

At top level of operation, the landscape architect should be able to identify relevant principles, apply them to complex masses of information, and then to formulate policies and strategies. At regional level, he should contribute to the shaping of national policies and be able to take into account the special characteristics and resources of the region in a more precise definition of aims, policies, priorities and resources to be allocated. This work will frequently be focused in a strategic document or plan. At local levels, the landscape architect is concerned with the detailed planning and management of the environment, with particular emphasis on creative design. This requires an understanding of the differing functions at other levels.

But the creative work of the landscape architect and planner demands a sensitivity to the aspirations of people – and those aspects of the surroundings which improve the quality of their lives.

Peoples and Ethos

Fundamentally and inevitably, strategies reflect a philosophy or ethos, but at all levels these are often the subject of bitter conflict. One helpful force is that, as we complete the first century of widespread mass education (however poor) and now have the potential of instant communication (even if it is not used properly), there are vast resources of human talent to be tapped and encouraged. And these are creating demands for personal and local expression of responsibilities of a scale and intensity unparalleled in history. As more local automony is obtained, so national governments and international bodies will be forced to construct strategies which fulfil practical needs at differing levels, to foster devolution and delegation, and to ensure a broad equity of treatment throughout their areas. Thus, we see everywhere trends towards forms of world government and multi-national collaboration – sectorially and geographically – while at the same time movements for local autonomy and for participation at the 'grass roots' grow ever more intense. And these two great world-wide trends are perfectly reconciled within the coherence which *could* be obtained from national and international strategies. It should be possible, although not easy, to devise strategies at European, national, regional and local levels for the environment. In fact, many governments, industries and other bodies already have some forms of strategy for specific aspects, as I have already indicated. Yet a strategy for the fundamental platform of our lives – land – is too

important to delay any longer.

As stated in the Shell film 'Environment in the Balance' (a classic for ten years and now – from 1979 – a new production), historically speaking we are in the 'stone age of technology'. Technology is developing faster than ever before – particularly in the field of communication and data processing. One of the most basic questions we need to consider is whether we allow technology to develop apace and possibly radically alter our natural heritage or whether we develop a strategy outlining the uses to which we apply the modern tools of society whilst retaining our resources for future generations. So for members of IFLA involved with strategies, I would commend the following four qualities[14] to form the pillars of their ethos:

Integrity: to infuse ecological concepts and true concern for the environment into one's lifestyle;

Humanity: to conserve the earth's resources and share them more equitably with all life on earth, today and tomorrow;

Determination: to arrest pollution and squalor, and to promote quality in one's surroundings;

Judgement: to choose wisely between competing and conflicting claims and values in order to promote the trusteeship of society for the environment.

In conclusion, our aim is to work with nature, achieving a balance between our demands for energy and minerals and our reliance upon living systems for breathable air, drinkable water and surroundings which enhance the quality of our lives. Although these needs are often in conflict with each other it is essential that a satisfactory equilibrium be found and this requires national and international strategies for the natural environment.

Based on such an ethos as I have postulated, I believe that these would lead to an improvement of our physical and social resources – to the benefit of mankind everywhere.

Acknowledgement and Caveat

I am grateful to the following for their observations on this paper: Dr P. A. Gay, Dr D. A. Goode, D. Diamond, D. M. Rowland, M. J. Rush and D. K. J. Withrington.

As I am closely involved in the work of the International Union for Conservation of Nature and Natural Resources (as a Vice-President), the Countryside Review Committee (a member) and the Nature Conservancy Council (Director General), it is not always easy to separate my own thoughts from those of the various teams in which it is my privilege to serve. Nevertheless, nothing in this paper should be construed as committing the Nature Conservancy Council or any other of the bodies with which I am associated, nor any of my colleagues, other than where there is a specific referenced citation.

References

[1] International Union for Conservation of Nature and Natural Resources. *A world conservation strategy*. Morges (Switzerland). To be published in September 1979.

[2] Nature Conservancy Council.
1975 *First report.* London, HMSO. (HC 499)
1976 *Second report.* London, HMSO. (HC 44)
1977 *Third report.* London, HMSO. (HC 53)
1978 *Fourth report.* London, HMSO. (HC 646)

[3] Scottish Development Department. 1974 *National planning guidelines.* Edinburgh.

[4] Ministry of Housing and Local Government. 1970 *Strategic plan for the South East.* London, HMSO.

[5] Nature Conservancy Council Act 1973, c.54.

[6] Ratcliffe, D. A. ed, 1977. *A nature conservation review: the selection of biological sites of national importance to nature conservation in Britain.* Cambridge University Press for the Nature Conservancy Council and the Natural Environment Research Council.

[7] House of Commons. Select Committee on Scottish Affairs. 1972 *Land resource use in Scotland: vol 1: report and proceedings.* London, HMSO. (HC 511-i)

[8] Department of the Environment.
1976 *Strategy for the South East: 1976 review.* London, HMSO.
1978 *Strategic plan for the South East: review: government statement.* London, HMSO.

[9] Ministry of Agriculture, Fisheries and Food *and others.* 1979 *Farming and the nation.* London, HMSO. (Cmnd. 7458)

[10] Countryside Review Committee. 1976 *The countryside: problems and policies: a discussion paper.* London, HMSO.

[11] Countryside Review Committee.
1977 *Rural communities: a discussion paper.* London, HMSO. (Topic paper No. 1)
1977 *Leisure and the countryside: a discussion paper.* London, HMSO. (Topic paper No. 2)
1978 *Food production and the countryside: a discussion paper.* London, HMSO. (Topic paper No. 3)

[12] Convention on Wetlands of International Importance Especially as Waterfowl Habitat, Ramsar (Iran), 1971. 1976 London, HMSO. (Cmnd. 6465)

[13] Convention on International Trade in Endangered Species of Wild Fauna and Flora, Washington, 1973. 1976 London, HMSO. (Cmnd. 6647)

[14] Arvill, R. 1976 *Man and environment: crisis and the strategy of choice*. 4th ed. Harmondsworth, Penguin.

NATURE CONSERVATION, NATURE IMITATION AND THE LANDSCAPE ARCHITECT

PROFESSOR DONALD KEUNEN

The species Man, *homo sapiens*, developed in an environment about which we can make some reasonable conjectures. The place was probably tropical Africa, the time scale about two to three million years. It was not the tropical forest but a more savannah-like type of landscape where man developed. One of his characteristic properties, his bipedal way of moving from one place to another, is certainly more convenient in somewhat open country than in dense forest.

Human culture could develop because of the structure of his hands. All other animals we know, either present or extinct, who tend to a bipedal way of living, show a more or less pronounced atrophy of the front pair of legs.

Besides the development of the hands the sophisticated method of communication was essential, which not only made concerted efforts, such as hunting, very effective but also considerably increased the capacity to learn, not only from one's own experience but also from collective experience.

As time progressed the dominance of man over other animals and over his environment as a whole became more and more apparent. Of course every animal changes his environment, by taking food, by producing refuse, by digging, nest-building and by dying in it. The characteristic of man is that he does so on a very large scale because of his use of instruments. In later times chemical industry has added xenobiotic substances to the environment. It is worth mentioning that when we speak about pollution the cause we are concerned with is chemical substances, but the real problem is, of course, the interference with some biological process.

About 15,000 years ago agriculture was invented, and that made the impact of man on his environment very much greater, and as his numbers grew and spreading continued the results began to have unexpected consequences. Most important is that certain effects of the process tended to become irreversible. Technological inventions made life easier and more comfortable and made concentrations of individuals feasible which, biologically speaking, are impossible.

At present large numbers of us are entirely dependent upon the achievements to technology, and all large concentrations of population live in a very fragile relation with the areas around them, in particular where access to food is concerned. Transport is vital and a few days of interruption can create havoc.

Most of our everyday thinking is concerned with ourselves and our immediate surroundings. We have not learned to think in long term and the concept of planning as a concerted effort is a comparatively new element in the history of mankind. Due to our technological might, the impact of what we do, however, does have great influence on what is far off, both in space and in time.

The cutting of hillside forests to increase agricultural surface can lead to serious disturbance of the water regime of a much larger area, mainly because the water now runs off the soil and does not drain through it, with consequent drying up of wells elsewhere, erosion, and silting up of deltas and consequent development of malaria.

The floods in Florence, some years ago, were, initially, the results of the wars between Rome and Carthage. The Punic wars were the time when the Romans cut down their forests for timber to build their fleet. There are many more of such examples, and some of you may be thinking of your own country under similar circumstances in the 16th and 17th century.

Technology, in every way, dominates our lives. But we can also see that in this completely technological world in which we, here, are living, the wish to be in contact with nature still persists. Trees along city streets, plants in the home and garden and on the balconies of blocks of flats, and the urge to get out of the town on free days are evidence of our needs. The persistence of out-of-town migration, in spite of the hardships of endless road blockages and queues for public transport underlines the strength of our urge.

It all goes to demonstrate that we are not adapted to the urban way of life and that the conurbation, or megalopolis of modern times is in direct conflict with our very nature.

It is in this context that conservationists and landscape architects come to find their allotted place in the way of things. They are both concerned about the recent developments and want to do something about it. They are both aware of the fact that the structure of man does not allow him to develop fully in an environment which is purely man-made, and they are both concerned with long-term problems of our way of living.

Their approach, however, seems to be quite different. Without wanting to make a caricature of either of the groups, we can say that conservationists primarily want to protect, to conserve, and to do as little as possible. They want to leave the area concerned alone, except for those activities needed to counterbalance the unavoidable influence of man.

Landscape planners, however, generally have to begin at the other end. They either find an area where the natural elements have been destroyed, and where they must begin to introduce living elements, or they are confronted with a more or less destructive plan and have to make the best of it.

But there is a further element, and that is that the landscape architect quite often has to be content with something that is not intrinsically natural but only looks nice, which pleases the town dweller, either in his park or his recreation area, while the conservationist wants the specific biological elements to function in their own environment. The conservationist wants to be able to go to an area with his botanical checklist and trapping equipment and to be able to register as many rare species as possible. The landscape planner will show you the comparative result of the initial desolate area, preferably photographed with one or two bulldozers, and then what he has made of it ten years later. It has then become something that is pleasing to the eye and possibly to the ear, it fits the soil and surface structure and in it, of course, natural processes may have helped or have been stimulated.

There is a second fundamental difference between the two. The conservationist will seek the support of recreationists, because he may hope that help will be obtained from that quarter. But in fact he would much rather do without them and the only person he wants to see in the reserve is himself, or his carefully trained assistant.

For the landscape architect, those who seek recreation are his first concern and he must constantly have in mind the problem of accommodating as many of them as circumstances allow.

Now experience has shown that the name *homo sapiens* is not well chosen, and that *insipiens* might, to a certain extent, be nearer to the truth. But a term which is less critical and more descriptive and objective is *homo faber*, the man who makes things. Making things, tools that serve some purpose, is an indomitable urge, and the fact that a certain amount of work has gone into something makes that object, *ipso facto*, valuable.

I believe this may be behind the appreciation of certain products of modern art. A lot of junk, which has lost its value completely, is welded together and put upon a pedestal; it thereby becomes a work of art. It has acquired a certain value, not only artistically but also in money, because someone has done something. For futurologists it might be worthwhile to consider what new forms of art might be the consequence of new techniques. Progressively more use of the incinerator to get rid of things, might reduce the options considerably.

One of the reasons why appreciation of natural areas is generally so low is that no great human effort has gone into their establishment. Besides it will retain most of its value by *not* doing something, and that, in the minds of many people, is something negative.

We observe some of this also in the spending of public money. Our cultural heritage has been supported, for quite some time, by public money from governments. It was the work of our ancestors which was being saved. Our natural heritage is much less worthy of support. It interferes with useful activities such as road building, agriculture, water impoundment for energy production, etc. Just think of public opinion concerning the killing of an animal or the cutting down of an old tree, as compared to the destruction of a minor painting of some second-rate artist.

The landscape architect in his profession, which he has chosen because of his inclination, is prone to act. His work follows in the wake of destructors, and he is there to either correct them, or possibly prevent them from doing their damage. But he must make sure that he does not fall into the error of thinking that doing something is indispensable under all circumstances.

I will give you two examples of the kind of thinking I am worried about, both from the Netherlands. I quote these, not to ridicule the profession as such, but as a warning where professional zeal may lead.

In 1932 the Zuiderzee was closed by a 40 km long dam. Consequently the brackish water was washed out and in the remaining freshwater lake, now called the IJsselmeer, a few large polders were constructed from 20,000 to 50,000 hectares each. The first of these was nearly entirely used for agricultural land, but as time progressed other land uses became more and more important. Gradually more trees were planted on less fertile parts, recreation was stimulated by appropriate design of the landscape, and then industry was introduced. Finally a satellite town for Amsterdam is now being built in the most south-western part of the last reclaimed polder. Incidentally, there is now much discussion going on whether the last of the planned polders should be made, and if so what to do with it. One of the more serious propositions is to build a new large airport there to replace Schiphol, which has become objectionable, with its heavy traffic load, to the inhabitants who have chosen to go and live near it.

The last polder so far became dry about ten years ago and is now under development. Along the north-western boundary an industrial area was planned. Situated in the centre of the country, accessible by road and water it seemed an ideal place to have such an area. The fact that it was the lowest part of the polder and would therefore require some extra provision, was no problem.

But before these extra provisions were taken care of, soon after the water level for the whole of the polder was stabilised at about 4 metres below the level of the IJsselmeer, it appeared that here was an ideal place for the development of a 'natural area'. It was a large, undisturbed marsh area with small differences in water depth where a diversified vegetation developed, partly open, partly closed and an increasing number of animals, particularly birds which are a prime indication of attractive natural circumstances, and are appreciated both for the professional biologist and the amateur.

Claims were made to set this area aside for conservation, but these were at first refused. After considerable discussion an alternative was suggested. If conservationists wanted a marsh area they could have it. In the centre of the new polder there was an area not particularly good for agriculture, and where no roads had, as yet, been planned. A dam could be put around it and water could be pumped into it at the required level while the further reclaiming of the future industrial area could then continue. Further discussions finally showed that this was not a very attractive plan. It was never officially proposed by anybody in authority, and soon afterwards dropped. Further deliberations led to the conclusion that not all the area was needed for industry and finally the decision was taken in favour of conservation. A large part of the area is now a nature reserve and developing well. It will continue to flourish as long as chemical pollution can be kept at a sufficiently low level.

The second example applies to the Waddenzee. In the early 'seventies a committee was set up by the government to study the possibilities to enclose parts of the Waddenzee as continuation and final act of the struggle of man against the sea in the low countries. The committee had not only engineers, but also agriculturalists, army representatives, general planners, economists and conservationists as members.

Different plans were put before the committee: large scale enclosure, part enclosure, small parts only in different versions and also zero activity. The great questions were technical feasibility, future use of the new polder areas, and comparison of the values in the present situation – mainly fisheries, recreation and conservation values – as compared to the future significance. Plans were made and put before different sub-committees. Large scale enclosure was not really feasible because the costs would be out of all proportion as compared to the possible uses. Possibilities for medium and small plans were considered. Agriculturalists were not interested. At present day prices of agricultural products the costs to acquire it are too high. Economists interested in increase of industrial production were not interested because it was too far away from the economic centre of the country in the west. The army could not use it because there were not sufficiently large tracts of usable soil, even for small scale manoeuvring.

Towns were not wanted there because the existing towns in the north can cope quite well with the expected growth of the population. Particularly in view of the changed demographical expectations – not 20 million but 15 million at the end of the century – no interest was shown.

So then another proposition was put forward. If nobody has any better use for this new area, why not make it into a nature reserve. So there we have come full circle. You have a natural area, quite valuable in spite of growing pollution by Rhine water, you destroy it by putting a dike around it and pumping the water out, and then at great cost you proceed to make it into a – second class – 'nature reserve'.

The plan obviously did not get the support it needed, and the final report of the committee advised to leave the Waddenzee alone as much as possible, except for perhaps a few minor changes. The government accepted the report and for the next few decades, at least, the Netherlands part of the Waddenzee will remain open.

Now let me be quite clear. I am not trying to say that landscape architects as a body are responsible for certain excessive manifestations of individuals. I refuse to feel responsible myself for some of the dicta of even prominent conservationists. I have given these two examples to warn us all against our tendency to do something while we should always first consider the possibility not to do anything at all.

The rôle of the landscape architect can be central if he is prepared to use other people's knowledge and succeeds in establishing a balanced integration of this knowledge in an overall plan.

Whenever ideas are put forward which imply a reduction of a natural area or when such ideas have resulted in activities which have already destroyed such areas, the landscape architect should use his skill to make something better. Better means something where man can find an environment which satisfies his ingrained adaptation to the environment in which the characteristics of his genetic constitution were formed.

We can no longer live in the savannah area, surrounded by trees and forest and predators and parasites, living in caves or just in a temporary lair, hunting in bands, armed with spear and stone. We need artificial caves, we practise agriculture, we use transport other than horseback and cart, but we still need some of our primeval environment. Conservationists may seem to believe that 'back to nature' is the very thing. They have their cars and their electronic watches and many more of the gadgets which we sometimes really can use effectively.

Landscape architects should not pretend to be conservationists. They are not. They should use the notions of the conservationists where they are applicable in a more integrated approach. They can learn from the conservationists. They must be aware of the very essence of man's nature and shape his environment to give him all the opportunities he needs for a full human life. By not interfering where interference opposes man's fundamental requirements he can give the best support to the cause of conservation which so many of us have at heart.

ENVIRONMENTAL IMPACT ANALYSIS

ENVIRONMENTAL IMPACT ANALYSIS MAURICE PICKERING

ENVIRONMENTAL ANALYSIS CLIFFORD TANDY

THE ASSESSMENT OF POLITICAL IMPACTS PROFESSOR A E WEDDLE

ENVIRONMENTAL IMPACT ANALYSIS
MAURICE PICKERING

To speak true, this subject is about civilisation.

We cannot be certain, finally that we, or civilisation, will survive, nor for how long but, man's duty to the mother earth is undisputed, fundamental, to every philosophical system the world has ever known.

Man's understanding of this memory has taken many forms in history.

> 'Nine-strata'd Hissarlik
>   a but forty-metre height
> yet archetype of sung-heights.
> Crux mounded at the node
> gammadion'd castle.
> Within the laughless Megaron
>   the margaron
> beyond echelon'd Skaian
>   the stone
>   the fonted water
>   the fronded wood.'[1]

Mount Fuji, Japan. An idealised view of the beautiful mountain. The moment is eternal, separated from the chronological chain of events.
Photo: Japan National Tourist Organisation. *Fig 1*

Sacred mountains, springs, trees were symbols of the powerful and life giving forces of the earth from which man himself was made.

Soon he learned to appreciate and venerate the created man himself, giving human form to gods and deity to men. Once the adulation had been tasted and found sweet, man desired more, so that gradually the seeking and maintaining of power became the sole object of his existence.

Although the assertive efforts of countless cultures have bequeathed unnumbered monuments, many of greatness and beauty, manifesting much loving skill in their creation, the path was, being earthly, bound to lead to nothing in the end.

> 'But the fruit that accrues to those men of small intelect is finite.'[2]

Ayers Rock in Central Australia. An abruptly intrusive monolith in an empty desert plain. Once sacred to the Aborigines it now boasts thousands of visitors each year, who leave behind them an airstrip, wardens, empty beer cans, orange peel . . .
Photo: The Australian Information Service, London. *Fig 2*

Through all this man has made, for better or worse, an impact on the earth. Until recent times this impact has been limited or localised. The Incas were not affected by the building of Troy, nor were the Bavarian forests. But the port of Liverpool was an effect of Africa and a cause of the United States of America, whereas the tiny atoll of Bikini had immediate and global repercussion.

It is this realisation, of the fragility of the biosphere, that has brought forth the expression of concern for environment and conservation. Complaints about the misuse of land are not all recent.

> 'England, bound in with the triumphant sea,
> whose rocky shore beats back the envious siege
> of watery Neptune, is now bound in with shame,
> with inky blots and rotten parchment bonds.' 16th C[3]

Sydney. The Opera House at Bennelong Point makes an impact on the environment of down-town Sydney as well as on the waterfront.
Photo: The Australian Information Service, London. *Fig 3*

'Things fall apart; the centre cannot hold;
mere anarchy is loosed upon the world.' 19th C[4]

Acapulco, Mexico. The first visitors were attracted by the empty shores near the tiny fishing village. In 1979 you could pay up to $75 a night for a room in a luxury hotel.
Photo: Mexican National Tourist Council. Fig 4

I too have wept for the agony and frustration of it all and asked the question why, if it is in the power of the individual to reason, is the communal intellect so blunted?

There is no ultimate reason why life on earth should not be good, no absolute condemnation to misery. That is of our own making. If we ask any sane individual to express what he wants of life it will invariably have something to do with happiness. Whether he thinks to derive it from riches or service or reputation is of little consequence. Happiness will be at the root of it.

If that is indeed the common aim, why should there be so much disputation?

Society relies fundamentally on duty. I have a duty to treat the other members of the society just as I would have them treat me. If I malign them, I shall be robbed. If I serve them, I shall be served. That at least is the natural justice of the situation but, it has all somehow become reversed so that we all begin to insist on my rights and the other man's duties, instead of my duties and the other man's rights.

In 1754 William Blackstone wrote, in the introduction to his Commentaries on the Laws of England:

'As therefore the creator is a being, not only of infinite power and wisdom, but also of infinite goodness, he has been pleased so to contrive the constitution and frame of humanity, that we should want no other prompter to inquire after and pursue the rule of right, but only our own self-love, that universal principle of action. For he has so intimately connected, so inseparably interwoven the laws of eternal justice with the happiness of each individual, that the latter cannot be attained but by observing the former; and, if the former be punctually obeyed, it cannot but induce the latter. In consequence of which mutual connection of justice and human felicity, he has not perplexed the law of nature with a multitude of abstracted rules and precepts, referring merely to the fitness or unfitness of things, as some have vainly surmised; but has graciously reduced the rule of obedience to this one paternal precept, 'that man should pursue his own true and substantial happiness.'[5]

The competition between good and bad impacts. The tree fails to hold the balance against rubbish during a strike of municipal workers in London. Fig 5

How then is man's substantial happiness to be obtained in practical terms? How might the laws of eternal justice be relevant to our study?

It is illogical to suppose that laws of eternal justice will operate in one part of the universe and not another; apply only to one species rather than the whole. We could not expect for instance that man is subject to one set of laws whilst all other creatures are subject to another.

Only a little observation is necessary to show that man is limited to earth. He comes from a seed fertilised and planted in the earth of the womb. He cannot exist without air, water, light and earth. This last is, of course, converted to suit his digestive need by the action of the previous three elements and contains them all. The apple we eat is earth, modified by the action of air, water and sunlight.

Man is subject to diurnal, lunar and solar cycles just as the other creatures. He is born, grows, reproduces and dies.

He is gregarious.

'The proof that the state is a creation of nature and prior to the individual is that the individual, when isolated, is not self-sufficing; and therefore he is like a part in relation to the whole.'[6]
and more recently,

'The concept of the public welfare is broad and inclusive . . . The values it represents are spiritual and physical, aesthetic as well as monetary. It is within the power of the legislature to determine that the community should be beautiful as well as healthy, spacious as well as clean, well balanced as well as carefully patrolled.'[7]

Whilst there is much sound philosophy to support a thesis of care for the earth and its resources, we find little in current practice that would encourage complacency.

The hope. The Birth of Venus by Sandro Botticelli. Fig 6

The reality. A Mediterranean Prospect by Peter Brookes.
(Radio Times, 12th April 1979.) Fig 7

The confusion by which Habermas[8] is supposed to be a leading thinker of our time, whereas his efforts seem to me to be to invent further justifications for supporting the present social order, offers neither hope nor reason.

The fact that John Kenneth Galbraith[9], self-confessed acolyte of John Maynard Keynes, finds that the end of his economic theories, upon which successive governments have founded their jaded fiscal programmes, lands him in an 'age of uncertainty', is sufficient to persuade me of their invalidity. Any economic system which fails to acknowledge work on land to produce wealth as fundamental, is bound to be a travesty.

If the power seekers seem to devise monetary measures to suit their own ends at the expense of the long term good, it must be no surprise to find that vociferous opposition arises in an attempt to redress the balance. Here a further foolishness presumes that unless a man joins himself to one side he must belong to the other. No room exists in the minds of the protagonists for the notion that there may be a third point that would bring matters into balance.

No criticism is implied of those who, like Fraser-Darling[10], Aldo Leopold[11] and Fred Bossleman[12] among many others who have drawn attention to what is wrong. God knows there is plenty, but I shall resist the facile course of rehearsing yet again the list of indiscretions committed by government and industry against the biosphere, because you will all know it well enough, and confine myself to this point:

In the end there must be a political response to public opinion.

If a nation changes its mind then its government cannot long continue the former policies, however it plans to survive. Now I say that the groundswell of environmental opinion which, in this decade, has grown to the point of producing lip-service at least from some political leaders bears careful scrutiny. A strike in Sydney, NSW, by workers to prevent the destruction of trees and open space on the harbour front in 1973(?) was salutary. The emergence of 'Ecology Parties' in France and Britain to campaign for electoral representation follows the thinking of 'Blueprint for Survival'[13] published in 1972.

Established politicians might hope to brush off this irritant but when the President, in his inaugural speech, invites the most profligate nation in the world to conserve energy, we may be sure that something is getting through.

Stephen Cotgrove in a recent survey of attitudes[14] gained his statistics by polarising his sample under the headings of 'catastrophists' or 'cornucopians' and, not surprisingly, got results to support his hypothesis of a community divided against itself.

Little will be gained, and much might be lost by fostering such a division. The procrastinating effect of extended disputes over these issues must bring land to an increasing state of dereliction. Certainly the Neronian attitude of some authorities is aided and abetted by a conflict of public views, and land held out of use for any reason is a crime against society.[15]

We cannot on the other hand, fail to notice that in life's competitive struggle, survival demands profit and risk. There can be few who would not admire the heroic achievements in constructing for and extracting oil from below the sea bed, or that the profitability which ensues from the winning of natural resources provides an economic climate in which the arts are more likely to flourish. Man does not commission the painter until his belly is full and his roof is sound.

Yet the enterprise can go too far. Where greed for profit, encouraged by usury, takes over, those involved will stop at nothing to achieve their gains. Ideas of conservation or ecological care sound strange and foreign to them, except it be to whitewash their operations.

The natural effect of such extremism is to produce anti-bodies in society who see it as their function to resist any and every enterprise whatever the benefits might have been. In this I would argue they are too often just as far off balance as those whom they criticise.

And the stagnation of deadlock becomes itself the main issue.

Ends and means become confused and prospects of rationality recede.

It is against this background that the demand, for some method of assessment of the effects of development on the environment, has emerged under the general title of Environmental Impact Analysis.

There can be little doubt that the state of the art, so far, is not very strong. The fact that it exists at all is something, without a doubt. Where, as in Australia and the USA[16], its use is mandatory, the results have been disappointing. The deployment of extensive and conflicting environmental impact statements has provided the legal profession with yet another field day at the end of which you may be sure that the word of law and common sense do not always coincide.

In Britain we have prided ourselves on our Planning Legislation, though as George Dobry[17] points out, it is the use we make of it that is at fault; that confusion of ends and means which employs much devious working and wasting of effort.

If there are some who engage in the tactics of inquiry to suit their own selfish ends, there are many for whom the issues involved in environmental impact are not at all clear. The question, 'who is to judge?' must remain prominent, if not crucial.

Whatever the shortcomings of the American practice the scope of assessment as defined in Section 102 of the National Environmental Protection Act seems to me to be wide enough to satisfy any situation. The five points required to be studied are:
1 The environmental impact of the proposed action.
2 Any adverse effects which cannot be avoided should the proposals be implemented.
3 Alternatives to the proposed action.
4 The relationship between local short-term uses of man's environment and the maintenance of long-term productivity.
5 Any irreversible and irretrievable commitments of resources which would be involved in the proposed action should it be implemented.

Wide though their scope may be they contain only the merest hint of what might be regarded as impact. Yet people have differing and totally subjective values. My partner is outraged by intrusive noise, while I, as a non-smoker, tend to suffer from dirty ashtrays. Whereas I believe we are all subconsciously offended by inharmonious detail, it is difficult to convince a drainlayer of the importance of co-ordinating his manhole with the paving and planting above.

These are three simple examples of environmental impact involving three senses in a daily routine way, yet the issues can also be much larger, as, for example, in the processing of nuclear fuels and wastes[18] or the careless carriage of toxic substance. Here the impact is on the scale of the biosphere and it is argued to threaten our very existence.

We cannot blame the legislators for the absence of definition. After all they only seek to provide a framework for judgement. If Europe[19] is inclined to be cautious in the wake of the American experience, it is only a reflection of the attitudes of the member countries.

The officially stated position of the British Government is hedged with caution.[20] It is still assumed that the process of thorough assessment will take up more time and professional resources than are available. This remains unchanged since the release of the Thirlwall-Catlow Report in 1977[21] which, by the way, brings a concise and rational approach to the process that I have not found to be bettered anywhere. Their check list is as follows:

Impact group	Sub-division
The natural environment.	The flora and fauna, insect life and organisms and ecological regimes in identifiable terrains or aquatic habitats.
The human environment 1. Aesthetic quality and the physical and natural environment.	Aesthetic quality in rural and urban areas including landscape quality and accessibility for its enjoyment.
2. Impact on employment.	(a) On the land including fishing and the hunting of game. (b) On other employment within the local area.
3. Impact on health, safety and convenience.	(a) On health through the apprehension of hazard. (b) On health through polluting emissions to water, land and the atmosphere, including solid waste disposal and radiation. (c) Nuisance affecting health, comfort and convenience arising from dust, grit, fumes, heat, light, noise, vibration and wind. (d) On pedestrian safety and convenience through changes in movement and traffic.
4. Impact on social and cultural well being.	(a) Arising from the breaking up or disturbance of existing communities or groups.

(b) Through disturbance and severance and changes in home and neighbourhoods.

(c) Through disturbance to or loss of recreational facilities.

(d) Through disturbance to the concept of man in the perspective of history either to long established patterns of living and working or to specific archaeological or historic remains.

The primary division between impact on the natural and human environment is most important. All too often it is not recognised. To hear eminent members of one's own profession straying off into 'pictorial qualities' when speaking of 'species richness' is, to say the least, worrying. But such an occurrence is far from rare and, I fear, denigrates the effect of the argument however valid otherwise.

Thirlwall and Catlow have put landscape as quality for human appreciation precisely where it should be. It is distinct from nature though composed from its physical elements. To say it in another way the emotion chiefly conveys the quality whereas the instinct connects with the nature. The intellect may, as now, be brought to bear on the subject matter of both things in order to formulate what we sense or feel but again that is distinct and frequently unable to do full justice to either. This tendency of man to confuse these separate functions of mind is a tiresome fact that leads to laboured explanations, and so-called learned conference papers such as this.

A number of people have attempted to classify landscapes into some sort of preference order[22] but personally I remain sceptical of trying to quantify a quality. When people stop to 'drink in' the quality of my London window boxes, I could not deny that the refreshment might be equal to a view of Mount Fuji – for that moment. Granted my window boxes are transitory in comparison to Mount Fuji but the moment is eternal and therein lies the quality and wholeness.

It would follow then that, if I deny the possibility of objective quantification of landscape as a quality, we might be left to fight the emotional rôle of landscape aesthetics without support. Such a platform is often found to be less than adequate against the reasoned arguments of engineers and the like with whom we have to bargain. Furthermore, in the area of Environmental Impact Assessment which is likely to deal with major issues we have a duty to ourselves as a profession to present our arguments in a convincing rational way. Whilst not seeking to make aesthetic judgements in themselves, there are a number of supporting methods of measurement that can be used to underpin our case.

Techniques of analysis such as Zone of Visual Influence[23] and Isovist method[24] are as useful to our arguments as are earth-bearing pressures to an engineer.

In planning there are techniques such as the Ordinal Method of Evaluation[25] and formula for tourist carrying capacity[26] which we should not neglect if they can give a firm foundation for our designs.

Although measurements like these might appear to promote qualities they never in fact attempt to measure quality directly.

The method I have proposed in 1977 which has come to be known as Pickering's Principle is for determining relative quantities of ecology and human impact. It has nothing to say about landscape quality, although I reckon my aesthetic arguments are stronger for the support which an ecological evaluation might give.

There are two quite separate and distinct orders of thought involved. First the Principle. Second the formula.

The Principle is the simple statement that:

Ecological Value is inversely proportional to Human Impact.

A principle is a fundamental or natural law. It is not man-made, though it may be discovered, and it ought to be self-evident. The law of gravity, as it is commonly known, is a principle by the application of which knowledge a heavy machine can be made to leave the surface of a planetary body or alternatively a building made to rest securely upon it. The principle is unchanging but the applications may be widely at variance.

In our particular context the statement means that where human impact is high, ecological value will be low and conversely where human impact is low, ecological value will be high. Ecological value is low in the city centre but high in the tropical rain forest.

The Principle works whether we like it or not. The wisdom of the situation lies in the willingness to make use of the knowledge for the common good. The same axe will hew timber, execute, murder, or hammer nails without question.

Knowing that his condition is dependent on the condition of the biosphere, man would require to have some measure of the effect of his impact on the biosphere in ecological terms. With the benefit of such a measure, man might choose to moderate his impact to ensure that ecological values were not unduly diminished.

The formula which I have devised is not the Principle but is derived from it in order to give some tangible measure to its effects. If this point cannot be understood there is no hope that we can progress to the detail. It is the *pons asinorum* of the thesis.

The emergence of the understanding that man responds to, and has impact upon, the ecosystem has been regrettably slow, and in some senses unpopular. He is less predictable than other species. His activities do not provide good steady material for a PhD thesis in ecology. It is left to a few rogues like myself to essay into the unknown.

Planning on the other hand, which is supposed to provide for people, has never paid much attention to the natural environment. True it infringes in economic terms when considering land values and the locations of natural resources and communications but this view is limited and, in an entrepreneurial fashion, sees the ruthless exploitation of the land as a virtue.

So it is that, having propounded the Principle, I find myself in a no man's land between planners and ecologists who have only recently discovered each other's existence and are disinclined to enter each other's territory. There is no formulated connection between them.

It was to this conundrum that I was by my station addressed. If ecology was so closely connected with man's economic activities, how could it be measured, applied, made useful?

I was aware of a number of methods measuring the ecology. They had even been the subject of a comparison study by Smartt, Meacock, Lambert, *et al*, who 1974-76 had applied different measures to the same terrain in order to compare the results.[27]

All of these methods were relatively long-winded. Two years at the very minimum with an average of four before results was common. Most required the use of sophisticated laboratory equipment in addition to the field work. None of the results was related to anything other than itself. In short, once you had a value, what did you do with it?

A preliminary analysis of the measures generally used shows a basis in one or more of four concepts: (i) the number of individual species, (ii) frequency of occurrence, (iii) area occupied, (iv) weight of material or biomass.

Apart from the development of computer models to handle this multifarious data, the science of ecology has taken on two main aspects during recent years. These may be broadly described as energetics and specialisms.

Energetics is really a way of looking at the biosphere, or parts of it, as a receiver and transmitter of extra-terrestrial energy. It is usual to find explanations on a large-scale basis. Broadly speaking the concept may be described by the example, that a plant receives energy from solar and other sources and transmits or transpires some part leaving the remainder stored as the tissue of its own body. This in turn is available for consumption by dependent creatures whose metabolism is not designed to fix sufficient of the directly radiated energy.

The researches of Woodwell, Dukeman and Whittaker during the International Biological Programme[28] are too well documented to need my review here, but their own observations both as to the difficulties of obtaining measurements despite their undoubted ingenuity, and the time span of their studies, make yet again the point of irrelevance to our day-to-day decision requirements.

Specialisms take the opposite road and concentrate the attention of the scientist upon the minutiae of biology. One species or one location might be selected for a life's work. The published papers of the ecological societies are full of such admirably presented studies. The British Ecological Society in an effort to codify all this diverse material began a card index[29] for members to record their interests in 1973. As such these specialisms are a most valuable adjunct to a general system but the detail can by its very nature only contribute towards and not frame the day-to-day decisions.

Satisfying though such methods might be in themselves they did not seem capable of answering the question with which we were constantly faced. How much development will this ecosystem absorb or, what will it be like afterwards? Nobody really knew. We had a series of experiences to go on and a deal of 'repair' work was being undertaken both in urban and rural situations. There was talk and occasional experiment in restricted access (eg Langdale)[30] and 'honey pot' planning which attempted to draw off the crowds from the more fragile habitat. But it was all rather *ad hoc*, rather hit and miss. You used your personal value judgement to decide what degree of provision or restriction to impose and likely as not this would be strongly influenced by site availability and budget, so it was a matter of luck if it worked.

I was looking for something firmer than that, I knew well my own variability which put one value judgement one day and another the next. Not that there was anything wrong with this in itself, after all I was aware equally that everyone else suffered the same variability syndrome; but if at least some of the matters were capable of repeatability from time to time or from place to place there would be an improvement both in the result itself and, where it had to be argued against other aspects such as engineering or political situations, the ecological case could be more firmly put.

Practice as a landscape consultant had over a period of twenty years stretched me further in both opposing directions than was comfortable. Knowing or instinct for the solution had sometimes worked when there was a sympathetic hearing but again and again it was not enough.

What I have attempted in the formulae is to measure both ecological value and human impact in such a way that for any given time and place, the one is numerically equal to the other.

The formula for ecological value takes into account the structure, extent, rarity and species diversity of the habitat. The formula for human impact measures the number of people, the time and space they occupy and their constructed artifacts. By the use of constants these two values are brought into balance.

It follows that, since human impact can be measured from plans, the resulting ecological value is directly predicted.

The plotting in the form of contour-like lines which I have called isopleths enables comparisons to be made between the existing state and any number of predicted states. Adjustments can be continued until the acceptable balance is realised. By this method the opportunity for optimum levels of development and nature conservation is enhanced. Economy and ecology become complementary instead of contradictory.

Such a measure as I have formulated is in the nature of a bridge between parts that have frequently found themselves in conflict, but constructing a bridge is one thing, crossing it is another.

The measurements and predictions derived from the formulae (which are really much simpler than they appear) can do no more than guide us towards a rational solution. They do not in themselves tell us what to do. The predictions they give can be ignored or overridden. Indeed I insist they are not the only aspect of environmental impact to be assessed, but they do offer for the first time, the opportunity of making rational decisions in these matters. We go in with our eyes open.

Against the presently emerging views of society towards conservation it seems to me that the landscape profession has the opportunity, perhaps the only opportunity it will ever get, to accept a fully responsible rôle. Society will still demand complete and rationally argued bases for its decisions.

Much of our training has been towards meeting these new demands but we all need to avail ourselves of new techniques in order to strengthen our hand.

Just as the final beauty of great architecture is supported by the application of unseen principles of engineering, so in time will the application of sound principles of ecology and economy support great and lasting landscape.

APPENDIX 1

Pickering's Principle
ECOLOGICAL VALUE IS INVERSELY PROPORTIONAL TO HUMAN IMPACT

so that

FOR ANY GIVEN LOCATION THE ECOLOGICAL VALUE (E) AND THE HUMAN IMPACT (H) MUST TEND TOWARDS EQUILIBRIUM.

The principle may be stated as: $E + H \longrightarrow 0$
where the index of Ecological Value,

$$E \equiv \log_{10} \sum_{1}^{n} \left[V^3 . E . R . S \right]$$

$$= (v_1^3 \times e_1 \times r_1 \times s_1) + (v_2^3 \times e_2 \times r_2 \times s_2) \ldots + (v_n^3 \times e_n \times r_n \times s_n)$$

in which:

v = number of vegetation horizons present
e = extent of habitat in hectares
r = rarity = $(100 - c)$, a percentage
c = $\dfrac{e \text{ (extent of habitat) ha}}{A \text{ (Area of land system) km}^2}$
s = species diversity (number of species present)

and the sum of human events, Human Impact,

$$H \equiv \left[1.5 \log_{10} \sum_{1}^{n} \left(\frac{P . t \text{ av/day}}{2.5 z} \right) \right] - 10$$

in which:

P = number of persons in occupation
t = average duration of occupation in minutes per day
z = zone of occupation in hectares

	E	H
Nature reserve (closed)	9·90	−10.00
Nature reserve (open)	9·80	− 9·49
Forestry (closed)	8·20	− 9·86
Forestry (open)	8·10	− 8·74
Agriculture	7·56	− 9·10
Public open space (woodland)	6·70	− 5·65
Public urban park (50 ha)	6·70	− 5·60
Private camp site	6·65	− 5·10
Playing fields	6·40	− 6·40
Riding school	6·10	− 5·95
Gravel workings (active)	5·60	− 6·55
City open space (1 ha)	5·15	− 3·85
Rural road	4·70	− 4·50
Private garden	4·30	− 5·05
Low density houses	2·00	− 2·43
Urban footpath	1·95	− 1·68
High density houses	1·60	− 1·45
Lorry park	1·50	− 1·30
Public building	1·30	− 1·15

Table 1. Corresponding Indices of Ecological Value (E) and Human Impact (H) for a variety of situations arranged in order of ecological value. (These values are used in the graph fig. 8.)

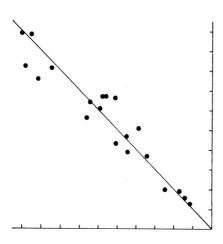

Correspondence between Ecological Value (E) and Human Impact (H). The graph includes all the values from Table 1.   *Fig 8*

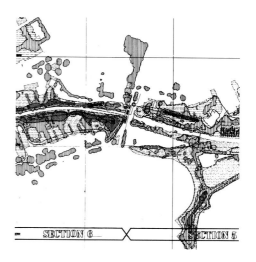

Isopleths plotted to show ecological values on a site in North London.   *Fig 9*

Example of ecological value=6.   *Fig 10*

Example of ecological value=2.   *Fig 11*

Bibliography
[1]Jones, David. The Anathemata, Ch 1. (The reference is to Helen's citadel of Troy.)
[2]The Bhagavad Gita. Ch 7, v 23. English translation by Swami Chidbhavananda.
[3]William Shakespeare. Richard II, Act 2, Sc 1.
[4]Yeats, W. B. Anthology.
[5]Blackstone, Sir William. Commentaries on the Laws of England. (Book 1, Section II).
[6]Aristotle. Politics 1.2. Ed. Jowett (1921).
[7]Douglas, Justice William O. Judgement: Berman v Parker 348 United States 26 (1964).
[8]Habermas, Jurgen. Toward a Rational Society. Max Plank Institute, Starnberg, Germany.
[9]Galbraith, J. K. The Age of Uncertainty, 1977. BBC London.
[10]Fraser-Darling, Sir Frank. Reith Lectures, 1969. BBC London.
[11]Leopold, Aldo. Round River.
[12]Bosseman, Fred P. In the Wake of the Tourist, 1978.
[13]Goldsmith, E., *et al.* The Ecologist, January, 1972.
[14]Cotgrove, Stephen. New Society. 22nd March 1979. London.
[15]Pickering, M. E. Profit and Loss from Derelict Land. Royal Society Lecture. Faculty of Building. November, 1977. London.
[16]The Environmental Protection (Impact of Proposals) Act 1974 Australia. The USA National Environmental Protection Act (NEPA) 1969.
[17]Dobry, George. Review of the Development Control System. HMSO London 1975.
[18]Parker, Hon Justice. The Windscale Inquiry. HMSO London 1978.
[19]Lee, N. and Wood, C. M. EIA. A European Perspective. Built Environment. Vol 4, No 2. London.
[20]Shore, Peter. Secretary of State for the Environment to the Press. February, 1979. London.
[21]Thirlwall, G. and Catlow, J. Environmental Impact Analysis. Research Report No 11 DOE London. 1977.
[22]Laurie, Ian. Classification of Landscape Values. University of Manchester, UK.
[23]Hebblethwaite, Ron. Zone of Visual Influence: Method developed at Central Electricity Generating Board, Cheltenham, UK.
[24]Tandy, Cliff. Isovist Method for plotting visual boundaries. Land Use Consultants. Fulham, UK.
[25]Jack Holmes Group. An Ordinal Method of Evaluation: Urban Studies 1972, Vol 9, No 2. UK.
[26]Staner, P. Harmful Ecological Consequences of the Development of the Tourist Industry and their Prevention. Paper to the Economic Commission for Europe. Dubrovnic. October 1975.
[27]Smartt, Meacock, Lambert, *et al.* Investigations into the Properties of quantitative Vegetational Data. 2 papers. The Journal of Ecology, Vol 62, No 3, 1974 and Vol 64, No 1, 1976.
[28]Woodwell, *et al.* International Biological Programme (current). United Nations.
[29]British Ecological Society, c/o University of Reading, UK.
[30]Lake District National Park HQ. Ambleside, Westmorland, UK.

ENVIRONMENTAL IMPACT ANALYSIS
CLIFF TANDY

Introduction
There is a comprehensive library of information on the origin of Environmental Impact Statements and it would not be advantageous to use the limited space of this paper to cover old ground. Some sources for references are given in the bibliography attached.

Like many good ideas the procedure of Environmental Impact Analysis has come from the USA as a new planning tool, but in fact it is largely a new name and a new format for the kind of analysis which landscape architects in the UK – particularly those working on industrial projects – have been doing for a long while.

Breaking it down to its simplest components, it is – in relation to a particular project – an analysis of the existing landscape, a study of the proposed developments, and investigation into the effects of the development upon the environment, and proposals to mitigate the undesirable effects by good landscape planning and design. In this context the word 'landscape' must be read in its widest meaning – including not only visual elements but every part of the character of a place which impinges upon the senses.

The EIA procedure was introduced as a means of formalising all aspects of this kind of study and it commenced with a 'check list' in the form of a matrix on which was recorded all possible elements on one axis, all possible effects on the other. By crosses placed in the relevant squares, impacts could be recorded and even the degree of impact by use of symbols. It was quickly found that one matrix was insufficient, and that separate charts were needed for 'constructional phase' and 'operational phase' of a project.

The USA introduced Environmental Impact Statements procedure following upon the passage of the National Environmental Policy Act in 1969 with the intention that information on the effects upon the environment of any new development should be available to the Council on Environmental Quality, and to the public before any action commenced. The result, unfortunately, was a flood of EIS documents with no machinery adequate to process them and no time even to read and digest them. Some became extremely elaborate with matrices containing more than 70,000 entries.[1]

It has been usual, under the British planning acts, for planning applications to include descriptions of the likely effects upon the environment, and landscape architects here have for many years, produced extensive reports containing an analysis of the existing landscape in terms of topography, geology, soil, water and drainage, climate, land use, and studies of the visual impact of the proposals together with noise, dust and traffic predictions. Such reports have mainly been prepared for large industrial projects whose applications were likely to be called-in for public inquiry.

Current Methods of EIA procedures

In the adoption of these procedures, the form of planning legislation and land use control in existence in any country is very important. Federal governments may have considerable variations between their States – even to some having no development control whatever. This is true of the USA where the demand for an EIA is Federal, but the implementation is State, or even local. Some States have, since 1969, introduced comprehensive legislation on EIA procedure, and its use has been extended beyond physical development projects to social and economic projects.

Australia introduced an Environmental Protection (Impact of Proposals) Act in 1974 which requires an EIS to be prepared only on large projects initiated by central government. However some States have begun to adopt EIA procedures for all new development proposals. Japan has introduced a procedure on a similar basis. Canada takes the same line with regard to federal projects, though the procedure does not rely upon a national Act, and the scrutiny of the impacts is carried out by the Department of the Environment of the Province concerned.

Recently France, Germany and Ireland have independently introduced modified EIA methods, and other EEC countries led by Holland, are considering their use while the EEC commission is investigating a method suitable for use throughout the Community. Chris Wood, (previously of Land Use Consultants) and Norman Lee, both at Manchester University, are consultants to the European Commission on EIA procedures, and have been formulating recommendations on the adoption of EIA by the European Economic Community.[2]

The feeling of the Community is that *no* new American type process should be introduced but that the current planning legislation of each member country should be widened to incorporate EIA procedures. In spite of the feeling of cautious approval, there is a long way to go before a common methodology is accepted by all EEC countries.[3]

In discussing 'Methods', Brian Clark[4] distinguishes between those which merely identify impacts and those which evaluate them. The *mechanics* of the six main methods are:

matrices	networks	quantitative methods
overlays	models	PADC method

Matrices start with the Leopold matrix[5] in which each square contains a score for *magnitude* and for *importance*. Later developments contain a scale of several degrees of disruption. Matrices have been extended to cover secondary and tertiary impacts and to relate *interactions* between elements. They can become too complicated and unwieldly to serve a useful purpose.

Networks are familiar as a management tool. They do not *identify* impacts but are useful in conveying information and comparing alternatives. With a large number of impacts computer processing is needed. Quantitative methods involve means of scoring (from factual data) the various parameters, then weighting these scores, and comparing them. Overlays (also known as sieve maps) are familiar to landscape architects through the projects described by Ian McHarg.[6] Simulation models have particular value in assessing complicated quantitative impacts from a single source on a range of alternative situations which are well covered by data surveys.

The PADC Method is that produced by the 'Project Appraisal for Development Control' research group at Aberdeen University, and is that described in the DOE Manual.[7] It is the system most favoured for use in UK and is referred to in more detail later in this paper.

Use of EIA in UK

In the UK there has been very limited guidance from the DOE on the use of EIA procedures. While on one hand it has published the Catlow and Thirlwall report[8] as an official document, and has followed it by a technical manual[7] by a research team at Aberdeen University, it has not made the procedure mandatory. It has indicated a policy that only certain large projects with complex problems and having national significance should merit an EIA, but has left it to the County Planning Authorities to instigate any use of the method.

It has not been laid down – or even tacitly agreed – whether the developer and his consultants, or the County should carry out the Study; nor has it been agreed who should bear the cost. So far we have in this country non-typical examples of both alternatives together with examples of joint co-operation in the Study, with shared responsibility for the analysis and joint working parties or committees to agree on the acceptance of evidence as *fact*.

The landscape planning consultant can therefore be engaged to take different rôles in this procedure. He can be the co-ordinator of the whole EIA on behalf of the developer, or on behalf of the C. Planning Dept. (commissioned or as staff). He may act for either party as a member of an EIA team co-ordinated by a Planning Officer, Consultant Planner, or Steering Committee. He may only be brought in for an independent opinion on a narrow field such as the analysis of the existing visual landscape, or the impact of a proposed building on visual amenity.

For the purpose of this paper, the widest rôle will be assumed, that of acting for the Developer to produce a complete EIA – on the basis that this position will include within it all lesser rôles. In such an engagement the landscape planner would be providing his own expertise, and that of his staff, and would have a management rôle in co-ordinating the study, but it would be unwise to assume that he could provide all services 'in-house'. A large input would be needed from specialists, from organisations with local knowledge, from the client's own technical staff, and from statutory bodies.

It is considered by the authors of the DOE Research Report[8] that the EIA procedure is complementary to, and will fit into, the present planning practice in the UK. It is intended that the completed EIA should be submitted as supplementary to a planning application, and should be available to a planning committee making its decision. It would also be an additional document submitted in support of an appeal made against an unsuccessful application.

It is not possible, yet, to determine the value of EIA's in Public Inquiries, as not enough of them have been tested. Theoretically the EIA procedure results in a record of the facts, agreed by all parties and listing the inevitable effects of the development together with means of mitigating undesirable impacts. This should, at the very least, limit the area of disagreement and prevent the time-wasting exchange of views between the experts representing the parties. In practice it seems likely that some witnesses will still wish to challenge the 'agreed views' and that an inspector is unlikely to prevent a member of the public from expressing his doubts at length by telling him that the particular point has been settled by a previous agreement on facts.

Quite recently (1978) the DOE has reversed its attitude of being very cool towards the Catlow & Thirlwall approach, to a mild approval, encouraging its use for a 'relatively few large and significant development proposals'.

Methodology

Because of the variable nature of the projects, the different demands of planning authorities, and the diversity of experience of the consultants, it is not possible to lay down any standard method of carrying out an EIA. In fact, to do so, would limit its value as a tool for broad investigation. However, there has come to be accepted a basic format which can be used, with modifications, for most projects. Generally it is in line with that advocated by the PADC research group.[7]

This has, as its main divisions:

1 Description of the project (including the need for the development).
2 Description of the existing site conditions.
3 Relationship of the development to present planning policies.
4 Impact of the project upon the environment.
5 Consideration of possible alternatives and reasons for choice – including possibilities for mitigation.
6 Secondary impacts needing a further EIA (eg, power supply to a project by overhead transmission line).

To attempt to list all the possible sub-headings would turn this paper into a mere catalogue, but mention must be made of a few: The project description 1 must include every possible aspect of its operation, and also of its construction phase. Much of section 2 is taken by the familiar form of landscape analysis followed by agricultural pattern, population and settlements, traffic and transportation and employment. It may also include a section describing the influence of the *environment* upon the *project* where this is a significant factor.

The alternatives considered should include not only various locations, but also layouts, methods of construction, means of operation, alternative energy sources, alternative forms of transport and routes, and different methods of waste disposal. All the viable alternatives should have their impacts assessed, and the possible lessening of adverse effects by the choice of other alternatives should be called to notice.

The major part of the EIA is likely to be section 4 which analyses the probable impacts, and this needs a fuller description: The first form of matrix used for the purpose of identifying environmental impacts was that devised by Luna Leopold – landscape architect – in 1971.[5] There have been other forms of matrices, check lists and networks, all intended to aid in identifying impacts and classifying them, as well as ensuring that no point is overlooked. Matrices have a value for this purpose, but it must be remembered that they have no real part in decision-making and are little more than an *aide memoire*. The open squares on a matrix may be used to register an impact by a simple / or X, or may – by key symbols – indicate the classification of an impact as short or long term, reversible or irreversible, beneficial or adverse, local or strategic, and also its degree of significance.

Once identified – by any method – impacts need to be studied and quantified. The list of possible impacts is endless but they may be grouped in a report under headings such as land use, ground factors, hydrology, visual intrusion, services, ecological impacts, traffic and transportation, employment, recreation, infrastructure, pollution (air, water, ground, noise and radiation) and safety.

A number of the impacts will be those which can be easily identified, but which need complicated investigation and study to evaluate them. For these it may be necessary to engage specialists, either to carry out the whole study and report upon such impacts, or at least to carry out investigations from which to provide data by which the study co-ordinator can express opinions. Some of the factors which need this approach are: air and water quality, pollution risks, noise and dust, radio-activity, traffic studies, vibration, subsidence risks, and dangerous chemicals.

This kind of impact needs study at two levels. Firstly, a measure of the ambient levels already existing in the local environment of the proposed site or alternative sites. The stations at which such measurements are taken must be carefully selected as representative of the population and visitor centres likely to be affected. Traffic counts, noise levels, need to be taken on several days and possibly overnight. Ambients involving climatic factors, air and water quality may have to be measured over a longer period to cover seasonal variations.

Secondly, predictions must be made, for each of the impacts, of the levels likely to be caused by the new development. Basic data on which to base these predictions can usually only be gained from measurement taken at similar projects elsewhere. Calculations applied to these figures will then convert them to levels likely to be perceived at the proposed site. Noise levels, dust deposit, traffic generation, employment, vibration and subsidence risks are capable of being reasonably calculated. Pollution risks are more difficult to assess and are more dependent upon expert scientific opinion.

Visual impacts – particularly where tall structures are concerned may require careful plotting of the area from within which the structure can be seen. Such an area is known as the Zone of Visual Influence. A sophisticated method of predicting its boundaries has been developed by the CEGB.

Much of the technical data in the project description must necessarily be provided by the developer's own staff or in-house expertise. The study co-ordinator must, however, question thoroughly every fact supplied, as there is a human tendency to overlook matters with which one is over-familiar, or which one has pre-judged to be irrelevant. Such attitudes are prevalent among technicians even without any intention to mislead or to conceal evidence.

On all matters included in the EIA the study co-ordinator should draw his own independent conclusions, whether the source of information be his own observation, data supplied by the developer, or opinions expressed by specialists, and he must be prepared to put forward the EIA conclusions at a Public Inquiry.

Example: NCB Coal Mine

As examples of EIA in practical use, this paper includes two projects from the practice of Land Use Consultants. The first is a coal mine in the Midlands for the NCB, and the second is a resource study on water supply and transmission for the North West Water Authority.

The coal mine study for NCB Western Area commenced in 1975 by a close liaison with Staffordshire County Planning Committee and officers who requested the developer to have an EIA prepared on the

County Planning Officer's own terms of reference (based at that time on the Dobry Report[9]), requiring evidence on:
(i)   visual appearance;
(ii)   waste disposal;
(iii)   traffic and transportation;
(iv)   foul and surface water drainage;
(v)   employment;
(vi)   noise and air pollution;
(vii)   likelihood of the project 'triggering off' other development.

The coalfield was of finite extent, bounded by faults and natural barriers, but within this area four possible sites were considered, and a landscape planning assessment of a 25 square mile search area was carried out. The EIA followed the format described[10], starting with a description of the project and the need for coal. The description of the existing environment covered landscape types, landscape quality (on a comparative scale only), agricultural land classification and 'sensitive areas'. Specific factors such as topography, soil, climate, hydrology, vegetation patterns, settlements, were incorporated into the general description, but detail analysis was made of the landscape of the Area of Outstanding Natural Beauty, and four historical landscapes which came within the search area.

Impacts of the project upon the environment were assessed under 18 heads grouped as follows:
    Appearance of buildings; Visual intrusion; Landscape quality; Land use.
    Waste tipping; The tip in the landscape.
    Transportation of coal*; Traffic issues.
    Drainage; Water supply; Recycling, discharge and pollution; Electricity supply.
    Labour requirements; Location of the labour force.
    Noise; Dust; Air pollution.
    Possibility of other industrial development.
    (* including farm severance).
Four possible alternative locations were reduced to two by engineering and geological constraints. The remaining alternative site was studied almost as fully as the first choice, and in order to carry out a proper evaluation, a hypothetical colliery layout, tipping design and landscape treatment was prepared. The same list of impacts was studied at both sites and comparisons were tabulated.

In addition, alternative transportation routes for coal, and even alternative methods of conveyance (eg, underground conveyor versus rail sidings) were considered and their consequences assessed. A full traffic study for road traffic (in-going materials and staff) was not included in the EIA, but has been carried out since by a firm of traffic engineers. Similarly the possibilities of bringing high voltage electricity supply across country to the colliery were investigated and possible routes considered, but if the project goes to a further stage, a separate public inquiry on overhead transmission lines may be demanded, and this would involve a separate EIA.

The final report was supported by 26 plans and sketches, photographs and a model of the tipping proposals. An interesting feature of the study was that representatives of the County and District Planning Departments attended working parties to consider specific matters such as the design of the waste tip, with the result that the proposal put forward in the planning application was one that had been jointly agreed. However, once the application was submitted, the planners reverted – quite rightly – to their normal rôle of public watch-dog, and studied the application objectively before placing it in front of their committees.

Example: NWWA Resource Study.

The second example is the environmental impact study on water resource development for the North West Water Authority which involved river intakes, aqueducts, treatment works and four major headwater sites at Haweswater, Borrowbeck, Hellifield and Morecambe Bay. In this project the NWWA *chose* to have an EIA prepared in order to make itself well-informed on the implications and alternatives. It had already taken a preliminary step in decision-making by selecting a short list of four sites.

This study was unique in that it was directed by a panel consisting of not only the Authority's officers and their consultants, but also the County Planning Officers of seven structure plan authorities. Under the direction of this panel the landscape planning consultants were responsible for the organisation and management of the study. The technical input from three firms of consultant water engineers was also co-ordinated in the study. Furthermore, it was a strategic study of alternative resource schemes which were only at a conceptual stage and therefore it had to be very flexible in its early stages when numerous variants were being adopted or eliminated.[11]

The four potential schemes had, between them, about 33 variants which were reduced to 14 in the final evaluation. These variants included reservoirs of different capacities and different rates of water supply per day. Matrices were used at first on which impacts were tabulated with five grades of significance. Study teams handled separate aspects of the appraisal, grouped under the following heads: Agriculture, Landscape, Terrestrial Ecology, River Ecology, Estuarial Ecology, Recreation. Separate studies were made on draw-down and aqueducts. In each of the subjects both existing conditions and changes likely to occur by the proposed development were studied. There is only space to describe one such subject within the scope of this paper, and so the Landscape Study is used here as an example.[12]

Briefly, the method used commenced by making an inventory of landscape elements on a classification system which included nine categories:

Landform	Surface cover	Networks
Edge elements	Mass features	Point features
Outward views	Water surface	Water networks

These categories were further sub-divided into 33 elements. Survey teams (from the structure plan authorities) measured, by area, length or number the quantity of each element within the visual envelope of each site. Networks were quantified as a 'density' of km per km^2.

For each location, topographical, geological, climatic, and visual descriptions were summarised, and also an assessment of 'perceived landscape' was made. The working groups met to exchange ideas and to clarify the terms of reference so that a common basis for all sites was achieved.

Landscape changes likely to be brought about by development were then assessed by measuring the amount of each element expected to be affected by development changes in each variant. Changes in 'perceived landscape' were similarly assessed but on a rather more subjective basis. In certain matters the selection of variants was influenced by the thresholds of landscape change identified.

The elements of the existing landscape were tabulated and expressed as a percentage of the whole envelope. Changes were not tabulated but recorded in some detail as comments upon the proposals for each of a select list of variants.

Similar methods were used in the appraisal of other subjects. It must be stressed however that in this *resource* study, comparisons were being made between the relative effects of variants at each site, and that no attempt was made to draw absolute comparisons between the quality of environment (existing or resulting) of the four major sites themselves.

Some of the studies were wide-reaching. Agriculture covered not only the existing rural land use, and consequent loss of land, but farm characteristics, productivity and employment, agricultural land values, farm-severance and the viability of farm units remaining after development. The Recreation Study differed somewhat, in that, in looking at future changes it had to consider not only the loss of existing recreational facilities, but the prospect of new – and possibly even greater – recreational potential resulting from the large fresh-water bodies likely to be created at any of the headwater sites. In this part of the work officers from the Regional Councils for Sport and Recreation participated.

Future Trends and Conclusions

Although momentum has been lost on the use of Environmental Impact Statements in the USA, and doubts have been cast upon both the effectiveness of, and the need for, the procedure in this country, it seems likely that the EI Analysis method is likely to remain for the foreseeable future as a part of the planning tool kit. It may *officially* be required only for large and complex projects of national – or at least regional – significance but the format of investigation is so useful that it may be used (without being named) as the basis of many analytical studies.

The risk – as for many good ideas – is that it may become too popular and used inappropriately. It is important to acknowledge that it is only an analytical tool, and not, in itself, a decision-making process. As Chris Wood writes[13] 'EIA is not, and can never be, a replacement for land use planning'.

The true purpose of an EIA is to assist Local Planning Authorities (and similar organisations in other countries) to make decisions. While Planning Authorities have competent professional and technical staffs, the actual decisions are taken by elected members and it is therefore necessary that, however technical the detailed studies, the conclusions should be written clearly and succinctly with the minimum of jargon. There may be a case, in complicated assessments, for keeping technical studies out of the final report and grouping them in an appendix.

Conclusions should, as far as possible, express likely changes in *everyday* terms relating them to circumstances and conditions with which the public are likely to be familiar. They should not, of course, pre-judge any of the issues.

References
[1]CEQ Environmental Impact Statements: An Analysis of Six Years' Experience by Seventy Federal Agencies. US Council on Environmental Quality, Washington DC, 1976.
[2]Lee, N. and Wood, C. Environmental Impact Assessment of Projects in EEC Countries in Journal of Environmental Management 1978. Vol 6, 57-71.
[3]Lee, N. and Wood, C. EIA – A European Perspective in Built Environment, Vol 4, No 2, pp 101-110, London 1978.
[4]Clark, B. D., et al. Methods of Environmental Impact Analysis in Built Environment. Vol 4, No 2, pp 111-121, London 1978.
[5]Leopold, L., et al. A Procedure for Evaluating Environmental Impact. US Geological Survey, Washington DC, 1971.
[6]McHarg, J. I. Design with Nature, Natural History Press (Doubleday), New York, 1969.
[7]Clark, B. D., et al. Assessment of Major Industrial Applications: A Manual. DOE Research Report No 13, DOE, London 1976.
[8]Catlow, J. and Thirlwall, C. G. Environmental Impact Analysis. DOE Research Report No 11, DOE, London 1977.
[9]Dobry, G. Review of the Development Control System: Final Report: HMSO, London 1975.
[10]Land Use Consultants: Environmental Assessment, Park Project, Stafford for NCB, Western Area. LUC, London 1977 (Restricted).
[11]NWWA. Environmental Appraisal of Four Alternative Water Resource Schemes. Report of EIS. Land Use Consultants, London 1978 (Restricted).
[12]NWWA Do. Technical Reports of Environmental Working Groups. LUC, London 1978 (Restricted).
[13]Wood, C. Environmental Impact Texts: An Assessment in Landscape Research. Vol 4, No 1, 1979.

THE ASSESSMENT OF POLITICAL IMPACTS
PROFESSOR A. E. WEDDLE

Introduction

In the last decade or so we have tried to focus professional and technical skills on the objective measurement of environment. How does it rank in quality, to what extent will development affect it, and what should be done to minimise adverse effects? The quest has been for scientific measures, to quantify proof, and so it has been believed, provide the decision-maker with a more secure basis for judgement. This we have called environmental analysis, in some cases taken to the stage of preparing formal reports or statements of the nature and degree of environmental impact likely to be caused by a specific set of development proposals.

I want to look briefly at the politics of environmental impact. Perhaps we should start by asking lawyers and politicians what they think of quantified evidence. Not much, I suspect. And what does the public inquiry inspector, or judge (Windscale) or reporter (Scotland) make of it, even with a technical assessor to guide him? Clearly it should carry forward in his report and so inform the Minister who under our British system makes an administrative decision, which may however be contrary to the recommendations.

Environmental issues affect people and are resolved by politicians and not analysts, scientific or otherwise. So as professionals how do we proceed? I suggest that we start by learning in a more systematic way how people respond not only in complaint or protest against potential environmental impact, but how they develop a group reaction which brings them into concert to pressurise the elected politician. We must then consider the following:

People as individuals and their response to proposals.

The *ad hoc* pressure group, seldom democratically elected and usually representative only of its own interests.

The political machine and its sensitivity to environmental issues.

For these we may need the assistance respectively of the psychologist, the social scientist, and the political scientist.

We should respond to the first two but need to influence the political machine, which is seldom innovative, and more responsive to vote catching to remain in office than it is to social attitudes unless these are expressed with vigour rather than quantitative evidence. Political attitudes can however shift strategically and lead to legislation to provide statutory powers to deal with emerging environmental problems. I regard this as a key stage in the transition from impact analysis to environmental synthesis.

The American Experience – Mark 1

To learn from recent history we can often turn to the United States, for examples as forerunners of events to be repeated in Europe. I want to go back first, not to 1969 and the early 1970's with their environmental protection legislation, but to California of the mid-19th Century.

In 1864 Congress made a land grant to the State of California of the Yosemite Valley, to be held for public use and recreation. One of the Commissioners was Federick Law Olmsted, and his 1866 report was clearly predictive of the long-term problems which could result from short-term increase of tourist facilities. State management proved Olmsted right, but in 1890 Yosemite was established as a National Park. This was not achieved, however, without a great deal of very high level political activity, and the realisation of the importance of politics and the need for combined efforts leading to the founding of the Sierra Club in San Francisco in 1892. Political skill was needed to resolve the conflicts between conservation and development. Development impact on soils and forests had made clear the need for legislative control. National progress was made with Forest Management legislation and in California thousands of acres of mountain forest land were brought under federal management.

Moving into the 1920's we see further evidence of the predictive and the political in California. Now with Olmsted Jr we find 1929 State Parks studies and a report which foresaw vastly increased use of the private motor car, and the need for controls. The report reviewed the political aspects of state park promotion, with a sensible understanding of the existing American system which could facilitate limited protection of environmental quality.

Coming on into the 1960's we can note political action at different levels. The Association of Bay Area Governments brought together a hundred San Francisco municipalities, together with special districts, state and federal commissions and boards, to constitute an advisory metropolitan authority. Most of its proposals were incorporated in city and county plans. Whilst this approach was motivated by general concern over development and conservation – an attitude of political awareness emerging nationally, but especially strongly in California – there were specific and more local ways in which community activity at the bottom of the organisational hierarchy could spark off action. One such action was that taken in 1961-63 to prevent continued filling in of the Bay itself by frontage municipalities and developers. It was a direct challenge to plans of the city of Berkeley to 'reclaim' 40,000 acres that lead to the commissioning of a study which examined the impacts, not only of this proposal, but the possibility of similar frontage works vastly shrinking the Bay. Legislation followed in 1965.

In 1970 California enacted its own Environmental Quality Act, extending to State-financed projects the Environmental Impact Statement requirements of the National Environmental Protection legislation which gave jurisdiction over Federally funded projects. Then in 1972 a California Supreme Court decision went some considerable way to extending similar requirements to privately developed construction projects.

It is significant that Michael Laurie, who has recently documented the Californian experience and to whom I am indebted for this information, takes the view that planners and landscape architects have not taken a leading rôle in initiating plans, but have played a secondary rôle at the level of implementation. He asserts that, 'Overall, initiation of legislation to preserve or enhance the landscape has been the achievement of lay groups, individuals and some politicians'.

My last Californian example relates to environmental impact studies for the Bay Area Transit system (BART). In the Appleyard and Carp (1974) report we find a description of a Socio-Environmental Impact Model. The report described a monitoring approach to ascertain 'before' and 'after' conditions consequent upon the development of a major metropolitan public transport system, certain to affect social and environmental conditions on a regional scale. The monitoring covers twin aspects – first the environmental change and second the population response. So impact is measured on the physical and visual environment, but the important extension is to assess reactions; in advance, during construction, and afterwards. Not only is the direct environmental impact measured, but the sensitivity of those likely to be affected is taken into account, and considered over a relatively long time scale.

The American Experience – Mark 2

The National Environmental Policy Act is well known. Now even those United States agencies which have always believed their recreational development to be to the public good in the environmental sense as well have their own impact appraisal divisions – Forest Service, National Parks, and so on. Appraisal systems are not without their drawbacks of course, including delays and the formalised 'confrontation' postures in which developers and opposers find themselves. In my view too little notice has been taken of the deeply penetrating influence which has brought about a massive shift in political attitudes. Consideration of the mandatory Environmental Impact Report is only the first part of the story. The second is the political and organisational response of *ad hoc* citizen groups who can respectably and, usually responsibly, make their views known. The third is of greater consequence in bringing about a shift in the land ethic of a whole nation. In Europe, and especially Britain since our 1940's town and country planning legislation, we can no longer hold land in absolute ownership. 'Fee simple' is only effective within the bounds permitted by development permission which is necessary for most kinds of change of use of land and for constructional development. The developer must make his case for consent, even where zoning indicates the appropriateness of his proposals. Except where land was already zoned by use and density the landowner in the United States assumed that the decision was primarily his, to be made on his own economic and other criteria, without too much regard for the public good. With so much development now subject to scrutiny, and so many well informed, properly organised and articulate citizen groups about this is yielding to the hitherto unthinkable view that general public and not private or single agency considerations should prevail. When we consider how fundamental to Constitution and ethos is the idea of the rights of the individual in the United States we can appreciate how startlingly influential this is. So we have a special kind of environmental impact; a concept of environmental protection with direct impact on the fundamentals of national and land law.

The British Experience

Some three or four years after the United States move to environmental analysis official studies were mounted in Britain, on the assumption it seemed that it might be necessary to adopt a system which included the formal Environmental Impact Report or Statement as evidence for planning approval for a selected range of major development projects. Two studies can be noted (DOE Research Reports 11 and 13), the first prepared by Catlow and Thirlwell, the second at the University of Aberdeen. The subject of impact assessment was given a good airing at an official symposium at the University of Canterbury in September 1975 when focus was very much on techniques developed for special aspects, with little overt attention to people or politics. Not all participants were in favour, and many major development agencies sent mandated delegates to raise the spectre of more planning delay to prepare statements and have them lengthily scrutinised.

Some of the material at the Canterbury Symposium was derived from slightly earlier studies commissioned by the Urban Motorways Committee. That Committee was established in 1970 in expectation of difficulties which might be faced with the new programme of urban motorway construction. In the event the problem to some extent obligingly went away, or at least did not get worse, because of the drastic curtailment of urban reconstruction by the mid-1970's. The studies were, however, very valuable in several respects. Actual motorway projects were analysed by consultants. In most cases the emphasis was on measurement of separate physical and visual problems. Some attempts were made at combining impact measurements to give an overall environmental index for alternatives. This soon revealed the difficulties, conceptual and statistical, of comparing or combining any but like-with-like. From the point of this paper the most interesting attempt was that to measure social impacts. Quite the most important outcome of the Committee's work, however, was the almost immediate political response. There was Government acceptance, with a White Paper to outline policy followed by legislation which included compensation provisions. The legislation provided for limits to 'acceptable' noise levels affecting residential properties adjoining major urban roads.

Meanwhile relatively little was heard about EIA, the Aberdeen report being released in 1976 and the other delayed until 1977. The Scottish study provided a useful handbook type report which contributed substantially to the development of analytical techniques. In both cases the emphasis was on appraisal of the project (or project alternatives) as proposed, rather than as design progressed. And little emerged on social or political considerations.

We were, of course, already using the 'public participation exercise' to elicit public opinion on rural road proposals. The crudeness of alternatives offered and the low response rate made some of these studies of very questionable value beyond giving objectors a better chance to object to proposals affecting them directly. But the polite form of protest was already being overtaken by action protest of a kind which chose to question fundamental methods and policies rather than possible alternatives. We moved to action politics, disruptive, distressing, and probably illegal. But the challenge was against the inquiry system and this ultimately brought about appraisals of road planning policy (Leitch Report) and some shift in Ministry methods at public inquiries.

Conclusions

So where do we stand today in the UK? What progress should we try to make in environmental impact work? Are we at the beginning of the road or at the end?

1. I venture the view that we are at the end of simple scientific 'objective' environmental analysis. We are at the beginning of the road in the social, professional and political sense and must be ready to proceed to what I shall call environmental synthesis.

2. The future lies in the sensible use of impact analysis as the project develops. Many planning agencies do this already. For example, in my own work for the CEGB as early as 1968 we were part of an appraisal team considering alternative sites for ash disposal from a major power station. In 1975 we undertook a sensitivity analysis of three counties to help determine the least difficult alignment for a 400 kV overhead transmission line. This was interesting because one half of the study dealt with sensitivity of the landscape, the other half with the likely sensitivity of residents and visitors; people were now taken more fully into consideration in an attempt to minimise impact.

3. More attention will have to be given to determining local political sensitivity. In cost/benefit planning studies it is necessary to ask 'costs and benefits to whom and how many?' In environmental impact studies the developer will ask 'impact on whom and how powerful?' being at least as concerned with the weight of response as with the severity of impact. And this will not be just to win planning inquiries but to produce proposals good enough to avoid them.

4. As professionals we need to work harder to relate our work to strategic political action. This should include better professional guidance available to Ministers dealing with physical aspects, of inner city problems for example. On rural, recreation and conservation fronts we must work towards a perceptive foresight of pending problems and the adoption of management rather than negative control systems to avoid them. We should cultivate a predictive attitude to environmental change rather than one which is simply analytical on the basis of past and present experience alone.

I do believe this can be done. It has been attempted for the Energy industries for example. A working group of the Watt Committee on Energy has been examining the land use implications of scenarios of future energy development to identify possible broad environmental impacts. Such regional impacts emerge as progressive eastward development of Midlands and Yorkshire coalfields, extending them into areas of high agricultural and scenic value, pressure for development of oil facilities in sensitive west and south west coastal areas, and of course sites for nuclear power generation in fine remote estuary locations.

Prediction to accurate levels will of course be difficult, but not I think as difficult as persuading politicians to accept imaginative prognosis on behalf of the electorates which they represent. And it is with this in mind that we may have to be more directly political towards those of an environmentally conscious public than the politicians who stand as proxy for them.

References

Appleyard, D. and Carp, F. M. *The BART Residential Impact Study*, in Environmental Impact Assessment, Ed. Dickert, D. G. and Domeny, K. R., University of California, Berkeley, Calif. 1974.

Aberdeen University Department of Geography, Project Appraisal for Development Control Research Team, *Assessment of Major Industrial Applications: A Manual*, (DOE Research Report 13), London, 1976.

Catlow, J. and Thirlwell, C. G., *Environmental Impact Analysis*, (DOE Research Report 11), London, 1977.

Advisory Committee on Trunk Road Assessment (Sir George Leitch) Oct 1977.

Energy development and land in the United Kingdom (1979). Report No 4, February. London: Watt Committee on Energy, quoted by Alistair MacLeary in *The Planner*, Vol 65, No 2, March 1979.

Laurie, M. A history of aesthetic conservation in California. *Landscape Planning*, Vol 6:1, 1979, Elsevier, Amsterdam.

ENVIRONMENTAL MONITORING BY REMOTE SENSING

ENVIRONMENTAL MONITORING BY REMOTE SENSING   DR J. L. VAN GENDEREN and P. A. VASS

REMOTE SENSING, AN AID TO LANDSCAPE MANAGEMENT   DR J. F. HANDLEY

MONITORING UPLAND LANDSCAPE CHANGE BY REMOTE SENSING   DR M. L. PARRY

ENVIRONMENTAL MONITORING BY REMOTE SENSING
DR J. L. VAN GENDEREN and P. A. VASS

Abstract
During the past twenty years, the state of the environment has become one of the major concerns of industrial societies. Continued growth in industrial development and in the waste from an ever-increasing number of sources, together with the need to preserve nature in its many forms have found attention focused on the burgeoning problems of environmental pollution and the demand for the early and reliable detection of vegetation stress caused by pollution, so that effective monitoring and control measures can be introduced. The paper outlines the various types of environmental monitoring which may be studied by remote sensing. The rôle of different remote sensors such as airborne cameras (including panchromatic, colour, colour infra-red and multiband systems), airborne thermal line scanners, side looking radar and satellite imagery for the identification and monitoring of the environmental pollutants and their effect will be evaluated.

Introduction
Advances in civilisation and technology have resulted in extreme and often drastic changes in the environment, thus it is a pressing necessity to provide a systematic global monitoring method for the environment to aid in the control of pollution events. Increasing pollution of the air, land and water are now matters of concern for everyone.

Pollution can be defined (Mellanby, 1973) as any direct or indirect alteration of the physical, thermal, biological or radioactive properties of any part of the environment by discharging, emitting or depositing wastes or substances so as to affect any beneficial use adversely, to cause a condition which is hazardous or potentially hazardous to public health, safety or welfare, or to animals, birds, aquatic life or plants.

One of the problems in carrying out pollution studies and environmental analysis is that most of the relevant parameters are not immediately visible to the human eye and others are so widespread that they cannot easily be appreciated. Remote sensing with its extensive range of imaging systems provides valuable information for the detection and analysis of pollution events (Giever, 1966).

Before describing the main pollution types and how these may be studied by remote sensing techniques, a brief review is provided on the basic imaging sensors of value in such investigations.

Aerial Photography
The photographic camera and the television camera, which operate in the visible range between ultra-violet and infra-red are still the most important systems in remote sensing for pollution studies. For many decades the vertical aerial photograph has been an invaluable aid in many fields of research and operational use. It provides a rapid, objective over-view of the environment, contains a high information content and has very good spatial resolution. Photography also provides an exactly-timed documentation of the environment for comparative studies of changes and development. The observation that objects photographed in the visible region of the electro-magnetic spectrum do not have the same degree of reflection led to experimentation with various film filter combinations, using multiband cameras which simultaneously exposes in different regions. Of the three most usual types of photographs taken by a multiband camera (viz black and white panchromatic, colour and colour infra-red) the colour infra-red film has been found to be the most single useful image type for vegetation damage analysis. However, normal colour film is able to detect discoloration of water caused by sediments and effluents, which are invisible on other film

types. Therefore, a multiband camera system is often the optimum sensor in pollution studies.

As most forms of vegetation have high reflectance in the near infra-red region, they take on a variety of red tones. This method of enhancement has aided the detection of vegetation and its quality in industrial and urban areas, in turn determining environmental quality. With a normal colour film, vegetation suffering pollution damage can only be separated from healthy vegetation when visible crown symptoms exist (Stellingwerf, 1969). However, with a colour infra-red film damage effects may be determined with or without visible crown symptoms in nature. Unhealthy, damaged or dying vegetation tends to deviate from the red colour towards cyan. Another important advantage of infra-red film is the easy differentiation of conifers and deciduous species of trees. As conifers are usually more sensitive to atmospheric pollution, this is an important extra asset of false colour film.

In addition, atmospheric scattering of visible and near infra-red wavelengths, due to reflection of dust particles, smoke, water vapour, sulphur dioxide, etc, does not affect colour infra-red film to the same degree as other photographic sensors, thus giving colour infra-red a strong haze and smog penetration ability, so valuable in studying industrial areas. This capability occurs as atmospheric scattering takes place mainly in the short blue-light wavelengths, which are filtered out of the colour infra-red images. Infra-red and visible radiation are often reflected and transmitted quite differently by vegetation and this has led to the development of vegetation keys used in the interpretation of aerial photography, van Genderen (1974), Murtha (1976) and Stellingwerf (1969). A key allows one to understand how and why the various vegetation types, both healthy and under stress, are recorded as they appear.

Thermal Infra-red Scanner
Airborne thermal line scanners are used to measure the infra-red radiation emitted from the Earth's surface and thus to measure the temperature and emissivity. The infra-red atmospheric windows of 3 to 5 and 8 to 14 microns are extensively used and the sensor can measure temperature differences in the order of $0.5°$ to $1°C$. Infra-red scanners can operate during the day or night and through haze and smoke.

As many pollutants are discharged with warm water, infra-red line scanners have been widely used to map rivers, estuaries and coastlines to study the distribution of this type of pollution. The most obvious application of infra-red scanners is to map the movement and mixing of cooling water being discharged from power stations. As many power stations are sited on estuaries with rapidly varying tidal conditions, the airborne infra-red technique has a great advantage over ship methods in being able to map large areas quickly.

Other applications of thermal imagery in the field of environmental monitoring include the detection of 'hot spots' – sites of internal combustion within slag or disposed waste tips, the location of underground mine shafts and cavities and the identification and monitoring of buildings surfaces and steam pipe heating systems for heat loss purposes as an aid in energy conservation measures.

Side Looking Airborne Radar
Radar has a particular application in bad weather areas, where cloud cover reduces the opportunity for conventional air photography. As the spectral band utilised is in the microwave it has the ability to penetrate through clouds and it can also operate at night. Radar systems do not, however, have the accuracy and resolution in terms of minimum target size discrimination that aerial photography has and they are mainly used to acquire small scale imagery of large areas such as for oil pollution along coastal waters. Due to the microwave back-scatter properties of land and water surfaces and the oblique view

given by imaging radar systems, they are sensitive in the depiction of surface roughness: this is especially useful in the detection of oil slicks where the oil film flattens out the normal wave patterns of the sea surface. Slicks appear on the radar imagery as dark or low signal return areas, as most of the microwave pulse is reflected away from the detector.

Satellite Imagery

Remote sensing techniques from satellites can effectively aid in the identification of regional changes in the environment brought about by natural or man-made phenomena because of two of its attributes. First, the satellite gives a synoptic over-view of the total environment: a perspective of the land, water and air seen as parts of an integrated system. Second, the satellite can provide a repetitive or seasonal look at certain types of steady, persistent or slow changes in the environment or abrupt alterations resulting from a disaster.

The most significant and widely used satellite mission to date, for earth resources surveys, has been the Landsat series. At present, two satellites are operating, namely Landsat 2 and 3, with information dating back to 1972 from Landsat 1. In principle, any area can be imaged every 18 days, but in practice, as in the UK situation cloud cover usually reduces the coverage. The main imaging sensor is a multi-spectral scanner which produces a continuous image strip format in each of four wavelength channels. The data can be supplied as computer compatible tapes for computer based analysis programmes, or as black and white photo images in various product types and scales. Colour images are made from combinations of individual black and white images by projecting each wavelength band through a particular filter.

The types of environmental monitoring and base-line mapping, in the UK and European context, that can be best achieved using satellite imagery include:

(i) Assessment and monitoring of changes of land use and quality associated with an extractive industry of a widespread nature, for example, the sand and gravel industry.

(ii) Classification of vegetation in different ecosystems of a region or National Park.

(iii) Mapping of features at a national scale, for example measurement of woodland, water bodies, urban areas, etc.

(iv) Regional mapping tasks for specific purposes, such as tourist maps.

The need and opportunity for the application of cost effective solutions of monitoring environmental problems at the regional level are greatest today and in the near future. Accordingly, for the effort to have a significant impact on environmental quality programmes, the use of satellite technology must be greatly accelerated.

Air Pollution and the Remote Sensing of its Effects on Vegetation

Air pollution is defined as the contamination of the atmosphere with undesirable solids, liquids and gases. In a strict sense, air may be considered polluted when any substances, foreign or additional to its normal composition, are added. This definition is much too wide, however, for the purposes of air pollution control and the term 'air pollution' is usually restricted to those conditions in which the general atmosphere contains substances in concentrations which are harmful, or likely to be harmful, to man or his environment (Mellanby, 1972).

Air oxidants, including sulphur dioxide, ozone, fluorides, nitrous dioxide, peroxacetyl nitrate (PAN) and copper oxides cause foliage discoloration, dropping of leaves and eventual death. Some of these symptoms are subtle and effect the same species selectively. An apparently healthy individual can be growing adjacent to a neighbour of the same species in its last stages of decline. Air oxidant pollution is frequently slight at first and can easily be overlooked if the wrong sensor system is used. Therefore, it is extremely important that the various remote sensing techniques, as described in the previous section, are evaluated for specific problems.

Smoke and Dust

The burning of fossil fuels, particularly coal and oil, is the greatest cause of air pollution in the form of dust and smoke. It has long been recognised that smoke in the air of towns and around industrial sites has an adverse effect on the photosynthetic processes in plants, by reducing the light intensity and hours of bright sunshine per day. Quality, as well as quantity, of light is affected since the absorption and scattering of radiation is greatest in the ultra-violet range. This fact makes the use of infra-red film, which cuts out these shorter wavelengths, extremely desirable in areas with high levels of atmospheric pollution.

The light energy available for photosynthesis is also reduced by the blackening of leaves by dust particles. These are usually heavy and settle out of the atmosphere quite quickly. The problems and effects on vegetation, as observed on aerial photographs, thus tend to be fairly local, being most acute close to the source, then decreasing rapidly. The reduction of smoke since the Clean Air Act has prevented the ubiquitous deposits of dust creating depressing scenes, but the damaging pollutant, sulphur dioxide, is not removed by burning smokeless fuels.

Sulphur Dioxide

Plants seem to be more susceptible to sulphur dioxide pollution than animals. Levels between 0·1 and 1·0 parts per million (ppm) have often been shown to cause obvious symptoms, such as leaf blotching and reduction in yield of crops. Coniferous trees grow poorly and even die in many urban or industrial areas. The degree of dispersion and dilution of sulphur dioxide is related to various factors, such as climatic conditions and the height of the emitting chimney. Depending on its concentration, the season and other climatic factors, the harmful effects of sulphur dioxide range from retardation of growth and exposure to death by poisoning. Susceptibility also varies with species, stage of growth and exposure time as well as being affected by environmental factors of air temperature, humidity, light intensity and water supply.

Although chronic damage of vegetation caused by sulphur dioxide fumes is invisible to the naked eye, its effects can be determined on colour infra-red aerial photography. As the pollutant affects the pigments (chlorophyll a and b) there is a loss of reflectance in the infra-red wavelengths. In general, the reddish photographic rendition of healthy trees and vegetation grades into magenta, purple and green as the loss of infra-red reflectance progresses. This has been reported by Dargie (1975), van Genderen (1974), Kirby (1977), Myers (1974), Olsen (1971), Remeyn (1972), Stellingwerf (1969), Sukhih and Sinitsin (1974), Weber and Polcyn (1972).

Murtha (1972) used Landsat satellite imagery to detect damage caused by sulphur dioxide fumes in an extensive forest area in Canada. The vegetation damage was most obvious on Band 5 as exposed areas or dry dead foliage have the highest spectral reflectance in the red spectral region and also the chlorophyll of green healthy vegetation absorbs in this region, so these areas appear dark. Thus, the contrast between healthy and damaged zones is greatest on Band 5. Satellite data should provide a simple means of mapping and monitoring large forest areas affected by severe sulphur dioxide fume damage, provided sufficient time has elapsed for the damaged forest region to take on the characteristics of the air pollutant damage.

Photochemical Smog

Photochemical smog results from the presence of large numbers of petrol engines producing exhaust gases. When a temperature inversion occurs the pollutants are trapped in high concentrations near the ground. Under conditions of high light intensity, ozone and peroxacetyl nitrates (PAN) are produced. It is a serious problem in many parts of the world. California is the region most often quoted as being affected, but it can occur anywhere under the correct conditions. It has been reported in many parts of the USA, in Japan, Australia and occasionally in Europe, such as The Netherlands and south-east England.

Ground level concentrations of ozone over 5 pphm will cause damage to plants, under pollution conditions levels can reach 40 pphm in summer and autumn. Pollutant effects include glazing and flecking on the upper surface of the leaves. The guard cells of the stomatal system rapidly close, reducing the intake of carbon dioxide, thus lowering plant growth. In very high levels of ozone the guard cells collapse and gape open. The semi-permeable membrane of the cell is affected, allowing leakage of the cell constituents. Necrosis of plants and defoliation of pine trees is common at these high levels. PAN is a very strong oxidant with drastic effects on the enzyme systems of the plant proteins, causing the denaturing of the cell membrane and collapse of the cell wall allowing the cell constituents to escape through protein holes.

Miller, et al (1969), Heller (1969, 1971), Wert (1969), Weber and Polcyn (1972) have reported on the effects of oxidant air pollution on ponderosa pine foliage in Los Angeles, USA, and how the foliar damage can be evaluated on colour films. The symptoms most useful in identifying affected pines were colour, low density and shortness of needles and high frequency of bare branches. Healthy pines usually have up to five years of needle retention, whereas smog-affected foliage may have only the current growth of needles, many bare branches are visible to the photo-interpreter and permit the positive identification of damaged trees.

Fluoride Pollution
Serious pollution today comes from brickworks and aluminium smelters. The two main pollutants are sulphur dioxide and fluoride gas. Sulphur dioxide from older brickworks with insufficiently high chimneys may damage crops in the vicinity. Newer works dispose of the gas more efficiently. However, fluorides, even at levels of 0·1 ppm or less can cause serious damage to plants. They are formed in the production of steel, bricks, clay-pottery, aluminium, ironstone, vitreous enamel and china clay.

In Norway, aluminium smelters were once built at the bottom of fiords, near the site of hydro-electric power and were surrounded by many square kilometres of dead and dying coniferous trees. The restricted topography concentrated the pollution effects in areas up to 30 kms from the source, with death of pine trees within 6 kms and a 25 per cent death rate at up to 13 kms distance. Very near to the source of pollution only tall herbs and grasses exist and often with signs of lead chlorosis. In Britain there have been reports of fluoride damage to trees and agricultural crops but the most serious effects have been on cattle. When fluorides are deposited on pastureland, the grass concentrates the pollutant leading to poisoning of the grazing animals, in the mild form present as mottled teeth, while in severe cases the skeletal bones are softened and eventually the animals die.

Most modern smelters have very high chimneys so local damage is reduced. They are usually built on undulating and well ventilated land with the following adjacent land uses – urban, residential and some horticultural cultivation.

Summary
Colour infra-red film at 1/3,000 to 1/5,000 scale are favoured for identifying various levels of air pollution damage to vegetation communities, crops and tree species. In most cases, these surveys are carried out using a two-stage system. The first stage involves the interpretation of simultaneous colour and colour infra-red aerial photography with a second stage of randomly selected ground check sites.

Water Pollution
Water pollution can be defined as substances, bacteria or other organisms present in such concentrations to impair the quality of water rendering it less suitable or unsuitable for its intended use and presenting a hazard to man or the environment. Some of the main types of water pollutants are:

(i) organic wastes – contributed by sewage and industrial wastes;
(ii) eutrophication – caused by the addition of plant nutrients that promote nuisance growths of aquatic plant life;
(iii) synthetic – organic chemicals, such as detergents and pesticides;
(iv) inorganic chemical and mineral substances – resulting from mining, manufacturing and agricultural processes;
(v) oil and marine pollution;
(vi) sediments – as a result of erosion caused by land development; and
(vii) heated effluents – from the use of water for cooling purposes.

Any two bodies of water that differ in quality have a unique distribution of reflected, emitted and absorbed radiation. These characteristics can be used to distinguish bodies of water and in some cases, to obtain information about the physical and chemical nature of the water. Most of the available techniques may be applied to the study of water pollution. Although only in rare cases is it possible to make a positive identification of a pollutant by remote sensing, the point of discharge can be detected, where the effluent goes and the general characteristics of its dispersion pattern.

Most pollutants in water can be detected on colour photography because of the discoloration of the water. Even when receiving waters are highly polluted, discharges at or near the surface are usually visible for at least a short distance from the release point. Colour infra-red film is only recommended for photo-interpretation of industrial sites when the photos are taken from high altitudes (more than 6,000 m) to minimise the effects of atmospheric haze. It is, also, a very useful tool for evaluating the condition of floating aquatic vegetation, algal blooms and shoreline vegetation, where determining the presence or

absence of vegetation is important. The ideal situation is the use of both colour and colour infra-red photography taken simultaneously from low and medium altitude missions (van Genderen, 1975).

The resolution factor of satellite imagery is an obvious problem in water pollution studies. Nevertheless, reports of the use of Landsat-1 imagery indicate that a great deal can be done with respect to water pollution analysis in spite of the limitations imposed. Water clarity is a distinguishable feature on satellite imagery. On colour composites clear water appears a deep blue, while water containing organic and suspended matter, a yellow or green colour and turbid waters as brown. In this way, sedimentation can be mapped. Orbital imagery can indicate surface currents, which may affect pollution dispersal and has been successful in the detection of oil slicks.

The distribution of relative surface temperatures can be plotted with infra-red line scanners. This will indicate currents and effluents, together with their degree of mixing. Infra-red line scanners can be used to monitor oil pollution as there is normally a temperature difference between the oil slick and the surrounding water. The thickness of the oil is indicated by the density of the recorded image.

Photography is, and will be, the most useful water quality remote sensing tool (Scherz, 1971). It is concluded from many studies that colour air photo-interpretation provides the most efficient and accurate means of locating outfalls and polluted waters (Meyer and Welch, 1975).

Organic Wastes
The commonest type of water pollution is by organic matter such as sewage. This has the effect of stimulating bacterial and fungal growth and these processes absorb oxygen and so de-oxygenate the water. Today, most domestic sewage is treated before discharge to inland waters but this is not universally the case. In many cities the population has outgrown the capacity of the sewage works, so the treatment is incomplete and some raw sewage is also discharged.

Many studies have been reported describing the monitoring of sewage discharge into streams and estuaries, by Klooster and Scherz (1974), Piech and Walker (1972), Scherz (1971) and Strandberg (1967). The main techniques have been the use of colour and colour infra-red aerial photography and thermal infra-red imagery. Colour photography has proved useful because of its water penetrating ability and hence it shows up markedly any discoloration and discharge structures. False colour tends to highlight any algal development along banks resulting from sewage discharge. As the sewage is usually at a different temperature to the river's water, at least at the point of contact, the dispersal pattern can be monitored for some way from the source.

Eutrophication
Nutrient salts are deliberately added to rivers in sewage effluents and accidentally when farm animal wastes are not properly disposed. Modern arable farming also contributes by adding nitrates and phosphates to water. Most of the increase in levels of nitrogen comes from arable land caused largely by the use of varieties of cereal which respond to large amounts of chemical fertilisers. Unfortunately, only about half the nitrogen applied to the land is taken up by the crop; the rest is lost and some contributes to eutrophication. Little phosphate, even when liberally applied in chemical fertilisers, is lost as it is usually bound firmly in the soil. However, phosphate levels have increased spectacularly since about 1952 and this rise is believed to come mainly from detergents.

Eutrophication affects the vegetation of running water, but its greatest effects are seen when this water is impounded in a reservoir or where the river runs into a lake. The most obvious result is an algal bloom. The main remote sensor used to identify eutrophic conditions is colour infra-red photography which can readily locate floating algal masses by its high infra-red reflectance. Thermal infra-red scanners are also useful in monitoring algae, since definite temperature changes are associated with their growth. Oswald (1967) suggested the possible use of thermal infra-red sensing in defining areas of potential algal blooms, which are frequently related to thermal discharges into streams.

Synthetic Chemicals
Unfortunately, there are substances in domestic sewage which, at present, pass through the treatment plant and pollute the effluent. The most notorious are the modern synthetic detergents. The main complaint regarding detergents is that they release large amounts of phosphates, which cause an increase in algal growth, and can be monitored by sensors as discussed in the section on eutrophication.

The pollutants so far considered have been substances produced by man or his industries, which have caused unintentional damage to the environment. Their control has been achieved by taking greater care over their disposal. Pesticides, on the other hand, are poisonous substances deliberately disseminated in order to exploit their toxic properties. They become pollutants when they reach the wrong targets. The presence of abnormal amounts of pesticides can only be detected using remote sensors if the toxic properties of the pollutant have removed the natural stream-edge vegetation or in extreme cases fish-kills have occurred. Understandably, the detection of pesticide pollution is a difficult task.

Chemical and mineral substances result from mining, manufacturing and agricultural processes. A major pollutant is acid mine drainage from coal seams. It can be a natural polluting agent, but most damage comes from the tailings of coal seams that have been worked by man. The acid is formed when pyrite, marcasite and sulphur compounds come into contact with water and oxygen. These substances turn the stream bed a red or rusty yellow colour and are extremely toxic to flora and fauna, which can easily be detected on colour photography.

Marine Pollution

Often it is assumed that the sea can absorb, unharmed, all the wastes discharged into it. However, pollution of at least some of the seas does occur, largely because noxious substances do not become equally mixed but remain concentrated in limited areas.

A large amount of raw sewage is discharged into the sea. Where long outfall pipes are used, so there is little risk of fouling the beaches, this system is reasonably unobjectionable. The organic matter breaks down and the nutrients are re-cycled. However, the discharge of sewage and other organic wastes is often too near to the land.

Today, the main concern is that the ocean may be polluted by poisons, which do not break down as rapidly as the organic materials. There are reports of discharges of heavy metals, including mercury and lead, of industrial chemicals such as polychlor-biphenyls and other organo-chlorine insecticides. There is little control of dumping of poisonous waste materials outside territorial waters and no international agreements on this subject. Fishing grounds are avoided and durable containers likely to prevent leakage, at least in the immediate future, are used. Several satellite studies have been conducted, mainly in the USA, on the detection and monitoring of pollution in coastal waters. Mairs, et al (1973) found that by utilising Landsat-1 MSS Bands 4 and 5 that they could identify the dumping and dispersion of acid, sewage sludge and dredge spoil. They also found an increased reflectance of the water made turbid by the inflow of sewage effluent. From sequential imagery it was possible to monitor the movement of those turbid waters that were flushed out by the tides and migrated towards the bathing beaches.

Fontanel (1973) cited the use of MSS Band 4 in locating a large mass of acid industrial waste known as 'red mud'. This substance, composed of iron and titanium oxides along with sulphur acid, was clearly visible in the dumping area between France and Corsica. Wezernak and Roller (1973) also monitored acid, iron and sewage sludge dumps in coastal waters. They found that the dumps were clearly visible on the MSS Band 5 and a comparison with the imagery from Band 6 gave a relative idea of the depth of the sludge mass because of the differences in penetration.

Oil is one of the most obvious pollutants of the ocean. It acts as a blanketing and scouring agent. The effect on birds and marine animals and plants is well known. It is stated that several million tons of waste oil are today floating on the oceans, often harmlessly, but still a potential danger if washed ashore or into a region where birds dive to catch fish.

Owing to the complex behaviour of oil on water, the susceptibility to transport and the physio-chemical anomalies associated with its presence both aerial and surface based sensors are necessary components of a complete and effective monitoring system. Ultra-violet, visible, thermal infra-red and microwave sensors exhibit capabilities potentially suitable for oil detection. The choice of sensor package must be made to fit, not only the prevailing, but the possible environmental conditions, which might be encountered at the site of the spill.

Laboratory studies show that oil gives a strong anomalous response to incident energy compared with uncontaminated water in the ultra violet. Conventional cameras providing a high degree of resolution may be used, since film emulsions are sensitive down to 0·29 μm. However, their use is limited to daylight and good weather. Scanning systems, including television, can be utilised. These exhibit poorer resolution characteristics, but they have the advantage of real time viewing capabilities. Oil products are known to reflect strongly in the ultra-violet, blue and red portions of the electro-magnetic spectrum. Thus, by selecting film and filter combinations in a multiband camera system sensitive to these wavelengths, contrast enhancement can be achieved, Reinheimer, et al (1973), Vizy (1974).

Thermal infra-red imagery of oil slicks has been found to be an effective tool for the identification of oil on sea water under certain conditions. Since thermal sensors do not depend on reflected energy for image formation, they do provide both day and night surveillance capabilities. Operating in a scanning mode supplies the important real-time data acquisition capability. Radar systems also offer day and night capability and, some, virtually all weather sensing. In addition, radar has the ability to cover large areas on a single image. However, it has two limitations: relatively poor resolution and the difficulty of providing real-time data.

The early detection and monitoring of oil in the marine environment will significantly improve predictions of its location, nature, areal extent and behaviour over subsequent time periods. The increased use of satellite imagery in oil pollution detection will be of importance in this aspect. The resulting assessments of the threat imposed, volume spilled, treatment required and the responsibility of any damage will, in turn, depend upon the accuracy and reliability with which the oil can be monitored under any weather conditions, day or night. Furthermore, it is imperative that any remote sensing system, or combination of systems, provide some degree of real-time monitoring. It is this capability that will play a key role in establishing the operational utility of any system to be used in an emergency response, where there is usually little time to react to the dynamic, rapidly changing characteristics of the marine environment.

Sediments

Problems of water pollution and environmental quality can, also, result from physical land development activities; for example, construction of a new housing estate, land reclamation, industrial land development, etc. Soils are disturbed, organic materials dislodged and transported into waterways and natural vegetation and soil humus which tend to retard rapid run-off, are removed, thus increasing the load of materials in the streams and rivers. Aerial photography taken prior to development will permit identification of areas where such problems can be anticipated. Photo-interpretation will reveal important features, including areas of steep slopes, unstable soils and protective vegetation that may be disturbed and the location of natural water channels and moist soil areas.

Heated Effluents

Life can only exist over a comparatively narrow range of temperature. If some activity increases the temperature so that plants or animals are harmed, this may clearly be considered to amount to thermal pollution. In North America there are several widely reported cases of rivers being heated almost to boiling point so that they are completely lifeless. Other cases of water at 50°C or above contain no fish and practically no invertebrates, though a few thermophylic bacteria may flourish. So far no really spectacular thermal pollution has occurred elsewhere, but increasing in-dustrialisation is having its temperature effects and these need to be examined. The most notable are where water is used to cool machinery, particularly electrical power stations.

A study of the effects of water pollution in West Germany (Schneider, 1972), was conducted for the Saar river, which flows through an industrial agglomeration near the city of Saarbrucken. Two flights were made with an infra-red line scanner at a height of 1,000 metres above the river surface at 5.30 am and 6 pm. Out of 17 outfalls for cooling waters, 15 were exactly determined on the thermal imagery. It was necessary to compare the imagery taken on both flights, as six thermal sources did not show up on imagery taken before sunrise, but were identified on the evening imagery. In contrast, only two thermal sources did not show up on the evening imagery, which were identified on the early morning data. These differences are probably due to processes in the plants.

There have been similar reported studies of thermal water pollution using infra-red line scanning in several other European countries, including The Netherlands, Sweden (Svensson, 1969 and Sellin and Svensson, 1970) and France. Kaminiski (1972) interpreted satellite imagery from Nimbus 1, 2 and 3, ITOS-1 and NOAA-1 and measured temperatures in coastal waters of the English Channel and the North Sea which seem to correlate with neighbouring industrial and urban agglomeration.

Multidate aerial photography will provide a continuing record of conditions and associated pollution problems in the aquatic environment. The frequency of coverage depends upon the nature of the site being monitored and the dynamic components being observed. Aerial photographic surveys of industrial localities along waterways will cover areas and facilities where pollution sources may originate, such as industrial plants, storage areas, waste treatment facilities and transportation structures. The presence of such complexes would alert the interpreter to suspect discharges or spills of hazardous pollution substances. Some outfalls occur only at certain periods of the day and unless the photography is taken at the time of active discharge, it may not be possible to detect water discoloration. However, the presence of discharge structures, pipes, holding tanks, canals and signs of residue along the shoreline are usually reliable indicators of a potential pollution source.

Aerial photography taken for water pollution surveys should meet certain criteria. The film-filter combination(s) should be suitable for making the necessary distinctions between the discharged substance and the receiving waters. Usually colour photography best meets this requirement. The scale of photography should be adequate for detecting and identifying features associated with pollutant outfalls and spills, such as liquid storage tanks, pipelines, sewage treatment plants, raw material and waste holding features, industrial facilities, shipping docks and structures. The scale range most suitable for such interpretations usually is about 1/5,000 to 1/10,000. Regional surveys for reconnaissance mapping are commonly obtained at small scales of 1/40,000 to 1/60,000, followed by larger scale coverage of selected areas, where concentrations of facilities usually associated with pollution sources are observed. It is generally accepted that one of the most advantageous uses of remote sensing for environmental quality control is in its application as a surveillance tool to detect and identify potential sources of pollution. That is, to provide the environmental monitor with information on the proximity of hazardous materials to waterways and on the integrity of structures designed to contain these materials.

Waste Disposal and Derelict Land Surveys

There are many applications of remote sensing in identifying, locating, mapping and measuring present and potential tipping sites. Just four examples are quoted below of remote sensing applications to various aspects of waste disposal studies.

(i)   Standard Black and White Panchromatic Aerial Photographs – aerial photography can provide synoptic coverage of individual waste disposal sites or for systematic coverage of all waste disposal sites in a particular area. The type of information that can be obtained by means of air-photo interpretation includes data on exact size and location of waste disposal sites, whether wet or dry, hydrological conditions in and around the site (at time of photography), nature of vegetation cover (density, type, height, etc), whether the site is in use or disused, above or below ground level, area of site, rock type, if any mineral is being extracted, number of houses within $\frac{1}{2}$ km or distance to nearest house, number of access points, general character of surrounding area, etc. The results of such a survey can be plotted on transparent overlays to be superimposed on available maps.

(ii)   Colour Infra-red Photography – by using this film type, detailed information on any one site or a particular region can be obtained to examine the effects of waste tipping on the surrounding area. The photography can be interpreted in terms of vegetation damage, effects that the toxic wastes may have on the ground-water table and/or drainage and hence on the surrounding area, detailed information on surface and sub-surface drainage conditions.

(iii) Volumetric Measurements – detailed volumetric measurements of any waste disposal/tipping site can be obtained in order to assess the capacity of a particular site or to examine the rate at which a site is being filled, if repetitive measurements are taken, contoured plots of the waste disposal site, volume computations using punched tape output from photogrammetric plotting instruments.

(iv)   Models – high density polyurethane land form models can be made. These can be used for detailed planning of the site and allow monitoring of the changes to be displayed.

Operational systems for monitoring derelict land have been developed and, also, for collecting and analysing data for land reclamation. Either very rapid surveys can be carried out by means of

small scale air photo-interpretation suitable for county level requirements, or much more detailed surveys of industrial and other forms of despoiled land. Remote sensing methods provide an economical, fast and reliable way of locating, monitoring and mapping derelict land studies and land reclamation schemes.

Environmental Impact Assessment

In any proposal for construction or development it is usual practice, both from a standpoint of engineering or economics, to prepare an analysis of the need for development and the relationship between its costs and benefits. More recently it has been recognised that there should be an additional detailed assessment of the effect of a proposed action on the environment, which usually involves an ecological cost-benefit analysis. When combined these investigations comprise an environmental impact assessment. The scope of an environmental data collection programme may range from an entire survey and inventory of base-line conditions in the case of a planned development to specific local investigations of existing facilities and their impact on the surroundings. Experience has shown the amount of time required to collect all the physical, biological, sociological and economic data has caused the suspension and, in some cases, the abandonment of many projects after considerable expenditure.

It therefore follows that the use of remote sensing methods to achieve rapid and efficient data collection is one of the keys to the orderly and timely development of a successful environmental impact assessment. As well as monitoring regional environmental conditions, it is also practical to focus on specific sensitive sites using the same remote sensing data and a similar method of interpretation and analysis. The data extracted from aerial photography or image data are informationally and temporally compatible, unlike other data collection methods, as even large areas can be recorded within a short time span. Remote sensing imagery contains the type of spatial information necessary for determining the number, location and type of field sampling system as well as yielding spectral data unobtainable from more conventional field survey procedures.

The use of an environmental impact decision matrix is one of the most effective ways in which large quantities of data can be systematically considered. However, often the relationship between measured environmental parameter and the physical character of the site is lost and it can become extremely difficult to convey results to the interested parties. Thus, remote sensing imagery with pertinent overlays of environmental factor distributions can overcome such problems by linking a data matrix with a visual presentation and an illustrative written text.

Remote sensing analysis contributes to the following stages in an environmental impact assessment:

(i)   Interpretation of base-line environmental conditions.

(ii)   Preliminary assessment of the impact of a proposed action.

(iii) Design of field data gathering programmes.

(iv)   Extrapolation of information from known ground sites to other areas.

(v)   Supplementing ground data in final environmental impact assessment.

(vi)   Providing a synoptic base for planning purposes.

(vii) Providing annotated image overlays to supplement decision matrices and written report material.

Remote sensing techniques when performed by experienced image interpreters and data analysts, can now provide an efficient and systematic approach to the collection of physical and biological information for environmental monitoring.

Summary

The collection of data necessary to establish a base line of environmental conditions, as well as studies to determine the extent of the impact from existing development has to date usually been carried out by means of laborious, time-consuming, and hence costly, field investigations. Remote sensing technology can provide a more efficient, systematic and less expensive approach to environmental data collection and field survey planning. A series of steps and procedures are outlined below and used as guidelines to indicate how remote sensing can be used to accomplish any of the following types of objectives in the field of environmental monitoring:

(i)   Collect data for land use mapping.

(ii)   Detect alien substances in the environment.

(iii) Identify specific pollutants and classes of pollutants.

(iv)   Monitor the source, movement and fate of pollutants.

(v)   Determine the effects of pollutants on the environment.

(vi) Analyse remotely sensed data to determine environmental quality, the susceptibility of the environment to degradation and provide data for comprehensive environmental management planning.

The first step in such an approach (after North 1971) is to define the area or areas to be surveyed and then to collect whatever environmental data are already in existence. While this ground truth data is being collected, a set of high quality aerial photographs of the study area should be flown. From this imagery skilled photo-interpreters would prepare land use maps. By measuring areas, it is possible to determine how much land is devoted to each activity. When these steps have been completed, the specific information can be extracted concerning the detection, identification and monitoring of environmental pollutants or land quality factors. Relevant information must be gained from the photography to serve both as a base line against which to monitor subsequent changes and for taking and implementing planning decisions. By careful examination of the photography, interpreters can carry out a cataloguing and inventory of effluents, sewage plant location, smokestack plumes, etc, thus, a base map of pollution sources and indicators can be compiled. Once the basic photographic coverage has been analysed, the requirements for further photography will become obvious. It is at this point that specific sensors, altitudes and film/filter combinations will be required.

The next step in determining environmental quality is to build up an information system and working model of the region. This involves the use of a computer to store the available environmental information. One method is to digitise the photo-interpretation map overlays on the basis of grid cells, thereby facilitating data extraction and comparisons with subsequent data sets. Another method is to code and store the data so that it can be related to enumeration districts, allowing the data to be correlated with other census information. Thus, remote sensing is a systematic approach, which facilitates the future use of data for other purposes. Each new set of data may be entered and compared with previously collected information.

The final stage in such a regional environmental monitoring study is to initiate corrective programmes. This involves decisions which must be made by administrators, resource managers, ecologists, planners, etc. Once corrective actions have been taken, it is usual to monitor the region to assess improvements. This, of course, can also be accomplished by remote sensing methods. Thus, if periodic coverage is acquired it can be used not only to produce new data but to assess the success or failure of the corrective programme.

Remote sensing technology provides an efficient and systematic approach to environmental data collection and field survey planning. The advantages of the modern remote sensors lie not only in the synchronous and synoptic observations of phenomena of regional studies, but in the combination of results from various sources, aerial photography, imagery, computer data and field work. There will no doubt be cases where the use of any one method will satisfy the demands made on individual research projects. However, the multi-informational remote sensing systems, where interpretation from the various sources is undertaken by inter-disciplinary working groups, will provide the best over-view of the environment.

References

Fontanel, A. (1973): Study of Pollution at Sea in the Western Mediterranean. Symposium on significant results obtained from the Earth Resources Technology Satellite-1 NASA SP-327, Vol I. Technical Presentations 1500-5.

Genderen, J. L. van (1974): Remote sensing of environmental pollution. Journal of Environmental Pollution, 6, 221-34.

Genderen, J. L. van (1975): Remote sensing of the Environment, with special emphasis on possible applications to the work of the Scottish Office. Paper presented to the Scottish Development Department, Edinburgh.

Giever, P. M. (1966): Needs for remote sensing data in the field of air and water pollution. Proceedings of the 4th International Symposium on Remote Sensing of Environment, Ann Arbor, Michigan.

Heller, R. C. (1969): Large scale colour photo assessment of smog-damaged pines. Proceedings of the Symposium of the ASP and Soc Photog Sci and Eng, New York, 15, 596-606.

Heller, R. C. (1971): Detection and characterisation of stress symptoms in forest vegetation. Proceedings of the International Workshop on Earth Resources Survey Systems, NASA, Washington 108-50.

Kaminiski, H. (1972): Detection of waste water effluents and of their surface spread in the English Channel, North Sea and the Baltic Sea, through the determination of the surface temperature of the sea by means of infra-red pictures taken by satellites, Bochum.

Kirby, R. P. (1977): Remote Sensing in the detection of Vegetation Stress with special reference to Dutch Elm Disease. University of Edinburgh, Research Discussion Paper No 12. 29pp.

Klooster, S. A. and Scherz, J. P. (1974): Water quality by photographic analysis. Photogrammetric Engineering 40, 927-35.

Mairs, R. L. and Clark, D. K. (1973): Remote sensing of estuarine circulation dynamics. Photogrammetric Engineering 39, 927-38.

Mellanby, K. (1972): The Biology of Pollution. The Institute of Biology, Studies in Biology No 38. Edward Arnold, London. 60pp.

Meyer, W. and Welch, R. I. (1975): Water Resources Assessment. In Manual of Remote Sensing edited by R. G. Reeves, ASP 1479-1551.

Miller, R. P., Parmeter, J. R., Flick, B. H. and Martinez, C. W. (1969): Ozone damage response of Ponderosa Pine seedlings. Air Pollution Control Association Journal 19, 435-38.

Murtha, P. A. (1973): SO_2 damage to forests recorded by ERTS-I. Proceedings of the 3rd ERTS-I Symposium, Volume I, Section A, Goddard Space Flight Center, Washington DC, 137-43.

Murtha, P. A. (1976): Vegetation damage and remote sensing; principal problems and recommendations, Photogrammetria 32, 147-56.

Myers, B. J. (1974): The application of colour aerial photography to forestry: a literature review. Forestry and Timber Bureau, Canberra, ACT Leaflet No 124. 20pp.

North, G. W. (1971): Remote sensing for pollution and environmental quality studies. Proceedings of the 7th International Symposium on Remote Sensing of Environment, Ann Arbor, Michigan, 973-87.

Olson, C. (1971): Remote sensing of broad-leaf trees under stress. Proceedings of the 3rd International Photo-Interpretation Conference, Dresden, 689-96.

Oswald, W. J. (1967): Remote sensing data evaluation of water quality. Proceedings of the 3rd Annual Conference on Remote Sensing of Air and Water Pollution, Sacramento, California.

Piech, K. R. and Walker, J. E. (1972): Outfall inventory using air photo-interpretation, Photogrammetric Engineering 38, 907-14.

Reinheimer, C. J., Rudder, C. L. and Berrey, J. L. (1973): Detection of petroleum spills. Photogrammetric Engineering 39, 1277-88.

Remeyn, J. M. (1972): Kodak Ektachrome infra-red film for vitality studies of Norway Spruce in the Netherlands, ITC Forestry Department Publication, 7-21.

Scherz, J. P. (1971): Remote sensing considerations for water quality monitoring. Proceedings of the 7th International Symposium on Remote Sensing of Environment, Ann Arbor, Michigan, 1071-87.

Schneider, S. (1972): Environmental control from airborne and space vehicles. Proceedings of the Symposium on Remote Sensing and Photo Interpretation-I, ISP Comm VII, Ottawa. 15pp.

Sellin, L. and Svensson, H. (1970): Airborne thermography. Geoforum 2, 46-60.

Stellingwerf, D. A. (1969): Kodak Ektachrome infra-red aero film for forestry purposes, ITC Publication, Series B, No 54.

Strandberg, C. H. (1967): Aerial Discovery Manual. John Wiley & Sons. 249pp.

Sukhih, V. I. and Sinitsin, S. G. (1974): Methods of interpretation of aerial photographs in forest inventory and management in the USSR. Proceedings of the Symposium on Remote Sensing and Photo Interpretation-2. ISP Comm VII, Ottawa, 535-40.

Thornburn, T. H. (1974): Environmental applications of remote sensing techniques – water quality and water pollution detection and surveys. Proceedings of the UN/FAO Regional Seminar on Remote Sensing of the Earth Resources and Environment, Cairo, September 4-15, 251-64.

Vizy, K. N. (1974): Detecting and monitoring oil slicks with aerial photos. Photogrammetric Engineering 40, 697-708.

Wezernak, C. T. and Roller, N. (1973): Monitoring ocean dumping with ERTS-I Data. Symposium on results obtained from the Earth Resources Technology Satellite-1 NASA SP-327, Vol I, Technical Presentations 635-41.

Weber, F. P. and Polcyn, F. C. (1972): Remote sensing to detect stress in forests, Photogrammetric Engineering 38, 163-75.

Wert, S. L. (1969): A system for using remote sensing techniques to detect and evaluate air pollution effects on forest stands. Proceedings of the 6th International Symposium on Remote Sensing of Environment, Ann Arbor, Michigan, 1169-78.

REMOTE SENSING, AN AID TO LANDSCAPE MANAGEMENT
DR J. F. HANDLEY

Metropolitan authorities are faced with the challenge of promoting urban regeneration whilst safeguarding the quality of surrounding countryside. An aerial survey of residential environments in Merseyside demonstrates the impoverished nature of inner city environments. Landscape regeneration is proceeding but the nature of the problem, as shown by a survey of despoiled and derelict land, demands novel approaches to landscape design.

Landscape restoration is also needed in the urban fringe where extensive derelict and despoiled land is a potential landscape resource. In open country air photography reveals a rapid deterioration in natural environments due to neglect and heavy public pressure. Remote sensing has assisted in the management of these damaged areas.

MONITORING UPLAND LANDSCAPE CHANGE BY REMOTE SENSING
DR M. L. PARRY

In the uplands of western Europe and the eastern United States increasing, and often conflicting, demands are being placed on a relatively sensitive ecosystem by agriculture, forestry, water catchment and recreation. On the landscapes which mirror this land-use competition there is evidence for an accelerating rate of change and this, in particular, has given cause for recent concern. An appropriate example of such 'landscapes under pressure' are the national parks of England and Wales, predominantly upland areas where the ranks of traditional 'land-users' (farming, forestry and water) are joined by recreation and conservation. This increase in pressure is disturbing, but we do not know precisely the nature of the consequent changes of landscape nor their pace. The problem can be most readily solved by the judicious combination of remote sensing and more orthodox forms of landscape study.

The types of landscape change evident in European uplands are wide-ranging. The most obvious are changes in the extent of rough grassland by reclamation (exemplified by the controversy in Exmoor National Park) and the process of afforestation or cut-over of woodland. Changes in the make-up of the semi-natural vegetation of moorland and mountain areas are no less important: the spread of bracken on dry-grass moorland since the 1940s is a problem faced by hill farmers throughout Britain. In some uplands there are signs of a substantial increase in erosion – by gulleying in hill peat, along sheep-walks and along footpaths and bridleways; and, in addition, there are changes to the upland landscape that derive from both the adjustment of hill-farming systems (deterioration of dry-stone walling, farm buildings and shelter-belts) and from the impact of tourist traffic, both on and off the roads.

Yet few of these landscape changes are adequately understood. Indeed, there are many instances in which we either do not know what changes are occurring, or what the scale of change has been because of our relative ignorance of the landscape before such change occurred. Moorland conversion and the spread of bracken are appropriate examples of this – we know they have occurred, and are now occurring, but to what extent, where and when is not at all clear. An unfortunate result of this uncertainty is that factions disputing the use of upland areas may take advantage of a weak and conflicting land-use record to substantiate their respective cases. There is, therefore, a need both to monitor contemporary changes of landscape and to monitor landscape changes of the recent past in order to provide a context for evaluating the significance of landscape change in the present and the future. The change may itself be seen to have several dimensions and it is logical that these should be measured in sequence. Thus, an initial survey of the location and distribution of landscape changes can enable an estimate to be made of their quantity; and, if these distributions can be studied in time-series, then a judgment may be made of their rate of change. More detailed studies may then follow on the process of change and its explanation.

The aim of this paper is to evaluate the use of remote sensing in monitoring these four dimensions of landscape change. I shall focus attention on the mapping and dating of change, because these are prerequisites for satisfactory description of process and its explanation. I shall deal firstly with the applications of remote sensing in monitoring contemporary changes of landscape and, secondly, with its utility for surveying changes in the recent past as a platform for contemporary studies.

Monitoring Contemporary Landscape Change

Three types of imagery are useful in the survey of landscape change in upland areas: (1) multispectral scanner data from Landsat and similar satellites, (2) small-scale, infra-red photography from high-altitude aircraft such as the U2, and (3) large-scale photography from low-altitude aircraft.

Satellite Imagery

Satellite imagery of the UK is widely available as a photographic print composed from digital information on sensor data tapes. These give a synoptic picture of broad land-use patterns at scales of about 1:250,000 but are unsatisfactory as a data source for land-use or landscape change at the local level. It is possible, however, to produce line-printer maps direct from the original, but corrected, digital information (composed of pixels of about half a hectare) at scales as large as 1:24,000. Urban land-use classes in the US have been mapped at this scale from ERTS-I MSS data to an accuracy of 90 per cent, although the number of classes is severely limited.[1] In rural areas it is possible to distinguish between deciduous and coniferous woodland, and between semi-natural moorland, permanent grassland and cropland. While some land-use types are not readily distinguished by their spectral signature, other (for example, heather moorland) are registered quite strongly. Indeed, it would probably be quite possible to adopt satellite imagery as the central source for monitoring year-to-year changes in heather moorland in the UK. With adequate ground control from existing base maps (and this is provided by the Second Land Use Survey of the late 1960s), the distribution of moorland conversion at 1:50,000 could be monitored with an accuracy of about 90 per cent.

This scale of survey, supplemented by agricultural census data at the parish level, would be capable of giving a regional picture of the extent and pace of farmland reversion or moorland conversion in upland areas. But it would be too small to be of use to National Park or ADAS officers – the smallest operational scale for these users is probably 1:25,000. Moreover, a large number of other landscape changes are not readily apparent at the required scale and with a reasonable degree of precision. It is possible that satellite imagery will, in the near future, satisfy a need for more comprehensive and accurate mapping but, in the meantime, this must be sought elsewhere.

High-altitude Photography

High-altitude photography offers the greatest promise. Colour infra-red photography of 1:160,000 scale taken from U2 aircraft provide the basis for the US Land Use and Land Cover Mapping Program which is conducted by the Geography Program of the US Geological Survey. Initiated in 1974, this survey had covered one-half of the US by November 1977 and will be completed by 1982.[2] The maps are compiled at a scale of 1:125,000. Only samples are published, the remainder being placed on 'open file' for purchase from the USGS Mapping Centres. The time-lapse between photography and availability of the data is only a few months, and exploratory work by the Geography Program has indicated that comprehensive rural land-use and landscape mapping could be achieved at 1:24,000 with an accuracy of 85-87 per cent.[3]

A survey of changes in land use since the data of initial mapping began in 1978 for small, selected areas. This is at present based on high-altitude photography but may, in future, rely on satellite imagery backed up by high-altitude photography for problem areas. The intention is to update the coverage every six or seven years and to present the data on land-use change on computer-mapped overlays of the original maps.[4] Area measurements of land-use change, and a wide range of associated information, will be available from a computer-based Geographic Information Research and Analysis System (GIRAS).[5]

I have outlined this mapping programme in some detail because it is evident that it has adopted a powerful combination of techniques – high-resolution, small-scale photography together with a flexible computer-mapping system and rapid publication – that would be valuable to the student of landscape change; and it is precisely this form of rapid and systematic monitoring of landscape change that is required in the UK and Europe because it could be implemented at the 1:25,000 scale and can yield information across the entire range of major land-use classes. A plea has recently been made for the construction of a data base of this kind – a nationwide UK coverage of high-altitude, infra-red photography, re-taken every five years – that would provide information for a wide variety of rural and urban landscape studies.[6]

Low-level Aerial Photography

The monitoring of contemporary landscape change requires a frequently updated information base, and it is an unfortunate irony that, in spite of the wealth both of airsurvey expertise and of airphoto demand, there is no comprehensive and systematically updated airphoto coverage of the UK. Thus individual landscape surveys need either to implement their own aerial surveys or to purchase existing photography, which, if not outdated, may frequently be of varying dates for different parts of the study area. Yet many types of landscape survey will, in spite of an inadequate airphoto coverage, find substantial advantage in the speed of aerial mapping relative to that of conventional field mapping. For example, changes in moorland in the Peak District and in the Lammermuir Hills in south-east Scotland were mapped and field-checked by the author at an approximate rate of 20 man-hours per 100 sq.km, which is perhaps three times more rapid than that which could have been achieved by field survey alone.[7]

Moreover, comparisons of the relative precision of airphoto-based and field-based landscape mapping generally reveal an equal degree of rigour. The uncorrected 'eyeballing' of stereoscopically-viewed data from (for example) 1:10,000 airphotos onto 1:10,000 topographic base-maps should be accurate to 95 per cent – though this figure will, of course, vary with the experience of the interpreter, the quality of the airphoto cover, the precision of the interpretation key and the type of landscape element under scrutiny. An accuracy of 98 per cent can be achieved at 1:5,000 with medium-order plotting instruments. Sample field checking has indicated that moorland changes in the Peak District and Lammermuir Hills, mapped from 1:10,000 panchromatic prints, are open to a maximum range of error not exceeding 10 per cent.[8]

Monitoring Recent Landscape Change

Information about on-going landscape change requires a reference point or context against which it can be evaluated; without one, the significance of change cannot be meaningfully assessed. Thus a small degree of change may, for one area, represent a radical departure from a landscape that has remained unchanged for centuries, while a substantial change in an area characterised by continuing adaptation (for example, the moorland edge in upland Britain), may not always be significant. In other words, the significance of landscape change (its direction, its time and its rate) depends very much on the stage upon which it occurs, and a plausible case can be made that monitoring on-going change without monitoring recent change is likely to yield information that cannot be fully evaluated. The remainder of this paper attends to the survey of recent landscape changes in upland areas.

Post-war Change in the Upland Landscape

A data source that is rarely employed in studies of landscape change but which is probably the most reliable available is time-series aerial photography. The United Kingdom has a coverage of standard, panchromatic aerial photographs taken by the RAF in the late 1940s or early 1950s, and by the Ordnance Survey or commercial air-survey companies in the 1960s and 1970s. Most areas have a coverage in duplicate, and many have a triplicate coverage. It is therefore quite possible to make a comparative study of a time-series of photography that records the state of the landscape at quite different dates. The comparison must be made with care because variations in both the season and the time of day of photography will produce misleading differences in vegetation and shadow. Differences in film and lighting will yield variations in tone, and differences in altitude and type of camera will produce variations in scale and in degree of distortion. However, given the use of comprehensive interpretation keys and stereoscopic study of the airphoto prints, a precise measurement of changes in landscape, land cover and land use

may be obtained. To illustrate this point an example may be taken from an area within the Peak District National Park.

Panchromatic aerial photography is available for the Dark Peak for the following dates:

RAF	April 1953	c.1:10,000
Meridian Airmaps	April 1966	1:10,500
Ordnance Survey	April 1976	1:26,200

Reproduced here are three prints for a sample area in Alport Dale, Hope Forest (Figure 1). They have been equalised in tone and scale to facilitate comparison, but it should be emphasised that, in the absence of stereoscopy and with the loss of detail in printing, only the most marked landscape changes will be apparent to the reader. Under stereoscopy, however, it is possible to locate and quantify reclamation and reversion of rough pasture and to evaluate the effect of afforestation on the landscape. Changes in peat coverage and increasing erosion are also evident. From evidence of this kind we can make a precise statement about the location, extent and pace of a variety of landscape changes in addition to those of vegetation or erosion – about the development of footpaths over the peat surface and its effect on drainage, about changes in the relative proportions of moorland, farmland and woodland, and about changes in walls, fences and buildings.

Figure 1: Landscape changes, 1953-76, from aerial photographs, at Alport Dale, Derbyshire.

Changes in the Upland Landscape since about 1870

Among the various forms of upland change that have been identified, the most important occurring today is the conversion of moorland to improved farmland and the (converse) degeneration of marginal farmland to rough pasture; and the survey of former changes of this kind have, for several reasons, a particular bearing on the present. Firstly, the argument over moorland conservation or reclamation has tended to focus on the longevity of the existing land-use and the opposing factions have frequently selected a version of land-use history that has suited their cause. If the argument is to centre on 'history' then at least let us have a full and factual historical record to hand.

Secondly, there is a real, but as yet uncertain, link between the present vegetation types of upland areas and their land-use history. For example, the airphoto evidence points clearly to a contrast in vegetation types between hill areas that have not been cultivated in the last 200 years (and which have an unbroken root mat and undisturbed soil horizons), and areas that have reverted from a once-improved state. This link is important to our comprehension of the ecology and capacity of the uplands today.

Finally, the chronology of recent landscape change in moorland areas can provide a basis for upland management policies. In the Peak District, the Planning Board has adopted the concept of 'core areas' and 'marginal areas' which can be defined from a survey of both past and contemporary locations of the moorland edge. In the 'core areas' (which have never previously been enclosed and improved) there should be a general presumption against agricultural conversion or afforestation. In the 'marginal areas' (the areas which had at some time been enclosed or improved and at other times been moorland) a more flexible policy has been agreed.[9]

The survey of former landscape change, in addition to that occurring today, is therefore valuable in a number of different ways. It is possible to reconstruct the history of reclamation and reversion at the moorland edge by comparative study of a time-series of OS topographic maps and by scrutiny of aerial photographs which record the landscape evidence for pre-OS reclamation and reversion.

The precise location and approximate dates of reclamation and reversion at the UK moorland edge from about 1870 can be identified from a comparison of successive editions of six-inch Ordnance Survey maps. OS surveyors and 'field revisers' identified landscape changes exceeding 0·25 ha and the consistency and accuracy of their work can be judged from a study of various editions of the OS 'Red Book' and (for post-war editions) by comparison with aerial photographs contemporaneous with the dates of field revision.[10] Dates of re-survey vary from region to region, for example those for the Peak District were 1871-80, 1894-1908, 1920-21, 1949-51 and 1959; and for the Lammermuir Hills were 1853-60, 1892-98, 1905-06, 1916-22, 1952-54 and 1961-64.

Primary reclamation of moorland (Figure 2). The study of sequential OS maps and aerial photographs enables the identification of the quantity, location and approximate date of the primary reclamation of previously unimproved (virgin) rough pasture. In the Peak District this amounts to 17,750 ha, or 54 per cent of the rough land remaining today.

'Permanent' reversion of improved farmland (Figure 3). It is also possible to map improved farmland which has reverted to rough pasture and which remains unimproved today. In this way we can establish the longevity of once-improved moorland and distinguish between regenerated moorland and 'moorland core' that has probably never been broken up, at least not by the mould-board plough.

The landscape changes that have been noted here are the most significant ones – *primary* reclamation of previously never-cultivated land and *permanent* reversion to rough land that remains unimproved to this day. We also have information on the very many interim fluctuations of temporary reversion and secondary reclamation that have occurred in the recent past, and recurrent fluctuations of this kind may provide a useful perspective on similar changes occurring today.

Changes in the Upland Landscape before 1870

For evidence of landscape change before the first edition of OS maps we must, once again, rely on the study of aerial photographs. With the assistance of detailed interpretation keys, by the scrutiny of duplicate and triplicate coverage of photography and by field checking, the distribution of plough land which had reverted to rough pasture by 1870 can be mapped to a locational accuracy and comprehensiveness of over 90 per cent. Moreover, a typology of cultivation ridges based

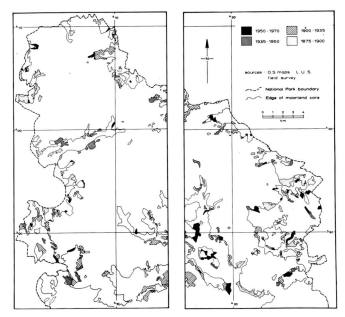

Figure 2: Primary reclamation and afforestation in the Peak District, 1870-1970.

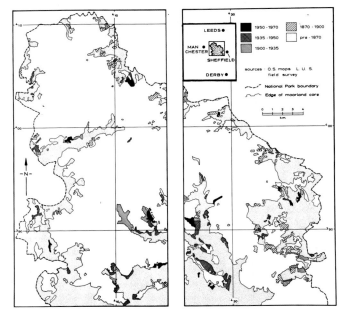

Figure 3: 'Permanent' reversion to moorland in the Peak District, 1870-1970.

on their morphology enables a distinction to be made between pre-1800 reversion and reversion occurring over 1800-1870 (Figure 4).[12]

The complementary use of aerial photographs and topographic maps allows some important statements to be made about the upland landscapes of today.

Firstly, it enables a distinction to be made between the never-cultivated moorland core and once-improved but regenerated rough pasture – the 'moorland fringe'. Further studies of the differences in soils and vegetation between these two types of rough land should be made to ascertain their ecological status, but there is a *prima facie* case for encouraging the conservation of the moorland core, since this area most closely approximates a natural landscape in ecological terms. The 'fringe areas' may deserve a more flexible land-use policy that, on the merits of individual areas, allows either for more permanent integration into the adjoining moor or for encouragement of improved agricultural use.

Secondly, and at the more local level, the OS and airphoto mapping offers a field-by-field reconstruction of the chronology of reclamation and reversion. This can provide useful background information for decisions concerning the response to be made to specific proposals by landowners for reclamation or afforestation. In such instances it might be desirable to encourage such developments away from areas which, according to all the evidence, have never been broken up, and towards identifiable areas which have a history of successful improvement.

Conclusions

The examples adopted in this paper have focused on the changes in the extent of moorland because this is probably the most substantial change occurring today on the landscape of British and European uplands. But I have stressed that the techniques discussed here would be equally appropriate for a variety of different landscape surveys.

I have also stressed the need always to evaluate present change in its temporal context. It is this line of thought that has prompted the development of an airphoto-based survey of recent moorland change in seven UK National Parks. This two-year survey is due to begin in October 1979 at the University of Birmingham with finance from the Social Science Research Council. The objective is to provide a sound basis upon which to evaluate the significance of on-going moorland change. But we should recognise that, if the landscape changes of the future are to be monitored effectively, there is a pressing need for a nationwide and systematically-flown airphoto coverage of the UK with a prescribed interval for up-date. Regularly updated, high-altitude photography of the kind available in the United States may be a prerequisite for landscape policies that are sufficiently sensitive of the landscapes they seek to manage and protect.

References

[1]Ellefson, R. *et al* (1974): 'New techniques in mapping urban land use and monitoring change for selected US metropolitan areas – an experiment employing computer-assisted analysis of ERTS-I MSS data'. *Intern Soc of Photogrammetry Proceedings of Commission No 7 (Alberta)*, Vol I, 56-63.

[2]Anderson, J. R. *et al* (1976): 'A land use and land cover classification for use with remote sensor data'. *Geological Survey Professional Paper No 964*.

[3]Fitzpatrick, K. A. (1975): 'Cost, accuracy and consistency comparisons of land use maps made from high-altitude aircraft photography and ERTS imagery', Final Report, Vol 6, Carets Project, US Geological Survey; Fitzpatrick-Lins, K. A. (1978): 'Accuracy of selected Land Use and Land Cover Maps in the Greater Atlanta Region, Georgia', *Jour Research US Geol Survey*, 1978.

[4]Anderson, J. R. (1977): 'Land use and landcover changes – A framework for monitoring', *Jour Research US Geol Survey* 5(2), 143-53.

[5]Mitchell, W. B. *et al* (1977): 'GIRAS: A Geographic Information Retrieval and Analysis System for handling land-use and land cover data', *US Geological Survey Professional Paper*, No 1059.

[6]Parry, M. L. (1978): *Information for Upland Management: A pilot survey of the mapping methods*. Report to the SSRC. Project No 5210.

[7]Parry, M. L. (1976): 'The mapping of abandoned farmland in upland Britain', *Geogr Jour* 142(1), 101-110; Parry, M. L. (1977): *Mapping moorland change: A framework for land-use decisions in the Peak District*, Peak District National Park, Bakewell.

[8]Parry, M. L. (1976): *op cit* 101-110; Parry, M. L. (1977): *op cit.*

[9]Peak Park Joint Planning Board (1978): *Peak District National Park: National Park Plan* (in particular Chapter 4 and Section 13.1). Identification of the 'core areas' and 'marginal areas' is discussed in Parry, M. L. *op cit* 1977 (also published as *A framework for land-use planning in moorland areas*, University of Birmingham, Department of Geography, Occasional Publications No 4.

[10]*Instructions for Detail Survey, Revision and Examination of large-scale plans* (The Red Book), 1952, Ordnance Survey.

[11]See Parry, M. L. (1977) *op cit.*

[12]This is described in Parry, M. L. (1977): 'A typology of cultivation ridges in southern Scotland', *Tools and Tillage* 3(1):3-19.

21 April 1953
RAF F21 58/RAF/1094: 0274

26 April 1968
Meridian Airways 27 68 157

30 April 1976
OS 76 015 364   *Sources of Fig 1 photographs.*

Key

1 Effects of afforestation:
   (a) pre-plantation vegetation of *calluna* and grasses evident in 1953 (at A); effects of enclosure on vegetation by 1968 and 1976;
   (b) plough-up preparatory to planting (at B_1, B_2 and B_3) between 1968 and 1976: *calluna* at B_1 and B_2, of improved grassland at B_3.
2 Pasture improvement (at C): Re-seeding prior to 1953, some reduction of *juncus* by 1968, further reduced by 1976.
3 Vegetation changes:
   (a) on valley side (c.15°) at D, increase in *calluna* 1953-68 and over 1968-76;
   (b) at E increase in *calluna* 1953-68-76; some pasture improvements at F; these possibly due to changes in control of grazing resulting from new fence at G (1953-68).
4 Peat erosion:
   Some headward erosion of rills at H_1, H_2 and H_3; deepening of rills at I_1, I_2 (detectable only under stereoscopy).

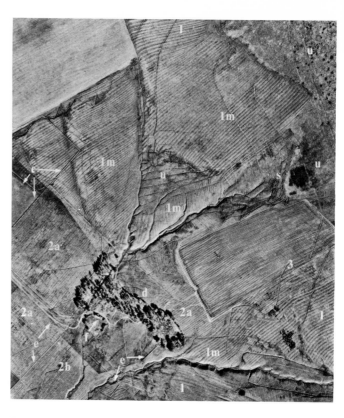

Figure 4: Vertical aerial photograph of reverted farmland in the Lammermuir Hills, south-east Scotland. Key: 1=irregular, broad cultivation ridges abandoned before c.1800; 1m= Type 1 modified by levelling and splitting after c.1800; 2a, 2b=straight ridges of regular breadth abandoned 1800-70; 3= Type 2 ridges overlying vestigial Type 1; E=post-1800 enclosure; F=post-1800 farmstead; d=recent ploughing for afforestation; S=open drainage (or 'grips'); u=never-cultivated moorland.

ECOLOGICAL CONSERVATION, COUNTRYSIDE PLANNING AND LAND ECONOMY

LANDOWNERSHIP AND LANDSCAPE PROFESSOR D. R. DENMAN

PROGRESS IN BIOLOGICAL CONSERVATION IN CAMBRIDGE DOCTOR S. M. WALTERS

ECOLOGICAL CONSIDERATIONS IN LANDSCAPE DESIGN AND MANAGEMENT – PART I EDDIE KEMP

PART II BRIAN CLOUSTON IN COLLABORATION WITH CHRISTOPHER WILD

LANDOWNERSHIP AND LANDSCAPE
PROFESSOR D. R. DENMAN

All civilisations have had their man-made landscapes, the good and the bad, some professionally designed, some the happy by-products of unrelated policy and some the layman's choice and fancy. Nothing happened by chance. Decisions were taken, then as now. And critical for the landscape is the question – whose decisions? While professionals and bureaucrats may have played their parts, the final word everywhere and at all times has been with the landowners. This universal truth is essential to a proper understanding of the making of landscape and yet is one seldom recognised. We, in our day, have become so accustomed to the planning processes and dialogue as to mislead ourselves into thinking of landscape and land use patterns as the outcome of planning decisions. Planners are at best negative in power and action. They may prohibit but not execute. They cannot initiate action and take positive decisions. This is no adverse criticism of them or their work – it is simply a fact of life. Only the holder of property rights has power to do. This basic theorem is the theme of this paper, as it is of first consequence to national and international landscape.

The question is also of primary consequence to the landscape architect. As a professional he acts for his client. If the client has no power to execute the ideas suggested by the architect, there is little point in taking instructions. It is not denied that landscape architects do on occasion work with the planners, those who draw up global plans for the use of land. What can be done and is done with the plans is of the first order of importance. So let us, at the outset, look a little more closely at the planning process and its achievement in our day.

Planning as practised in this country is no sure safeguard of the beauties of landscape nor a means of enhancing them. This is not to say that planning has failed. Doubtless, it has achieved much. What is clear is that it has not, and presumably cannot, protect us from an ugliness, creeping and growing over the landscape, which we all deplore. There is a fault somewhere that we need to find and rectify. Some years ago hopes were raised that the remedy was to be found in wider public participation in the planning process. Hope is withering on that vine; the wider and wilder the public voice, the greater the confusion and delays in the planning process. Is there then something else, something that has been overlooked all down the years of this planning and planned age? Have we misunderstood the power syndrome that determines land use and landscape? I believe we have. We have misread the credentials of planning and paid too little attention to those of landownership.

Planning is not a philosopher's stone, the depository of a hidden, an inherent wisdom. It is not a force but a process. We are all planners after our style. We plan our holidays, our homes, our income tax dodges. Planning is no more than a process of rational thought making for order. God said: let there be light. Hitler said: let the Jews of Warsaw perish. Both were planners, after their way. In short, we can plan both good and evil, beauty and ugliness. The outcome of a planned decision cannot go beyond the power of the planner to decide, nor achieve more than his ability to judge can warrant. The so-called planned landscape is no more than a mirror of man's wisdom, wiles and weaknesses.

Planning is the rational ordering of forces beyond itself. This truth cannot be over-emphasised. That waste is dumped in green fields and over pleasant land, that 40 per cent of the population of the Eastbournes and Budleigh Saltertons are retired folk, that the farmers plough up Exmoor and the military range on Dartmoor, are not, in the first instance, the result of decisions taken by officials with overwhelming planning powers. No one deliberately says: here is Eastbourne, just the place for a 40 per cent retirement ratio; here is heather, let it be ploughed for wheat; here are the glories of tor and skyscape, the land Edward I gave to the Black Prince, let us therefore make a military base of it. These and all other land uses are the result of forces of demand which somehow need to be met. Waste must be disposed of; land is needed for wheat as man needs bread; the army must exercise itself somewhere; old folk should be free to live where they will. From these imperatives come demands addressed to landscape. Behind the land use patterns and landscapes are forces of demand and supply.

It is the supply side which hitherto has been so little studied and understood. Planning jargon speaks of planners 'releasing land' for this or that purpose; as if the planners owned the land. Planners do not, in the first instance, control the supply of land for various uses. Supplies are in the hands of those who hold the property power over land. These powers may be in private or in public hands. Wherever they lie, it is these powers that are critical and which have been so consistently overlooked and misunderstood. Public control of land use may direct the use of them in a negative, prohibitive manner. But it can never initiate action. All ends have beginnings. All landscape decisions start with the owners of the land.

Conscious landscape design and execution are not the confrontation of change but the containment of it to such ends that the new shall improve upon the old. This ideal lies deep in the hearts of all of us. Difficulties arise at the surface where one man's notion of what should be abolished, retained and improved upon differs from the notions of others. The judgements that have to be made are subjective, value judgements. It is not my purpose here to go deeper into this philosophical aspect of design. I simply remind you of it on my way to making a main but less recondite point.

In coming to this main point which is not unrelated to what has just been said, I want to use a citation from a recently published report of the Devon Conservation Forum, under the title *Planning Urbanisation in Devon*. Among many other pertinent observations, the Report referring to new housing estate layouts and landscape says:

> Very seldom, in fact, do the designers of the new housing estates appear to give deliberate thought to creating a 'sense of place'. Most of the new dwellings could be found in suburban estates anywhere in Britain. Local building materials have given way to imported and alien materials which can appear out of place. Many new developments have also been marred by the insensitive use and siting of street furniture, especially the large and obtrusive street-lighting columns. The absence of trees, the excessively wide residential roads and pavements and the monotonous layout and design all tend to heighten the dreary feeling of many new estates.
> (para 2.17)

Ask the Landowners

The writers assume that what they see as lacking in the new urbanised landscape is an environmental quality which if present would be patent to all; as if there were some universal, transcendental standards by which and without question, matters of landscape aesthetics are to be judged. The assumption is questionable and the wanting of accepted dogma here is a difficulty we have to face.

But let that problem stick on the wall for a bit. Let us suppose, as the assumption implies, that there are natural, universally accepted standards common to all opinions by which the landscape of new urban layouts can be accepted or condemned. Even so there is no evidence to show that the investigators sought out those who had had the property rights in the land, the private and the public holders of them, to ask them why the policies of development that produced the new landscapes had been accepted and pursued. Why were the layouts stark and treeless and the street furnishings overbearing and crude? Was it because the landowners responsible had had different standards by which they judged what for them was good landscape; or were they simply indifferent to the outcome of their policies for the quality of the environment; or had they no alternative, given restraints and limitations unknown to the uninformed observer? Truly to understand the reasons for the changes that have in the past taken place and in the present are taking place, explanations must be sought from public and private landowners in whose power the authority for decisive decisions lies. Why is the land used for waste disposal? Ask those who own it. This lesson will be brought home to us if we read the recently published reports on the plight of the inner cities. The waste land, the neglected sites, the boarded-up houses which compound ugliness on ugliness are in nine cases out of ten owned by local authorities or government departments or corporations. Only they can tell why these lands are in the state we see them. Not infrequently the explanation, so the reports tell us, is financial: to sell the land for development would mean loss to the ratepayers; in other cases short term dereliction must wait upon long term street widening or other improvements. It is little good drawing up landscape schedules and making designs if what is proposed runs contrary to what those who own the land can and will do with it. Dialogue on landscape in the future should reach out to the landowners, small and great, public and private.

The Need for Dialogue

For the sake of the dialogue that ought to be, I suggest we consider the following facts.

Land values. Changes in landscape which the conservationist and other idealists object to, whether radical, as when crude urbanisation invades the countryside, or more superficial but no less objectionable as the removal of hedgerows and other pleasant features of landscape, are often justified in the eyes of the landowner on financial grounds. For the farmer, hedgerows and isolated trees can stand between loss and profit in the current cost account of an enterprise; as do the amenity refinements on housing estates for the developer. May I suggest that we urge landowners in the interest of good landscape to look beyond the immediate current costs of an enterprise and consider the economic advantages of multi-land uses and the land market's response to amenities. The demand for sporting facilities in today's countryside is such that in some places the capital value of sporting rights is greater than the freehold values in the land. Removal of trees and hedges, while of short term benefit to the farming enterprise, can impair the long term values of the sporting rights, rights which are as much property in the land as the more substantial rights of a corporeal freehold. One has only to compare prices and particulars of houses and homes in any estate agent's window to see what emphasis is placed upon landscape, gardened landscapes and so on as the justification for higher than normal land values. Ever since the Human Environment Conference of the UN at Stockholm in 1972, the world-wide case has been made for a change in attitude to values. Maximising profit by the destructive use of land and other resources in the short term can impair long term capital values and do so to a degree greater than the immediate short term advantage. It would be informative to compare market demand, prices and purchasers' attitudes towards landscape. It can be shown, I believe, that there is nothing to lose financially in understanding good landscaping and its judgements and following them in the management and development of land. In the balance sheets where capital values count, landscaping can be shown to pay.

The natural ally. Nowhere in the world, aside from this country, is the private ownership of rural estates, by their tenure and tradition, inclined more naturally to landscaping. Some years ago I was encouraged and enabled to make an extensive study of the motives which in those days held the rural landowner to his land. The results from some 1·75m acres (we thought in acres in that time) were analysed to show which of a number of different attitudes and motives were the most frequently recorded. The arid motives of income, investment and tax relief (which meant something in those days) fell far behind such outlooks as residential attraction, social responsibility, inheritance and amenity enjoyment. Each one of these last four is on the side of a proper regard for landscape in the countryside. Many of the frustrations of today which beset rural landowners do not arise from a change of mood or manners; they are induced by the climate of envy and false values which has come to cloud so much of our political thinking. The land has its own time scale. Time heals damage, but at nature's pace. A hardwood copse once felled will only come again when a father sows for his sons to reap. If the heather of Exmoor, its ecology and the symbiosis of living things could, after the plough, be restored with the annual advent of spring, we would not have heard so many words of deep concern expressed in the recent

enquiry. Landscaping with its ordered containment of change is best served of those who have the command of time. The sense of inheritance which belongs to the highest order of private landownership matches up to the need. And so with residential attraction. I once enquired of a landowner of modest acreage in Gloucestershire why he spent so liberally to maintain the cottages, shops and open places in the village on his estate – financially, in terms of the current account, a loss maker. His reply was indicative of the landowning outlook: I live here. Admittedly these sentiments are personal and in the practical outworking of them it is often one man who has his way over broad acres of shire and long stretches of shore. There is nothing wrong in this if the actions are in accord with the aims of proper landscaping. We suffer today from the false values of collectivism. The private landowner is not expected, encouraged or enabled to take the social responsibilities his fathers took for granted. By and large, he is still willing to do so. He is the natural ally of the landscape architect, who needs all the friends he can get. Those who come naturally to his cause should be recognised, wooed and worked with.

Inner knowledge. Because time and the passing of the years have played so great a part in the creation of those things which make for prized landscape, the landscape architect has a close affinity with the people who have written history into the physical landscape. Apart from the professional antiquarian and historian it is the landowner who in the majority of cases knows most about the historical events which have moulded the landscape. This is not necessarily a question of broad acres. We all know houses, detached and in rows, whose claims to care and conservation lie as much in the evidence of their title deeds as in their ancient timbers and masonry. He who owns the place is usually in the best position to know most from the records. Here again, the landowner and the landscape architect are or should be walking the same road together. I have spent a life-time among these ancient walls and architectural splendours of Cambridge. Only those who know the long and inner history of things appreciate why an ancient roof truss is preserved to do its age-old job; or a mulberry tree in Christ's College Fellows' Garden is held up by iron struts. To the uninitiated, it is no more than a very old mulberry tree that is seen – that 'Paradise Lost' was written beneath it has to be explained by the landowners, the College authorities who know. Visitors who do not share our history sometimes display a dangerous impatience towards the old piles we prize so much. Only we, the landowners, can convert these heathen, through our full possession of a knowledge of the past, if such be the effective revelation they need. There have been times when we know the cause is lost. One such was the occasion when in the 1960's the Warden of Wadham College, Oxford, was sitting at his window open to the spring lawns. Across the green came a visiting American professor from The House, accompanied by his wife and small son who had opted for the 20th century. The boy looked up to see the Warden sitting at the window and was heard to say to his mother; 'Say, Mom, these ruins are inhabited'. These ruins are inhabited! Why? Ask those who live in them. Ask too that they may continue there.

Farming and the conservation of quality. The ruins are inhabited: yes! and in consequence a central heating system makes cosy the medieval chambers. Good landscaping accepts and indeed makes for change; preservation petrifies, in the proper sense of the word. To keep our thinking in right perspective we should carry our imagination back to the countryside as it used to be – without hedgerow, fence and the physical divides of severalty. The landscape we so much cherish today was created in the teeth of social opposition three hundred years and more ago. Parliament had to force the pace of change, using the Enclosure Acts to do so. Agriculture was changing. The open fields had to go to make way for new techniques which meant planting hedgerows and erecting new scattered homesteads. These changes were, if anything, relatively more fundamental than are those which our latest mechanised agriculture demands.

The changes of long ago drew the features of the landscape we in our generation have come to love. They were not at the time conscious efforts at conservation. They were technical devices accepted as necessary in the cause of profit and food production. And more important still, it was the landowners and farmers going about their daily business who brought them about. Admittedly Parliament helped; but only when asked to do so by those in command of the land. And so today. We may object to the new field patterns, where the caterpillar tractors and ploughs have ripped the carpets of green from the bare earth, the asbestos and pyrex and the mammoth shed where once the thatched barn stood. Yet when all the plaints are made, the beauty of landscape lies in the tidiness of the well farmed land. The spontaneities of tillage and husbandry not consciously done to beautify or conserve generate the qualities that please and which we must conserve. Time and again of late visitors from the new countries, from the USA and Australia, have remarked to me in wonder and delight on the well-kept fields and neat farmsteads of our up-country. Such virtues are spun of the daily round; they are a work-a-day fabric. The innumerable acts of husbandry, management and maintenance should not be controlled by a public bureaucracy. Any attempt along these lines, albeit in the name of landscape, would lead ultimately to a totalitarian control of the countryside. There are limits beyond which public control over the countryside cannot go, if the very qualities we would wish to see are to be kept. Because these qualities are the outcome of the spontaneities of daily action by farmers and landowners, it is to those folk that you who practise the profession of landscaping must look. Farming ideas constantly change, as they did at the time of the enclosures. But they are farming ideas. Time will make familiar, perhaps even dear, what in its newness jars today. If your profession is to contain landscape change to its own best ends, it must be *en rapport* with the landowners and farmers responsible.

No-one Owns Land

All that has been said so far points to landowning as the seat of decision-making and hence as having a direct authority over landscape issues. The message cannot rest there. There is something more to be said, concerning landownership itself. Strangely, in the eyes of the common law, no-one in Britain owns land as such. Estates and interests in land with their rights, many and few, are the subjects of ownership. A man owns a fee simple estate in the land as his neighbour owns a leasehold. When we refer to landownership we mean the holding of all manner of rights in the land as property. That seat of decision-making which we call landownership is not occupied solely by freeholders in possession of their farms or of landlords letting off shop and housing tenancies. Anyone who owns a limited interest as a tenant is included. We are not then referring simply to those whom the man in the street calls owners. Tenants have to take decisions as owners of limited interests and their decisions can be as vital to landscape issues as are the decisions of the holders of estates of freehold. A man's estate in the land determines what he can do with it. A tenant owning a leasehold may be bound by leasehold covenants which preclude his doing things he otherwise would have done – actions which might or might not be prejudicial to landscape. The dialogue spoken of earlier needs to be with all kinds and degrees of owners.

The wider the range of ownership types, the greater the variance of response to landscape questions can be. While there is much to be said for estates of large physical extent; among other advantages, on such estates land use policies can be single-eyed over broad stretches of countryside. But the wider the physical extent of ownership, the more the risks of encountering monopolistic rigidities. A large landowner opposed to landscaping considerations can do far more damage than can a small landowner; although with the right outlook the former can do the greater good.

Conservation of Private Property

In this context we come to the question of public ownership of land. Obviously in no society can the state own all rights in the land; by such a formula all citizens would become trespassers. Nevertheless to vest all freehold estates in the state is a feasible although horrendous prospect. Should such land nationalisation ever be experienced it would spell disaster to the landscape. The state as owner of all freeholds would create an absolute monopoly over the land. The notion that the state as owner would be more conducive to the interests of sound landscaping is misleading. A government department has .usually a definite task to perform as owner – agriculture, education, defence and so on. The prime purpose for the department being in existence determines its priorities. To oppose what the department has been set up to do, even if the opposition is in the name of landscape, can mean formidable confrontation.

That is not to say that a government department as landowner is indifferent to the claims of landscape. Some of the most startling successes in landscaping have been achieved by the Department of Transport, responsible for new motorways. The Forestry Commission

also is exemplary in its attitude and actions, although primarily responsible for afforestation. In the present state of the political postulates in our mixed economy, the amount of land in public ownership is relatively slight. It is far from the monopolistic control that would result from a universal state title.

Furthermore it is difficult for a government department to act spontaneously, unfettered by the red tape of officialdom and its regulations. Landscaping, especially in the countryside, is surely an art and is best served without too much coercion and the regulations of bureaucratic control. Some years ago I was engaged in a study of the use of access agreements and access orders as sanctions to public access over private land. The evidence pointed strongly against all formal agreements and doubly so against access orders and towards leaving alone the *ad hoc*, unchartered access which takes place at the nod of the landowner. The recent move to try and make all commons statutorily open to the public could be disastrous for the very existence of the commons as essential adjuncts to farming and to the conservation of their traditional functions. The conservation of private property in land with its variance, flexibility and voluntary responses is essential to a worthy landscaping profession.

Mutual Benefit

There could be, indeed needs to be, a two-way traffic of mutual benefit here. Private ownership of freeholds is under direct attack from the extremists in the radical camps; but it is also facing a more subtle erosion from the pressures of excessive capital levies by the tax authorities. Creeping land nationalisation is in the long run just as damaging as the more outright versions. I am sure that the demands landscape and conservation policies make on some estates, although they may impose limitations on the immediate financial rewards, are in most cases as nothing compared with the disrupting financial burdens resulting from capital transfer tax and capital gains tax. As we have already said, in the long run landscape policies are often rewarding in their sustaining effect on capital values. In the present state of affairs there is a golden opportunity. It needs careful study and discussion but I believe an equation can be found which would conserve the interests of the private estate owner in his land in exchange for his embracing sound landscaping principles in the management of it. We have a kind of precedent in the dedication scheme for private woodlands. This is no place to work out details but I would leave the thought with you that policies could be devised to relieve those estates of immediate capital tax levies whose owners were prepared to dedicate management to the highest ideals of landscape design. The obligations would be painless for those whose traditions are not that way and who lament the present threats because they prevent their using their inheritance to conserve all that it has stood for.

Last summer the Duke of Hamilton had to offer 1,000 acres of the High Parks Estate on the outskirts of Hamilton in Lanarkshire to the government in payment of estate duty. These warm, well-nurtured lands and far-flung forests have pride of place among the scenic splendours of southern Scotland, haunted as they are in the presence of the 12th century Cadzow Castle. The scenic valleys are what they are today because of the care and sacrifices of the Hamilton successors in title over the years. How can the cause of landscape be served by taking these lands from those who by precept and policy deeply care and understand, and putting them into the impersonal pound of the State? It would pay the nation to forgo the tax and leave the lands in Hamilton hands under covenant to continue their traditional policies. The present fiscal policy can, if persisted in, lead to a countryside bankrupt of the charm of quiet parks and homes of elegance, of the ways and manners that care. Today's glories will be tomorrow's ruins, as Sophie Andree and Marcus Binney so ably warn in a recent publication. The heritage they see tumbling into ruins has been left to our generation and to those who shall succeed us, by landowners who were free to express a quality of thought, care and sense of landscape. The coming generations must be enabled somehow to stand where their fathers stood and to care as they cared. If mass man, the denizen of our collectivist age, wants to enjoy the age-long beauties of the landscape and countryside, he must respect and recognise the rights and responsibilities of individual man who lives there; or else there will be no beauty to conserve and for either to enjoy.

PROGRESS IN BIOLOGICAL CONSERVATION IN CAMBRIDGE
DR S. M. WALTERS

Introduction
The conservation of nature and natural resources is a relatively modern idea. The prevailing mood of the leisured class in Victorian England, at least as we now see it, was one of naïve optimism and a belief in the inevitability of 'progress', with which went an unreasoned assumption that 'nature' was inexhaustible, or at least infinitely renewable. This belief was demonstrated in so many ways, not least in the attitude of the nineteenth-century 'sportsman', hunter and collector. Before the end of the century, however, other voices began to be heard, and the first nature reserves came into being through the philanthropic concern of a few naturalists who saw how fragile 'nature' was, and how rapidly her variety and richness could be seriously impaired by unthinking development.

The contrast in mood today is very obvious. In the last decade in particular, the real possibility of environmental disaster caused by man's so-called 'progress' has received so much publicity that we are in danger of over-stating our legitimate concern. At any rate, a return to unthinking Victorian optimism is impossible, and a clear gain is the rise of a concerned and informed public opinion, prepared to listen to the case for biological conservation. We have seen, since the Second World War, the creation of the Government Nature Conservancy (now the Nature Conservancy Council), and also the rise of a powerful voluntary conservation movement which in its various societies and trusts can now number more than 300,000 members in Britain (see Sheail 1976 for detailed history). This movement for the conservation of nature can and should be judged by its concrete results: I propose to illustrate these results in the Cambridge area, and assess their value and their long-term importance.

Direct Nature Conservation
To a naturalist whose interest is in the wild plants and animals of the countryside, 'progress' usually appears destructive, and sometimes quite crudely so. Inevitably, therefore, the pioneer action of public-spirited naturalists who wished to preserve for future generations the 'wild places' they themselves enjoyed was directed to the purchase and establishment of nature reserves which could then be protected from gross interference. The two great Fenland nature reserves in the Cambridge area, namely, Wicken Fen near Ely, and Wood Walton Fen near Huntingdon, are both old reserves established by private initiative, and their history illustrates the growth of the nature conservation movement.

Fenland Reserves: Wicken Fen as an example
At Wicken, the first land bought was given to the National Trust in 1899 and constituted one of the earliest properties of the Trust. Wood Walton Fen, on the other hand, was given by the naturalist Charles Rothschild to the newly-formed Society for the Promotion of Nature Reserves in 1920. Whilst Wicken Fen is still wholly administered by the National Trust, Wood Walton is now leased to the Nature Conservancy and administered as a National Nature Reserve. Without these two Fenland reserves, there would be virtually nothing remaining of the vast peat fens of Eastern England, so they have a unique value as survivors of a former vegetation and landscape, with great interest for the historian and archaeologist as well as for the biologist. To complete the picture, Cambridgeshire also possesses the National Nature Reserve of Chippenham Fen, administered by the Nature Conservancy but much less well known than the two older and larger Fenland reserves. Since it is not possible to describe all three Fen reserves, a few words on Wicken Fen must suffice to show something of the interest and value of these protected sites.

Rather more than 700 acres (280 ha) in extent, the Nature Reserve of Wicken Fen is a compact block of peatland on the edge of the small 'island' of mineral soil on which the village of Wicken is situated. It is divided by the waterway of Wicken Lode into a northern area, the Sedge Fen, and a southern area called Adventurers' Fen (named after the 'merchant adventurers' who risked their money in the seventeenth century in bringing the newly-drained peatland into arable cultivation). These two main areas of the present reserve have had very different histories. The Sedge Fen has survived undrained to the present day, partly because it was (and still is) used for regular production of crops of sedge *(Cladium mariscus)* for thatching, and partly because it provided a convenient low-lying area on to which flood water could be turned by the Drainage Board in winter and

spring. Adventurers' Fen, on the other hand, has been drained, and most of its peat has been lost, so that the present land surface is some 6 feet (2 m) below that of the adjacent Sedge Fen. Arable cultivation was attempted on Adventurers' Fen as recently as the Second World War: when the land was returned to the National Trust, a new lake and large reed beds were created there, providing an outstanding bird reserve with protected habitats of reeds and open water. Together these two contrasting areas provide a unique range of plant communities rich in plants and animals now much reduced everywhere by drainage and arable cultivation. (Figs 1 and 2.)

Figure 1. Wicken Fen: view of Wicken Lode.

Figure 2. Wicken Fen: sedge field.

The importance of Wicken, however, extends far beyond the sphere of the naturalist and biologist in the strict sense. Recent years have seen an enormous increase in the use of the Fen by members of the general public, and by school parties and groups from teacher-training colleges, and its contribution to a broad general education at elementary and advanced levels has been increasingly recognised. Geographers, historians of rural England, and those interested in our countryside and its changes during the centuries, find in Wicken an abundant source of material.

Woodland Reserves: Hayley Wood as an example
The city of Cambridge is conveniently situated at the junction of three very contrasting landscape and soil types. To the north stretch the Fens at or below sea-level, where arable agriculture reigns supreme, and where, as we have seen, three nature reserves are virtually all we have left of undrained peatland. The higher ground surrounding Cambridge on the other three sides can be divided into the broad belt of upland chalk which runs diagonally to the south-east of the city, and the clay country to the west. It is on the claylands that our remaining semi-natural oak-ash woodlands survive. One of the largest of these is the nature reserve of Hayley Wood (Fig 3) purchased in 1962 by the Cambridgeshire and Isle of Ely Naturalists' Trust and wholly administered by this local voluntary conservation organisation. Seventeen years after Hayley Wood became a nature reserve, it is now amongst the best-studied of all English woodland, ranking with the National Nature Reserve of Monks Wood near Huntingdon, and sharing with that wood the distinction of having a whole book devoted to its natural history (Rackham 1975).

The wood covers 122 acres (49 ha) and is roughly square,

occupying a flat hill-top at 260 ft (80 m) above sea-level in west Cambridgeshire. The soil is an impermeable clay, and much of the surface is so flat that winter and spring flooding is a regular feature. Dr Rackham's researches have shown that as early as 1251 the extent of the wood ('Boscus de Heyle') was virtually the same as it is today, and we can be reasonably confident that we have a piece of original woodland, in the sense that the ground was never cleared during Roman or Saxon settlement. The wood in fact constitutes a remarkable 'living document' of interpretable history going back to Norman and even Saxon times, its individual features (ditches, banks, rides, even coppiced trees) being in many cases datable by historical evidence. Such woodlands are being studied increasingly from a combination of specialist angles, and this new discipline of 'historical ecology' now has a vigorous life of its own.

Hayley Wood is an immensely valuable nature reserve. It provides, because of its relatively large size and its undisturbed history, an excellent base-line from which other more disturbed and artificial woodlands can be interpreted. By studying it, we can at least have some idea what kind of climax woodland might have covered the heavy clay-lands before the main Saxon clearances began – although, of course, the detail of the modern wood, its structure and composition, are the product of centuries of human use and interference. Moreover, experimental management, for example of coppiced areas, rapidly yields much information needed to interpret the history of coppice-with-standards woodland in general. This process is building up a surprisingly large body of ecological information which produces a fascinating picture of a highly complex, interdependent plant and animal community in which, for example, the flowering of the Oxlip *(Primula elatior)*, a very local plant for which the wood is famous, is seen to be dependent on the incidence of grazing by a herd of Fallow Deer *(Dama dama)* which make Hayley and other local woods their home.

Chalkland Reserves: the Devil's Dyke as an example
Unlike the heavy claylands which, until recently, were very difficult to clear and bring into arable cultivation, the belt of light chalk soil which runs across south Cambridgeshire carries no semi-natural woodland at all. Whatever natural tree cover was there in pre-historic times had largely disappeared by the end of the Romano-British period, and probably many centuries before, and all existing woodland on the Cambridgeshire chalk is of relatively recent, artificial origin. For centuries the chalklands were covered by a close-grazed turf on which flocks of sheep were reared. This chalk turf itself was largely ploughed up in the period of the Napoleonic Wars, and its characteristic rare plants and animals survived only on sites where the grassland was unploughable. Cambridgeshire is fortunate in having two impressive archaeological features which survived the Napoleonic agricultural revolution; these are the Fleam and Devil's Dykes, two great parallel earthworks thrown up in post-Roman times as military defences across the open belt of chalk.

On the Devil's Dyke (Fig 4), now preserved as an archaeological and biological site, the top and steep side of the earthwork are clothed with grassland which until recently was kept close-grazed by rabbits, which had replaced the original sheep-grazing after the conversion of the main ploughable chalkland to arable cultivation. With the advent of myxomatosis, however, rabbit-grazing declined and hawthorn *(Crataegus)* and other wild bushes naturally invaded. The rich chalk flora (and the associated insects such as the rare Chalk-hill Blue butterfly, *Lysandra coridon*) survives only where the scrub does not invade, so that conservation on the Devil's Dyke (and indeed elsewhere on chalk grassland sites in England) involves some artificial management to prevent or reverse the natural scrub succession. Thus, on the Devil's Dyke nature reserve of the Naturalists' Trust, volunteer work parties cut out sapling bushes and mow the grassland to preserve wild species such as the rare and beautiful Pasque Flower *(Anemone pulsatilla)* adopted as emblem of the Trust.

Breckland Reserves: Cavenham Heath as an example
The Breckland of East Anglia begins on the borders of Cambridgeshire and Suffolk as one travels east from Cambridge. It has been famous for its rare plants and animals since John Ray first recorded scientifically the flora of the Cambridge region in 1660, and generations of naturalists have visited this sandy heathland to see the rare Speedwells *(Veronica spp.)* and other plants largely if not wholly confined to the Breckland in the British Isles. The Nature Conservancy Council and the Norfolk and Suffolk Naturalists' Trusts now separately or jointly own or lease important nature reserves in this area, of which the National Nature Reserve of Cavenham Heath

Figure 3. Hayley Wood: ancient boundary oaks.

Figure 4. Devil's Dyke: biology students at work.

Figure 5. Cavenham Heath.

is the nearest to Cambridge and one of the largest (Ratcliffe 1977; Fig 5).

Breckland heath nature conservation, like chalk grassland, involves management to prevent natural woodland succession, especially by Birch *(Betula)*, now that rabbit-grazing is no longer effective. Moreover, many rare Breckland plants are annuals, more or less dependent on traditional agricultural practices for their continued survival . . . as indeed are rare animal species of the Breckland such as the Stone Curlew *(Burhinus oedicnemus)* which breeds there. Management of some Breckland reserves therefore involves 'old-fashioned' ploughing followed by a fallow period when the 'Breck' or 'broken' land is re-colonised by weedy species. Breckland heaths are clearly artefacts of man, because (as the Forestry Commission has amply demonstrated!) even the most impoverished Breck soils can carry mature forest; we know, however, that they represent some of the earliest human forest clearance going back to Neolithic times. The story of Breckland, even more than that of the other land types in East Anglia, involves geological, archaeological and biological research of a particularly intricate kind going back thousands of years. The Nature Reserves are an essential part of the evidence we need to understand the Breck today.

Other Protected Sites

Although the existence of sizeable nature reserves provides the best guarantee that rare species and rare types of vegetation will not become extinct, many smaller areas of ground, often thought of as 'waste land' by the developer, are of very great importance to the biologist. In recognition of this, the Nature Conservancy Council draws up and submits to the Planning Authority for each county a list of 'Sites of Special Scientific Interest' (SSSI's) which merit a measure of protection. Such sites, which may be of any size, are often the places where particular rare species grow; it is the concern of the County Naturalists' Trust to protect these smaller sites by agreement with the owner or tenant, and (where possible or appropriate) eventually by acquisition or lease to devise a more permanent protection. Roadside verges and ancient hedgerows are of particular interest and concern; in Cambridgeshire a measure of protection can be given to selected sites of this kind by notifying them to the County Surveyor's Department.

Education and Biological Conservation

Until recently, it was possible for teachers of field biology to assume that the countryside could supply their needs, whether for field studies or for demonstration material. With the advent of modern mechanised and chemicalised agriculture, however, this is no longer true, especially in lowland England. Nature reserves and other protected areas take on a new function, as the places where field studies can be pursued by educational parties, and the 'educational nature reserve' comes into being. It is, of course, true that the larger national nature reserves such as Wicken Fen can act both as protective and educational reserves – though the balance between the two rôles needs careful adjustment, especially when rare species sensitive to disturbance are involved – but increasingly County Trusts are acquiring special educational reserves which cater explicitly for field studies. An excellent example is provided near Cambridge at Fulbourn, where a small reserve leased on a private estate is extensively used by school biology and local history classes (Fig 6). In such reserves there are no particularly rare species, but the variety of wildlife and the management employed are sufficient to ensure that reasonable study and collecting does not deplete the biological interest. In such reserves, very important lessons on the value of nature conservation can be taught together with the more traditional biology. For example, the need for legal protection of rare or local species of plants or animals can be explained in the field, and followed up by classroom or other demonstrations using slides, posters, etc. In all this field, the County Naturalists' Trust plays an important part.

Study and Protection of Rare Species

Part of the problem of biological conservation concerns the fate of rare species. In the early days of the movement nature reserves were often established precisely because several nationally rare plants or animals occurred at the particular site. The late development of ecological science, however, often meant that conservationists did not understand the problem of the protection of rare species, and in several cases a particularly well-known rarity has declined and died out on a nature reserve under the eyes of the management committee. (The fate of the Swallowtail Butterfly, *Papilio machaon*, at Wicken Fen is perhaps the best known local example of this.) This whole subject needs much more explanation than I can give it here, but I can at least indicate recent progress in the establishment of a special project for the study of rare plants.

The Nature Conservancy Council Contract

In 1974 the Cambridge University Botanic Garden received a contract from the Nature Conservancy Council to study and, where appropriate, cultivate reserve stocks of all the nationally rare vascular plants (ie flowering plants and ferns) still to be found wild in the Eastern Region of England, a region for which Cambridge is a natural centre. The project is two-fold: the appointed scientific officer studies all known remaining populations in the wild and records carefully all relevant details, especially population size, whilst the conservation propagator in the Botanic Garden raises, from seed or cutting as appropriate, a stock of each rare species. These reserve stocks have several functions. Firstly, and most obviously, they are an insurance against total extinction. Of course, we hope that one or more wild habitats can be protected, but there are certain categories of rare plant such as the arable weeds for which it is difficult if not impossible to preserve the 'wild' habitat when land use or agricultural practice changes. (An extreme case of such a species is the annual weed grass *Bromus interruptus* last seen in the wild in a Cambridgeshire

field in 1972, and now known only in cultivation.) Secondly, stocks of rare plants provide material for legitimate research or commercial needs, rendering unnecessary any further depletion of the wild stocks. The Cambridge Botanic Garden is now supplying in this way samples of the British flora for medicinal research by the Pharmaceuticals Division of Imperial Chemical Industries. Thirdly, rare plants in cultivation, especially those occurring locally, are very important indeed in educational displays on the themes of nature conservation. This year (1979) sees the establishment of a new Conservation Display Bed in the Cambridge Botanic Garden in which a selection of the rare wild plants we have in cultivation can be exhibited and their interest explained.

Ecological Study of Rare Species

The protection of a rare species requires an understanding of its ecology. Unfortunately, each species has its own particular requirements, so that there is no short cut, although of course certain generalisations can often usefully be made. It is therefore encouraging to report that there is a real increase in scientific investigations of rare species, and the information received is being increasingly applied to the management problems of nature reserves and protected sites. Studies of rare fenland plants such as the Fen Violet *Viola persicifolia* (*stagnina*), reveal how important, for example, is the long dormancy of the seed and the precise conditions favouring germination and seedling establishment. We can now ensure the survival of this species at the Wood Walton nature reserve by appropriate management.

The Future of Biological Conservation

Everything we have talked about so far could be said to involve 'rearguard actions' which at their best might stave off extinction for some wild species for a limited time. Is such action of any real value? Ought we not to accept (as all previous generations have had to) that 'progress' brings destruction and dull uniformity? Does it really matter if most plants and animals follow the Dodo into extinction? There are no easy answers to these questions. One consideration, however, seems to me to be of very great importance. No-one knows what the pattern of the English countryside will be in the twenty-first century, nor can we predict whether we shall still be dependent on large-scale arable agriculture for our food supply. If there *is* another revolution in agriculture, might it not create a new 'waste-land'? In this case, our nature reserves will be the reservoirs from which recolonisation by surviving wild species can proceed. Even if this does not happen, and concrete, barbed wire and chemical agriculture dominate the landscape, the nature reserves can survive, their contents more and more valued by the generations to come – for it is generally true that we value most those things which are obviously rare and fragile.

Figure 6. Fulbourn Educational Nature Reserve: old oak.

References

Rackham, O., 1975 *Hayley Wood: its history and ecology*. Cambs and Isle of Ely Naturalists' Trust, Cambridge.

Ratcliffe, D. A. (ed), 1977 *A Nature Conservation Review*, Vol 2, p 132. Cambridge University Press.

Sheail, J., 1976 *Nature in Trust*. Blackie and Son, Glasgow and London.

Acknowledgements

Photographs 1, 2, 3, 4 and 6: W. H. Palmer; photograph 5: Nature Conservancy Council.

ECOLOGICAL CONSIDERATIONS IN LANDSCAPE DESIGN AND MANAGEMENT – PART I
EDDIE KEMP

In Autumn 1971 the author began to create a botanic garden for the University of Dundee upon 10 hectares of neglected agricultural land. The main function of the garden was originally to produce plant material for teaching in the Department of Biological Sciences and also to provide accommodation for populations of plants grown for research.

In planning the garden, however, it was considered that a plant sociological unit would enhance its educational value at all visitor levels – academic, school and lay public. This unit, most of which is already constructed, consists of reproduced Scottish vegetation types, arranged in a naturally occurring sequence, from sea level to mountain top. The layout begins with a pool (eutrophic) by the south boundary of the site and nearby there are the beginnings of sand dune plant communities containing *Elymus, Ammophila, Salix repens* sub-sp *argentea, Hippophae* and *Rosa rubiginosa*. From the pool, a path leads northward up the slope through Scottish woodland types, oakwood on the right and ashwood on the left, in which some of the shrub and field layer species are already established. As we ascend, these woods give way to Scots pine and birch and beyond these there is a mound symbolic of a Scottish mountain. At the summit, below a semi-circular ridge, a lochan (tarn) has been constructed and from it flows a stream fed by spring water, tumbling down the hillside in a series of waterfalls from small pools (oligotrophic).

Although originally conceived only as an educational feature, other functions of the unit soon became apparent. Thus the huge volumes of teaching material formerly obtained from the countryside are now, in the interests of nature conservation, obtained within the layout. Another function, the need to provide accommodation for locally endangered species, was suggested by recent publicity (Simmons, *et al* (ed) 1976) regarding the rôle which botanic gardens could fulfil in preserving stocks of these plants and was further emphasised by the numbers of rarities in the region which were available for rescue from civil engineering and forestry operations. Accommodating these rarities in their appropriate plant associations within the unit is environmentally as well as visually more acceptable than attempting to grow them by the usual horticultural methods and is indeed necessary for those dependent upon others for survival.

It is not suggested that the plant sociological layout is a substitute for field study, but such a demonstration is not available in nature without travelling considerable distances and it is, therefore, a time-saving introduction to local ecology and more effective than viewing museum dioramas or projected slides. Nor is it suggested that preservation in a garden is a substitute for conservation in the field, but that preservation is better than extinction. Furthermore, the availability of cultivated stocks of endangered plants relieves pressure upon them in the field by compulsive plant collectors. In Britain, for example, commercially available material has undoubtedly saved the remaining naturally occurring plants of *Salix lanata* and distracted collectors from the Arran sorbuses, *Sorbus arranensis* and *S. pseudofennica*. It is, however, the value of the layout as a reference feature for landscape designers and managers which is relevant to the present discussion.

In nature, the colonisation of bare ground usually begins with the lower plants, the algae, lichens and mosses, followed by herbs, then shrubs and finally the trees. But to accelerate the establishment of the woodland associations, the trees were introduced first, and since large trees are necessary for the immediate creation of these associations, most of them were of semi-mature size. In the spring of 1972, 6- to 7-metre tall trees were transported from one of the fragments of native Scots pine forest, the Black Wood of Rannoch and in 1975, seventy-five Scots pines of north-eastern Scottish provenance and of similar height were also planted. The Scottish pinewood is therefore the most established part of the layout and is already becoming ecologically sustainable with a minimal maintenance requirement. Seedlings of *Juniperus communis, Vaccinium vitis-idaea* and *Empertum* have sprung up; *Calluna* and *Vaccinium myrtillus* are well established and also *Goodyera, Trientalis* and *Pyrola media*. Many fungi have appeared from the pinewood floor litter and among the higher plants, also inadvertently introduced with the balls of soil attached to the trees are *Genista anglica, Galium saxatile, Viola riviniana, Oxalis acetosella,* and the pines

themselves have begun to regenerate. Although the length of the layout from the pool to the north slope of the hill is but 140 metres, there is space for lateral extension, eastward and westward. In the earliest plant sociological layout known to the present author, that of Professor Tuxen at Hanover, there were about 45 associations in 1·5 hectares and ten of these were forest associations.

The early management of the Dundee layout has been dominated by the very high proportion of weed seeds in the soil and without modern herbicides the staff of three and the curator would have found maintenance impossible. Even with these herbicides, there are limits to their application in regulating the composition of the associations. For example, there are many herbicides for eliminating dicotyledons from among monocotyledons, but none which is selective against monocotyledons and leaves the dicotyledons unharmed. A recent development, the 'Croptex' glove is proving useful in singling out for treatment with herbicides individual unwanted plants growing with others in dense clumps. A pad of fabric on the palm of the glove is wetted with a translocated herbicide, glyphosate, so that when the plant is grasped and the glove pulled along it, herbicide is deposited. The grasping action re-charges the pad by pumping herbicide from a small container attached to the operator's belt. This method is especially valuable in eliminating plants with underground perennating organs.

The woodlands will require thinning as they develop to regulate the amount of light reaching the lower layers of vegetation and some of the plants in these layers will require controlling in order to secure adequate representation of the constants in the associations. For example, a recent management operation was the suppression by cutting of vigorously growing *Calluna* in order to increase the representation of *Genista anglica* which has since begun to regenerate by seeds in the cleared patches.

After a lapse of seven years, it is becoming obvious that information regarding the time required to establish *de novo* the various plant associations and experience in their management, have an application in landscape rehabilitation work as well as in deciding the composition of new plantings. Where there is less urgency than in the Dundee layout, smaller trees could be planted and then managed over the years to permit subsequent colonisation or planting with shrub and field layer species. This calls either for a personal knowledge of the local plant ecology on the part of the designer and manager or liaison with the Nature Conservancy or the botany department of the nearest university. The need to conserve existing habitats is constantly being emphasised, but they nevertheless continue to be exploited for other purposes and their wildlife destroyed. In consequence of this, attention should be drawn to the possibility of creating new ecologically authentic scrub and woodland habitats to replace those which have vanished. Even areas such as motorway verges could be important wildlife habitat gains if appropriately planted, but again, the planting requires local ecological knowledge. For example, the present author saw recently the extensive planting of *Rhododendron ponticum* on a motorway verge, despite the fact that, not far away, this plant is a noxious weed to foresters since it prevents regeneration of trees by cutting off light to the seedlings and is very costly to eradicate. In the district concerned, there are several stands of moribund *Juniperus communis*, material of which could readily be propagated vegetatively if a local nurseryman were contracted to do so. The resulting juniper plants would probably cost less than the rhododendrons and would certainly be ecologically more appropriate.

At a recent conference on ecology and landscale design at Wye College, Kent, Mr R. A. Ruff of Manchester University mentioned the saving that could be made by not levelling, by not filling in ponds, by not lowering the water table by draining; in other words, not to ignore the potential of a site as it stands. If such a site preparation policy were combined with the approach to planting outlined by the present author, we would clearly be offering the future a wider choice of undepleted biological diversity.

References
Simmons, J. B., *et al* (eds) 1976. *Conservation of Threatened Plants. (NATO Conference Series 1, Ecology, Vol 1)*, Plenum Press, New York and London.
Tuxen, R. 1953. *Etablissement et Entretien d'un Jardin Phytosociologique. Colloque Internationale des Sciences Biologiques. Sur l'Organisation Scientifique des Jardins Botaniques*, pp 251-254. UISB Sér B, No 13, Paris.

ECOLOGICAL CONSIDERATIONS IN LANDSCAPE DESIGN AND MANAGEMENT – PART II
BRIAN CLOUSTON
IN COLLABORATION WITH CHRISTOPHER WILD

Before the end of the eighteenth century, towns contained little public green space. During the late eighteenth century and in the nineteenth century developers consciously integrated green spaces into urban areas. These green spaces were mostly formal areas, for example the London squares and parks such as Regent's Park. Other examples are the classical victorian parks such as Birkenhead Park, and Liverpool's Sefton and Princes Parks. In Britain we copied on a much smaller scale Haussmann's tree-lined Paris boulevards and the small formal open spaces fashionable in the Victorian town.

As towns spread, tracts of common land and areas of what might best be described as 'no man's land' became integrated into the fabric of our urban areas. Important examples include the great commons such as Wimbledon Common, Clifton Down and Southampton Common. These extensive areas of land were essentially unmanaged apart from traditional grazing and they contrast sharply with the more formal Victorian municipal parks which were based on careful intensive management of the landscape, the maintenance of exotic plant species, large areas of mown grass and the frequent use of bedding plants.

In every town, areas of land, often quite small areas, were neglected by man and overlooked by the development process, or simply left as areas of 'useless' land. I am thinking of canal banks, the corners of industrial sites, stream corridors and railway embankments. In these areas a particular plant community developed of its own accord without man's interference. Many of these plant communities have matured over time to become some of the most ecologically interesting wildlife habitats in our cities. Similarly, plant communities have developed as part of the landscape of the countryside due to man's disinterest, abandonment or neglect.

The value of such areas is great, especially in the context of our cities today. They represent 'reservoirs' of plant species and wildlife habitat which are often becoming increasingly rare in Britain. Psychologically, such areas have a value in that they offer urban man contact with nature which has too often been lost in the 'planned' environment. Because they are continuously growing and changing they provide visual interest and perhaps most importantly, such plant communities are largely self-sustaining and require very little maintenance.

Left to itself, a plant community will develop on virtually any neglected site in these islands. The range of species found in the community will depend to a large extent upon the prevailing soil and hydrological conditions, seed sources and the movement through and into the site of birds and animals. Starting from bare ground, these communities will develop through clearly defined stages towards a climax vegetation which in Britain will generally be deciduous woodland. There will be a gradual development from ground cover plants through scrub and immature trees, to fully mature trees with a rich understorey and a variety of ground cover plants. Ultimately such a climax vegetation would, given a large enough area and without man's interference, be self-sustaining. The speed of build-up of such a community varies enormously and is often very rapid in the initial stages, but under natural conditions, very slow to reach the final climax.

Examples of the tremendously rapid build-up of such plant communities could be seen in the bomb-damaged sites so common in our cities after the last war. Even more remarkable is the way in which sites completely devoid of topsoil and composed entirely of brick and rubble are colonised by plants almost immediately. For striking examples of this we may look to the work done by German botanists and landscape designers on the waste lands of Berlin.

It is clear from Edward Kemp's description of his work at Dundee that man can create plant communities very similar to those which would develop naturally. Furthermore, we can exert considerable influence both in determining the speed at which the community develops, the range of species within the developing habitat, over development costs and subsequently over the cost of habitat management. Plant communities based on naturally occurring plant associations, since they are essentially self-sustaining, require considerably less maintenance than the manicured landscape of the traditional municipal park or the vast areas of grass too often found in modern housing estates.

At present we are faced with many, often extensive, areas of land in our cities which are either vacant as a result of the demolition of inner city slums, or are earmarked for development at some future unspecified time when finance is available and a suitable developer can be found. The desertion of many inner city areas by former residents and frequently by small industrial concerns has vastly increased the number of available sites waiting for development.

Clearly there is a wide range of sites within our towns and cities which could be developed as ecologically balanced plant communities requiring minimum maintenance and re-introducing natural woodlands and shrubs into areas where they have been absent for too long. In addition, in developing such plant communities on the wastelands of the inner city there is the visual benefit of landscaping unsightly areas and the benefit of creating at low cost an infrastructure of tree planting into which future development may be integrated.

However, before discussing the creation of such plant communities, and the adaptation of existing landscapes to incorporate ecologically based plant associations requiring minimum maintenance, perhaps we should consider examples which already exist. We should also consider the desirability of adopting such a policy and think about the likely implications of both development costs and maintenance.

Motorway and Trunk Road Maintenance
We are all familiar with the development of our motorway and trunk road network and with the policies adopted by the Ministry of Transport in seeding extensive areas of road verge with grass. Until the constraints on public spending in the early 1970's many miles of motorway and trunk road verges were close mown, uniformly green and tidy in comparison with the botanically rich and colourful roadsides of country lanes which often received virtually no maintenance. The odd congratulatory letter to a County Surveyor referring to the neatness of the verge was usually sufficient to spur him on to greater provision in his budgets for mowers and men.

The close mowing regime stopped when the constraints were applied and motorway maintenance authorities were directed to restrict mowing to a narrow strip along the road's edge. In the intervening years ecologists have found that large parts of our motorway verges have become more species rich and have begun to be invaded by shrubs and tree species which reflect the naturally occurring plant association of the area. Motorway verges are now increasingly important as reservoirs of wildlife habitat, the more so because they are linear features linking many other areas of habitat into a continuous system. There is little we can do at this stage to alter the range of tree species with which part of the motorway verges were originally planted, since in many cases the trees are now semi-mature. However, the introduction of a long-term policy aimed at the establishment of natural plant associations appropriate to the specific location should be aimed at with the two-fold intention of enriching the range of wildlife habitat in our countryside and reducing maintenance costs. There would appear to be considerable grounds for optimism that such a programme would be successful if one considers the example of railway embankments. These were generally constructed in the last century, often using any available material which sometimes included colliery spoil and shales. With no planting and no maintenance these embankments have, over the years, become species rich ecologically valuable wildlife habitats.

A decade ago, any hope that road and motorway verges might be allowed to develop into ecologically rich habitats seemed remote. It took economic constraints to change Ministry policy – to the benefit of the overall landscape. Perhaps we should ask how much richer roadside habitats could become if an ecologically-based planting programme were adopted, and how much money could be saved on implementation and maintenance costs.

Oakwood Development Area – Warrington New Town
An example of the landscaping of a large scale housing development based on ecological principles is that of the Oakwood development at Warrington. Six thousand houses are to be built on the site of a former ordnance factory which was demolished in the late 1960's. The area is largely surrounded by naturally developed plant associations of oak/ash/elm woodland; an area of peat moss colonised by birch; topsoil dumps which have been colonised by willow and birch, and scattered areas of well developed oak/ash woodland with a hawthorn and willow understorey. Within these woodlands, the proposed building site which consists of brick rubble, mud and sand, is being planted over several years with a mixture of birch, alder, oak and ash together with a selection of understorey shrubs. The aim is to establish

something similar to a climax woodland as quickly as possible by speeding up what would be the natural progression of habitat types in advance of housing development. Eventually the species chosen will grow to a full climax woodland ecologically related to the surrounding woodlands and requiring the minimum of maintenance. The planting will form part of a rich and varied series of semi-natural woodland habitats surrounding and running through the housing area. We have here an example of a planting plan based on the principles of the natural association of plants and minimum maintenance closely related to a new housing area.

Durham University Woodlands

The University of Durham manages extensive areas of woodland, in and near Durham City, which total about 54·16 ha; of these about 0·17 ha are situated on the Cathedral banks. These woodlands are predominantly managed on an 'ecological' basis with the intention of maintaining a semi-natural association of tree, shrub and ground cover plants. Maintenance is generally limited to the minimum lopping and felling of mature trees; occasional cropping of poorly grown trees, underplanting of tree species and keeping footpaths open. Mature trees are predominantly oak, ash, beech and elm. Understorey shrubs include hawthorn, willow, bramble and holly which are allowed to grow on. A rich ground layer flora has developed which varies as would be expected, according to the type of mature trees found in different parts of the woods. The result of such policies has been to produce and maintain a visually attractive woodland which is frequently used for amenity purposes. In Great High Wood, an area of about 16·6 ha, the underplanting policy is aimed at producing an oak/birch woodland which approaches the association of plants which would be found in a naturally developed woodland. The wood itself is used for outdoor experiments to measure the population of rodents and other mammals in semi-natural woodland.

The average workforce needed to maintain 54·16 ha of their woodlands is 1½ men per year, a figure which compares favourably with the Forestry Commission's staffing ratio, and is considerably less than that needed to maintain an equivalent area of grass or ornamental woodland.

Ludworth Colliery Spoil Heap

My fourth example is somewhat different in that it illustrates public attitudes to a part of the environment that has been allowed to develop a natural association of plant species. Ludworth village, about five miles east of Durham City, has a derelict colliery spoil heap composed of inert spoil and waste shale. Over the last forty to fifty years, since the tip has been derelict, an interesting flora has developed which offers an important insight into the natural colonisation of derelict areas. The tip is unusual in the extent to which colonisation of inert material has taken place by small herbs and grasses. It is also unusual in that plants which favour acidic soils grow in some places, and other typical of calcareous soils grow on different

parts of the site. In addition, the area is rich in insect species. The site particularly benefits from the presence of a nearby marsh where several rare plants including the fragrant orchid grow. According to the Nature Conservancy Council the site may be unique to County Durham in view of the variety of habitats and the relatively short time taken for them to develop naturally.

The importance and attraction of the site is such that local residents have formed an association to protect the site and prevent its 'reclamation' to agriculture – a most unusual attitude in a County which has been so much scarred by industrial dereliction in the past, and where tip reclamation projects are normally received enthusiastically.

Fashions in landscape design change but the landscape architect is concerned with living plants which are all, to a greater or lesser degree, related to natural plant associations. All landscape schemes form an extension to the network of wildlife habitats and plant communities which exists throughout our environment. We have seen that natural plant associations will develop spontaneously in some of the most inhospitable parts of Britain extending the network of wildlife habitats; providing psychological relief and visual interest which can capture the imagination and support of people.

This short paper is not the place to discuss in detail the techniques of establishing such plant communities; for that we must look to the experience of Dutch landscape architects in the great forest parks of Amsterdam, and to the work of Alan Ruff of Manchester University. Essentially the establishment of such communities on virgin land is dependent on planting trees and shrubs selected on the basis of size and species appropriate to the conditions of the area to provide mutual shelter and allow ground layer plants to develop. Subsequent maintenance is aimed at speeding up the development of the climax community by thinning and introducing appropriate species at the correct stage of development. In practice this requires a low level of maintenance and is considerably cheaper than the work necessary to maintain grassed spaces.

In conclusion, I would like to return to one of the points I raised earlier in this paper; the centres of our cities. We are now faced with the problem of improving the environment of large areas of inner city land at present vacant and likely to remain so for some time. Here, I suggest, is an opportunity to put into practice the principles of ecologically based planting. We should begin to consider the landscaping of such sites in terms of the natural associations of plant they can support – such a policy would produce results vastly different from the all too common policy of grassing empty sites. How much better it would be to create a landscape framework of natural plant associations – with all its advantages – in advance of development. The key sites, I would suggest, for a series of pilot schemes would be those which link existing green spaces, canal banks and riversides sites where new planting would form continuous extensions to the network of semi-natural environments within our cities and create a robust, dynamic and visually interesting framework into which future developments may be introduced.

DESERTIFICATION AND WETLANDS

DESERTIFICATION AND WETLANDS MAJ-LIS ROSENBROIJER

COMING TO TERMS WITH THE DESERT SHLOMO ARONSON

DESERTIFICATION AND WETLANDS
MAJ-LIS ROSENBROIJER

Synopsis

As a world phenomenon desertification is increasing. In certain parts of the Sahara the boundary line of desert zone is advancing at the rate of 17 kilometres per year.

There are many causes for the increase of desertification. There are climatological factors and the wind moves the sand. There are long range factors operating to dry out the land.

Man himself is a great factor in desertification in many ways, one being the burning of forest areas to produce short-term agricultural areas which then turn into desert areas. Grazing practices lead to desertification. Timber-cutting may lead to desertification.

Ancient Greece was forest-land. The forests were cut down and erosion followed.

At present 43 per cent of the land surface of the earth is desert.

Chile and Argentina are at present threatened by desertification.

In Egypt 6 per cent of the area is agricultural. There is a process of urbanisation. It is feared that urbanisation will take over agricultural land. It is better for town settlements to be built in desert areas rather than in agricultural areas.

The traditional mode of expanding the agricultural area in Finland, in addition to clearing forests, was to drain swamps.

COMING TO TERMS WITH THE DESERT
SHLOMO ARONSON

The desert areas of the earth were conceived of by mankind until very recently as hostile and separate worlds. They were described in almost all ancient Egyptian, Greek, Roman and Arabic literature as a feared and antagonistic world full of danger and mystery. Ancient Jewish writing divided the universe into three separate parts: one third seas, one third deserts, and one third land.

Deserts usually formed a barrier between civilisations and empires. Napoleon Bonaparte said after his ill-fated Middle Eastern expedition that of all obstacles which create the boundary of an empire, the desert is the hardest one to bridge. Mountain ranges, like the Alps, come only second, and big rivers third.

In the second half of the 20th Century mankind's outlook has changed dramatically and the desert areas have begun to be seen as immensely valuable and important for human settlement.

Our rôle as landscape architects is to facilitate the onthrust to the desert, which is backed by a tremendous amount of money and a distinct change in priorities. Our task is two-fold: on the one hand to prevent irremedial damage which such development may cause, and on the other hand to create habitable conditions for the growing needs of mankind.

The desert is one of the most fragile ecosystems in the world. Each brackish water hole has a crucial importance to living things for many miles around. A single rain or flood will have a measurable influence on the next year's vegetation. Each mature tree becomes a habitat by itself. Thus any change in the existing pattern, however slight, should be very carefully thought out.

There is no rain to obliterate or soften the impact of man in the desert. Heavy machinery tracks can remain in desert conditions for tens or even hundreds of years. The encampment of the Roman garrison at Masada in AD70 is still clearly seen in the Judean desert. The visual remains of Rommel's campaign are still to be seen in the Western Desert. Thus all the important landscape questions which we are dealing with daily in temperate zones, such as road construction impact, minimising earthworks, cuts, and fills, have even more significance in desert conditions. Mistakes can not be glossed over with trees and groundcover. It simply can't be said that a hideous result of poor design, such as an ugly fill, will be covered over with vegetation after five rainy seasons.

Being 'watchdogs' starts, not when the contractor is on site, but at an earlier stage, over the drawing boards, especially of our colleagues the highway engineers, who for lack of the usual constraints which exist in built-up areas such as land ownership, costs, public objections, etc, have a dangerous golden opportunity in deserts of doing the ideal 'best' job. There suddenly seems to be the possibility here, the only place nowadays, where an engineer can possibly try to fulfil the American highway standards of the 'sixties – the ideal dream for limitless growth. This is something we must be very careful of, for over-growth in the desert is invariably deadly.

It is possible to live in the desert well. Many groups of people have done it successfully in the past, and some in the present. I believe that the way to do it is not by forcing ourselves on the desert, relying solely on modern technology and high energy solutions such as air-conditioning or desalination of sea water. The way must be based on solutions or techniques which embody understanding of the desert and working with its natural systems. A technique like this should be based on what I will call the 'multi-track system' as opposed to a 'single-track system'. A 'single-track system' is one in which only one problem is solved in the design effort. A 'multi-track system' is one in which as many effects as possible are considered along with the primary goal in order to reap all the benefits possible from any one development.

For example, let us look at the ravine system in the Negev. The primary goal in developing the ravine system was erosion control in a semi-arid zone (250 mm rainfall per annum with 'loess' type soil). A single-track approach would have been to build an expensive concrete dam someplace upstream, make a fancy brochure, and get a loan from the World Bank. The multi-track approach not only served to control erosion, but also to take full advantage of other benefits which might result from the process. Instead of the concrete dam, the ravines were moulded into a softer form with bulldozers, without, however, changing their courses. Small earth or stick dams were constructed for catchment areas. The ravines were then planted with trees and bushes. The results of this simple procedure were the creation of narrow, sinuous forest belts which run along wadi contours, which provide a new habitat for wildlife, and change the scale of the vast desert. The desert which before was so desolate, was thereby structured, and began to take on the appearance of manageable spaces. It became more beautiful. The forest benefits not merely from the 250 mm annual rainfall, but from a quantity of water which is as much as three times that amount since it is in a drainage entrapment area. Trees and plants which would be unable to survive otherwise, are able to flourish there. The new forest is a major habitat for wildlife which had been unable to exist in the area before. Lastly, but not least, the planted ravine systems stop the erosion of a potentially good agricultural land. The beneficial impact of this solution is easily seen to be far greater than the mere building of a dam to stop erosion.

Another example of the multi-track approach is the Yatir Forest. Yatir Forest was conceived twenty years ago as a typical semi-arid forest like those seen in many countries around the Mediterranean such as Iran, Greece, Italy or Spain. One of the characteristics of such forests is that of being monoculture, of very few species of trees covering big tracts of land without much regard for different orientations, soils, slopes or other local physical conditions. In a way, forests such as these are manifestations of man's will to change their environment by force, with energy and dedication. Philosophically this stems from the same forceful optimism of the 'thirties and 'forties which produced the TVA in the United States. Remarkable and admirable as these efforts may be, they may fail in the long run because of the single-mindedness of their conception.

In the case of the Yatir Forest, after the first thirteen years of this 'single-track' approach by the Israeli Afforestation Commission (JNF) it was felt that a different approach was needed. A new concept was developed, and for the last six years all new plantations of forest have been done in accordance with these concepts. Instead of planting a blanket of conifers, four elements are intermixed to create a more complex and viable ecological system. These elements are: conifers – still the dominant tree in harsh conditions; broadleafed trees, mainly *Pistacia atlantica*, in the ravines where soil conditions allow; field crops such as barley and wheat in small meadows; and some large areas, some of them of special natural beauty or interest, were left in their natural state. This mixture is not only visually much more pleasing, it was also found to support much richer wildlife, and it created much more 'edge' space, which has been found to be the choice location of use for most vacationers.

The ancient Hebrews and the Nabateans who lived 2,000 years ago in the same desert, the Negev, understood perhaps better than anyone how to come to terms with the desert. They had flourishing cities which were self-sustaining in food and even provided food for caravan trains. This was accomplished in the desert solely by the wise channelling of floodwater into prepared terrace fields, by building small stone mounds and ridges to increase run-off, and by damming the valleys with small stone dams.

Twenty years ago the Afforestation Commission of Israel (JNF) began to use a similar idea, copied in this case from a current Bedouin practice of re-forming small ancient dams to entrap run-off. In the beginning they made square, utilitarian catchment areas with heavy equipment. This they planted in uniform rows with one species of tree, generally *Eucalyptus occidentalis*. When this proved successful in providing adequate water to support the trees, the system was developed into bays which were more naturally shaped to the topography, and quite a few different types of trees and shrubs were introduced. The bays were later developed into a series along the ravines in order to make a continuous belt. This proved to be even more successful visually and ecologically because it created a bigger system with much more variety.

These are a few examples of a fruitful approach to planning in the desert. The results of this approach are not so much a function of the amount of money put into the project, but more a function of the amount of understanding and innovation put into the design! In fact, putting a lot of money into a desert project which relies upon the most advanced mechanical techniques and artificial systems can be not only economically unfeasible, but can also involve massive ecological damage which is virtually irreparable. If the desert planner always keeps in mind the *necessity* of combining goals in any project so that the maximum human benefit can be taken out of the simplest project, with the minimum of expensive and fragile supporting systems, he will already by a big step ahead toward the success of his design.

BIOLOGICAL AND ECOLOGICAL CONSERVATION

CONSERVATION OF WILDLIFE AND VISUAL RESOURCES IN THE AMERICAN COUNTRYSIDE

SALLY SCHAUMAN

ROLE OF THE LANDSCAPE ARCHITECT IN BIOLOGICAL AND ECOLOGICAL CONSERVATION

HANNO HENKE

THE CONSERVATION OF WILDLIFE AND VISUAL RESOURCES IN THE AMERICAN COUNTRYSIDE
SALLY SCHAUMAN

Background

More than forty years ago, the Soil Conservation Service (SCS), was established as an agency within the United States Department of Agriculture. Working directly with private landowners in more than three thousand local conservation districts, SCS has attempted to reduce all types of soil erosion. This work has been accomplished primarily by providing technical assistance rather than by direct funding or cost-sharing programmes. In providing technical assistance directly to private landowners, SCS is unique among Federal resource agencies. Many other resource agencies manage or regulate Federal lands. Since the agency is neither a land regulatory agency nor a land management agency SCS must accomplish its mission by persuading land users to adopt conservation practices designed to prevent soil loss and reduce sedimentation, thereby preventing the pollution of water resources.

The need for conservation on private lands is great because the amount of privately owned land is large. Approximately three-fifths of the more than 2·2 billion acres of land in the United States is privately owned and controlled. More than 1 billion acres of the American landscape is under cultivation or in permanent grassland pasture and range. Almost all of the 500 million acres of cropland is in private ownership.[1] Clearly these agricultural landscapes are significant resources in the content of world food needs. The conservation of these soil resources for food and fibre production is the primary mission of SCS.

The food and fibre production potential is only part of the total resource value of such agricultural or countryside landscapes. In recent years, SCS has widened its technical focus in recognition of the fact that soil conservation is related to a wide range of natural resource conservation efforts. The modern approach to soil conservation is to identify the range of related resources, such as wildlife, archaeological, and visual within any landscape unit and to deal with the interrelationship of these resources in a multipurpose conservation programme. The work of SCS biologists in fish and wildlife habitat management and SCS landscape architects in landscape resource conservation are indicative of the present SCS conservation approach.

Fish and Wildlife Habitat Management[2]

The countryside landscape provides a significant resource for creating and maintaining a variety of fish and wildlife habitats. Conservation practices installed in these landscapes, primarily to control soil erosion and to reduce sedimentation, can be managed to provide a better fish or wildlife habitat. For example, SCS has assisted landowners in building more than 2 million small ponds to control erosion. When these ponds are planned and built according to criteria developed by SCS biologists, such areas can provide fish habitat and an element of wildlife habitat more valuable than comparable acreages of woodland, cropland, or grassland. SCS biologists provide practical suggestions for the water and edge characteristics, and vegetation types that will improve the quality and quantity of habitat available for fish, animals, and waterfowl. A single conservation practice alone seldom will provide adequate habitat elements; but with some modifications, cropland conservation practices such as stripcropping, minimum tillage, field windbreaks and field borders will provide increased food, cover, and water for animals and birds. Using standards developed by SCS biologists, fish and wildlife habitats on rangelands and pasture lands will be enhanced as well.

In addition to cropland and rangeland conservation practices, SCS biologists assist land users in identifying, improving, and maintaining

specific areas to be set aside for wildlife. For example, a major part of the waterfowl habitat in America exists on private lands usually associated with agriculture. These habitats provide valuable wintering, migrating, and breeding areas for waterfowl and associated habitats for other wildlife and fish. In a recent year, it was estimated that more than 600,000 acres of wetland were managed for wildlife by private land users.[3] As one views the pattern of conservation in the American countryside, the work of SCS biologists is not apparent, but increasingly important as conflicting land uses impact our limited supply resource – landscape. Providing fish and wildlife habitats often aids the work of SCS landscape architects by improving the countryside landscape resource.

Landscape Resource Management

SCS landscape architects are concerned with conserving the countryside landscape resource as a defined composite of ecological, social, and visual resources. SCS landscape architectural policy and technology are relatively recent. The first landscape architectural position on the Washington staff was created only in 1973. Since that time other landscape architectural staff positions have been filled and all landscape architects are engaged in developing techniques to assist land users in conserving the landscape resources.

One of the first problems SCS landscape architects encountered was the lack of landscape architectural understanding within the agency, a typical professional problem encountered with any new client. For example, many SCS technical specialists saw the landscape only in terms of their own discipline. One of the first tasks of SCS landscape architects was to educate their colleagues as to basic design and visual perception principles by developing training materials. These training materials lead SCS personnel through seeing exercises – seeing the parts of the landscape as elements, as patterns, and as a whole and seeing changes to all components. SCS landscape architects are beginning to discover that while these training materials were designed strictly for agency use, parts of the materials are useful as general education for public groups who have difficulty in visualising future landscape changes. The agency expects to add other basic training materials because SCS landscape architects believe they can make substantial progress in landscape resource management; but only if concomitantly, they educate their colleagues and the public land user as to visual resource principles.

SCS landscape resource management (LRM) is the application of landscape architecture to the wide variety of SCS conservation activities. LRM follows the traditional design process of:

1 Inventorying and investigation.
2 Planning and design.
3 Implementation and construction.
4 Post implementation and post construction.

We believe we can provide technical guidance for land users themselves to apply LRM in some uncomplicated situations; but we also know we must identify the complex situations where professional expertise will be mandatory. As a first step in sorting out these situations, SCS landscape architects published a document known as SCS Technical Release 65, 'Procedure to Establish Priorities in Landscape Architecture', October 1978.

In this document we devised a method of evaluating the landscape as to the three factors we believe contribute to landscape resource value: visual resource quality, landscape use value, and visibility. By first identifying relative values of each of these factors and then by superimposing these values, we are able to designate a composite value of the resource in a specific location. Finally, the combined values are ranked to indicate priorities for applying landscape resource management and to clearly designate areas where professional landscape architectural expertise will be required. While this procedure was designed to manage the use of landscape architects within the agency, we believe it can be adapted by communities to find those special areas within the countryside that deserve prompt action to conserve valuable scenic areas and open spaces. The latter use of Technical Release 65 is important in view of emerging concerns for American countryside. Public awareness of countryside landscape resource conservation in America is only now gaining momentum, the literature is scanty, academic research is meagre, and public policy is unclear.[4]

By some standards the American countryside may seem vast and boundless. This is far from true, equally accessible to viewing by the vacationer and indigenous regional countryside visual resources, for some unique countryside open spaces are in short supply and are in danger of complete conversion to other uses. Thus, we are not only reducing the amount of prime agricultural land for food and fibre production; but we are also eliminating a special landscape resource for succeeding generations. In the future, SCS landscape architects will continue to provide direct technical assistance and to develop training materials, audio visual presentations and technical documents. All of these will be designed to relate and apply basic landscape architectural concepts to the conservation of the American countryside.

References:
[1]Data compiled in 1974 as illustrated in US Department of Agriculture, 1978 Handbook of Agricultural Charts, Agricultural Handbook No 551, Washington, DC. November.
[2]This section after Thomas, Carl H. 1978. Co-ordination of wildlife habitat management with grazing and other range management practices, paper presented at the SCS National range workshop, Rapid City, South Dakota, June 27, 1978. Mr Thomas is the Chief Biologist in the Soil Conservation Service, Washington, DC 20013.
[3]Davis, R. M. 1979. From the Administrator. In protecting wetlands and wildlife, a reprint from the Soil Conservation Magazine, SCS, USDA, Washington, DC.
[4]For example, the first conference on preserving rural landscapes sponsored by the National Trust for Historic Preservation was held in April 1979 in Annapolis, Maryland.

THE ROLE OF THE LANDSCAPE ARCHITECT IN BIOLOGICAL AND ECOLOGICAL CONSERVATION
HANNO HENKE

The aim and the task of the landscape architect are to influence, through landscape planning, man's take-over process of nature in such a way that during economic development his spiritual and physical natural support system is retained and sustainably secured for future use. The paper presented here is divided into three parts. The first part shows from what standpoint and for what areas the landscape architect has thus far tried to contribute to the mentioned objective. In the next part the, in many countries, independent development and spatial expansion of nature conservation is dealt with and points out how nature conservation overlaps with the task of the landscape architect due to their mutual objective. Through the integration of both fields into a planning system with sectorial planning and comprehensive land use planning, the possibilities for biological and ecological conservation are shown in the third section by using the ecological effect assessment as a planning instrument. To counteract the vision of a desolated landscape by the year 2000, landscape architecture has to concern itself to a much greater degree with biological and ecological conservation than it has up to now.

The position and the task of the landscape architect within society derives from man's relationship with nature, meaning his natural environment, which due to his ongoing take-over process is subject to constant change. Because of dynamic economic-technical development within a short time span, man's environment, reflecting his needs, cannot anymore historically evolve in a self-regulatory sense and makes planning by the landscape architect, among others, necessary. Whereas at the beginning of the profession's development the need of a small privileged class to have nature adapted in gardens and parks according to the aesthetic conceptions of the time was pursued, through the course of time the landscape architect has taken over a more and more comprehensive responsibility for a broader public. Where man has most intensively altered or destroyed nature, that is, residential, urban and industrial agglomeration areas, 'nature' is reintroduced and developed on the basis of the spiritual and physical needs of the public. In residential areas the landscape architect plans gardens, play and sports grounds, green open spaces and parks, and for urban areas develops open space and green belt concepts. For major engineering works, for example, industrial plants, transportation sites and mineral excavation areas, he participates in determining the site's location and plans the integration of the project into the landscape as well as the reclamation of the impact. Because of these work areas, the landscape architect is placed in a close relationship with architects and city and regional planners, on the one hand, and due to his primary work material – plants – with horticulturists and nurserymen on the other hand. In horticultural and nursery enterprises the plant material is cultivated

and to a great extent bred to suit specific site conditions and the aesthetic needs of the public. When the landscape architect's work is confined to this realm, however, it cannot really contribute to biological and ecological conservation.

As the landscape architect develops into a planner of man's natural environment in which not only, as in the beginning, the aesthetic needs are of importance, but also a number of human ecological interactions in the man-environment relationship are the focus of landscape planning, a spatial expansion of the landscape architect's work area takes place – from the urban and agglomeration area to the open landscape (countryside). With this development an essential broadening of the content of the landscape architect's work to fulfil societal needs occurs. In the urban and agglomeration areas in which nature is extremely altered or destroyed by man, the landscape architect's task is to reintroduce nature, as far as possible, primarily on the basis of society's present needs. Whereas in the economically used open landscape which functions to a great extent by bio-ecological processes, it is his task to secure the bio-ecological potential for future generations. Since, on the one hand, the demands of future generations are not known and, on the other hand, a great part of the bio-ecological potential is irreversibly lost through unrestricted economic-technical development, biological and ecological conservation is of great importance as a prophylactic measure to prevent desolation of our landscape by the year 2000. The landscape architect can achieve this far-reaching and important goal only in close co-operation with the nature conservation field which is primarily responsible for this task. The extent to which biological and ecological conservation is implemented by nature conservation and landscape planning varies to a great extent from country to country due to the historical development of both fields. Also, the harmonisation of each field's protection or planning instruments to achieve the mutual objective is only in an embryonic stage. The requirements for joint biological and ecological conservation by nature conservation and landscape planning will now be dealt with.

The objective for nature conservation and landscape planning is to sustainably conserve nature and landscape as the natural support system for man. Due to the dynamic process of the transformation of nature by man, nature and landscape are in constant development and, therefore, continuously altered. The protection of nature, in the historical succession of conservation of the biological and ecological potential of nature and landscape, involves as a first step the exclusion of man. This means that economic use of nature by man is not permitted. Through this, a protected area system reaching from species protection to ecosystem protection and requiring property rights, an independent administration and sectorial planning can develop. A comprehensive protected area system should contain at least one sample of each representative and unique ecosystem. The foundation for a single protected area is a differentiated flexible area system based on the ecosystem's functionally linked sub-complexes. At least five sub-complexes, each having its own spatial delineation, are necessary for the protection of an ecosystem. These sub-complexes are:

vegetation-ecological
animal-ecological
pedo-ecological
hydro-ecological
climate-ecological.

These are to an extent studied within protected areas by the respective scientific disciplines. However, their functional interactions as an ecosystem have yet to be dealt with. In practice, the vegetation-ecological or animal-ecological core areas of an ecosystem only fall under strict protection in the most favourable cases. Over a period of time the protected area system's existence is endangered by the intensification and alteration of land uses outside protected areas through the interrelationships of ecosystems. In this phase it becomes necessary to extend protection of ecosystems to economically used land. In the case where man is excluded from nature it is the aim to secure the development of representative and unique natural ecosystems, while in the case of economically used land the aim is to protect, manage and develop the biological self-regulatory ability, meaning the capability, of transformed ecosystems. The conservation of transformed ecosystems is intended to prevent direct and indirect effects from land use changes on the natural ecosystems of protected areas. The greater the adaptability and, therefore, the stability of transformed ecosystems, on the one hand, and the more comprehensive the compensation measures for use originated impacts, on the other hand, the less harmful the effects are on protected areas. For this aim the natural resources which enable the highest possible self-regulatory ability of transformed ecosystems, such as

climate, air quality
water areas, wetlands
soil, soil fertility
vegetation cover
wild flora and fauna

have to be determined, protected, managed and developed. Through the realisation of such biological and ecological conservation as independent sectorial planning, a contribution is made at the same time toward securing the usability of natural resources for other types of land use planning, for example, agriculture, forestry and recreation. Only in connection with economically oriented land uses can sectorial planning for nature conservation ensure that by the year 2000 our landscape will be able to fulfil the then relevant land use demands.

Area protection is the instrument for fulfilling the two objectives for nature conservation, which are, the sustainable securement of:

1 Natural species and ecosystems by species and ecosystem protection.
2 The capability of transformed ecosystems on economically used land as a support system for species and ecosystem protection and the usability of natural resources.

For the conservation of natural species and ecosystems, strict protection including management is required. However, for the conservation of the capability of transformed ecosystems this is not possible because dynamic land use changes would be eliminated. In addition, for the securement of a high natural self-regulatory ability it is only possible to protect the essential components – meaning the natural resources – of transformed ecosystems to a certain degree. In the case of a land use change, protection can be achieved by assessing its effects, that is, how much they impair the capability of transformed ecosystems and the interlinked natural species and natural ecosystems of protected areas.

If the effects will cause serious changes in the transformed and natural ecosystems they are termed impacts and, thus, have to be prevented. The better sectorial planning for nature conservation is established and the more equal its position is in relation to other sectorial planning, the better the chance that its objectives can be put through in the planning process. As a result, in practice, this can mean that a planned land use has to either be omitted or implemented in an altered, less impairing way and the remaining effects have to be eliminated through compensation measures specified by the nature conservation authority. The implementation of this type of procedure for assessing the effects caused by land use changes is a planning process through which the landscape architect can provide an essential contribution to biological and ecological conservation for a liveable landscape in the year 2000.

The basic requirement for effective work by landscape architects is a planning system constituted by law which includes sectorial planning and comprehensive land use planning on a local, regional and national level. In the historical evolution of land use planning, economically oriented sectorial planning, such as, agriculture and transportation, in general, develops before sectorial planning for nature conservation, which is a civilisation follower. After the establishment of such sectorial planning an initial step can be made toward comprehensive conservation planning via the assessment of ecological effects of individual land use changes. The ecological effect analysis and assessment of land use measures can either be carried out by the originator of ecological effects or by the affected party, namely, primarily, sectorial planning for conservation of nature and natural resources. In either case the landscape architect is engaged in solving the problem. As already mentioned, the landscape architect up to now has been involved in the restoration of the natural environment, due to urban and industrial construction work, in conjunction with economic interests which are the originators of impacts. It has been his goal to satisfy, as far as possible, the public's current spiritual and physical needs for nature. This is still the landscape architect's concern, but he is in a stronger position as a result of an increasingly aware and powerful public and a decreasing availability of visual and natural resources. The latter makes it necessary to pursue economically oriented land uses in such a way so as to sustainably secure the usability of natural resources. In an association in which the landscape architect is the contractee of an economic interest, a conflict of interest, in general, will not be brought up resulting in very slow progress toward securing the biological and ecological potential of the landscape for future generations. The situation is different when the landscape architect is engaged on the side of the affected party. In this case, conflicts will be brought up and solved on the basis of an analysis and assessment of ecological effects of each land use change on the long term survivability of a protected area system and the capability of transformed ecosystems. This procedure, applied during the planning process, makes it possible to omit a use measure or to implement it in an altered less impairing way and to have the remaining effects eliminated through compensation measures. Up to now the landscape architect only planned compensation measures without being able to take a clear nature conservation standpoint. Only by influencing economic development and growth can the ecological and biological needs for society in the year 2000 be fulfilled and desolation of the landscape prevented.

If the landscape architect wants not only to satisfy the current needs of the public for a natural environment for which the contractor, to a great extent, determines what is sufficient, but also wants to contribute to the sustainable securement of the landscape's biological and ecological potential for future generations, landscape architecture must cultivate a close relationship with nature conservation in order to be able to take a firm position *vis-à-vis* economic interests. However, such a relationship is viewed with some reservations by many nature conservationists because the landscape architect has been looked upon so far, primarily as an associate of economic development and growth. It is, therefore, the task of the professional organisations in different countries and their international federation, IFLA, to develop a strategy for a closer liaison with institutions responsible for conservation of nature and natural resources.

References

Bundesminister für Ernährung, Landwirtschaft und Forsten (1976): Gesetz über Naturschutz und Landschaftspflege (Bundesnaturschutzgesetz – BNatSchG) vom 20. 12. 1976 – Bonn: BML.

Ellenberg, H., Fränzle, O., Müller, P. (1978): Ökosystemforschung im Hinblick auf Umweltpolitik und Entwicklungsplanung. Bundesministerium des Innern, Forschung im Bereich Umweltgrundsatzangelegenheiten, Abschnitt Ökologie, MAB.

Haber, W. (1978): Raumordnungskonzepte aus der Sicht der Ökosystemforschung. Akademie für Raumforschung und Landesplanung, Wissenschaftliche Plenarsitzung 'Die ökologische Orientierung der Raumplanung', 19 Oktober 1978 in Saarbrücken.

Henke, H. (1979): Untersuchung von Verfahrensweisen zur Erstellung planungsorientierter ökologischer Raumgliederungen. In: BDLA-Schriftenreihe (i. Druck).

Hanke, H., Krause, C. L. (1979): Study on Environmental Effects for Conservation Planning. In: Special Report No 2, National Committee for the UNESCO Programme 'MAB' of the Federal Republic of Germany.

Holling, C. S. (Ed.) (1978): Adaptive Environmental Assessment and Management. Chichester, New York, Brisbane, Toronto: Wiley IIASA International Series on Applied Systems Analysis No 3.

Jeffers, J. N. R. (1978): An Introduction to Systems Analysis: with ecological applications. London: Edward Arnold.

Odum, E. P. (1977): The Emergence of Ecology as a New Integrative Discipline. Science Vol 195, No 4284.

RANN (1977): Regional Environmental Systems. Department of Civil Engineering, University of Washington, Workshop 20 – 24 June 1977, Assessment of RANN-Projects.

LANDSCAPE ARCHITECTURE EDUCATION

HUBERT B. OWENS

The roots of the profession of landscape architecture reach back to the earliest pre-historic civilisations through the Greek and Roman Classic periods, and the Medieval and the Renaissance periods. It is necessary for the practitioner to have a sound knowledge of the history of the profession, particularly its development since the Renaissance, especially the era of de-formalisation of public and private properties, the coming of the Industrial Revolution and all the influences which have effected the visual, aesthetic and technical considerations man has used in designing outdoor environments through the years to the present.

As landscape architecture is practised today, it has come into its own primarily during the 20th century. The term landscape architect was first used in the 1860's. The first professional association of practitioners – the American Society of Landscape Architects – was founded in 1899; and the first baccalaureat degree course was established at Harvard University three years later. Several colleges and universities in other countries had been teaching ornamental horticulture/landscape gardening courses for many years but these curricula were not planned for their graduates to assume responsible rôles parallel to those of competently trained architects and engineers, as was the Harvard course.

Those of us in the United States who have served as pioneer educators at the University level and acquired a number of years experience as teachers and practitioners recognise that there are two important kinds of education for which teachers and practitioners alike must recognise and promote:

(a) University students.
(b) The public.

University Curricula

For almost a century, members of instructional staffs and administrators of American universities have given close attention to curriculum content. Course content of curricula in the various universities is revised and updated periodically to keep pace with changing times.

1. Accreditation by the National Commission on Accrediting and the Committee on Education of the American Society of Landscape Architects for the Bachelors and Masters degrees. Currently there are 45 university accredited programmes with a total of approximately 5,000 students enrolled in the United States.

2. Council of Educators in Landscape Architecture (CELA) in the USA.

An organisation of the teachers in all the universities which offer landscape architecture training. It is administered by a set of officers, which comprise an Executive Committee, and a number of working committees. It publishes a newsletter periodically, and holds an annual meeting.

Curriculum organisation and accrediting (certification) methods to achieve minimum landscape architectural educational standards differ in the relatively small number of nations with university programmes. Nevertheless, it should be the objective throughout the world to train students to become competent landscape architects who can adequately handle small, medium, and large scale projects, wherever they may practise.

The Public

The term is used in this instance to include all citizens except landscape architecture teachers. Most university level courses have come about as the result of a demand for this specialised training from parents of students, civic and political leaders, philanthropists, etc. Without the support of such citizens it is difficult for landscape architecture programmes to become established and to be sustained.

1. Legal protection of the practice of the profession. Enactment of legislation for licensing brings official recognition of the profession, and protects the title and practice.

2. Schoolchildren. Savannah, a beautiful, well planned city in Georgia, has a programme which serves as a 'cradle for public education'. It is known as the Massie Heritage Classroom, and is operated by the Board of Public Education of the City of Savannah and the County of Chatham. The programme focuses on the rich historical and architectural heritage within the USA's largest National Historic District. The staff working with students, grades 4-12 on a field trip basis with pre- and post-activities in the classroom, proposes to train up a generation of perceptive and responsible citizens appreciative of the special environment in which they live. The idea of training in a minimum amount of time, grade and high school students to learn the types of architecture, kinds of trees in the parks and streets, become conscious of paving patterns, street furniture, etc, in their city is a splendid way to get citizen participation in civic development in later years, as well as to guide talented young people to choose an environmental design profession for university training.

IFLA's Educational Programme

The Federation aims at establishing programmes in professional landscape architecture in developing nations, preferably in one or more universities where a curriculum in architecture is presently offered. Support of the instructional staffs at existing universities for exchange professorships, student scholarships, overall counselling, and for moral aid is important.

The position of an IFLA Co-ordinator of International Education was created by the Grand Council in September 1978. Twenty years ago IFLA established a Committee on Education. This Committee made a world survey of landscape architecture education which was published. It is actively functioning today. It is intended that the Co-ordinator will deal largely with promotion of education in the developing nations, and the Committee on Education will continue its service to the established programmes in universities located in nations which are affiliated with the Federation.

HISTORIC LANDSCAPES

HISTORIC LANDSCAPES PROFESSOR RENE PECHERE

HISTORIC LANDSCAPES IN BRITAIN PROFESSOR B. HACKETT

HISTORIC LANDSCAPES
PROFESSOR RENE PECHERE

The name 'Historic Landscape' must be clarified. It must be examined from the point of view of our profession and the rôle which the latter can fulfil in this field.

The members of the IFLA have a task to perform in the field of gardens and landscapes. But where *historic* gardens and landscapes are concerned, there is a need for a specification requiring knowledge closely linked with the history of art and even with archaeology.

Therefore, before coming to an agreement on the question of 'who does what?', it would seem to be useful to dwell upon the different aspects of the 'Historic Landscapes' problem.

In the field of historic gardens properly so called, a series of actions has been carried out following the initiative taken by the IFLA in Sardinia, in 1968. This initiative has been completed by collaboration with ICOMOS and the creation of a joint committee. This collaboration has made possible:

(a) the organising of four conferences, in Fontainebleau (1971), in Granada (1973), in Zeist (1975), and in Krömeritz and Prague (1977); a fifth conference is planned for Bruges (1979);

(b) a definition of historic garden;

(c) the drawing up of national and international lists;

(d) the drawing of attention to gardens in danger;

(e) demonstration of the importance of the landscape architect in collaboration with art historians;

(f) participation in certain rescue operations.

As far as historic landscapes are concerned, the IFLA has also taken an initiative, which was confirmed at the Istanbul Congress in 1976. It is essential that a distribution of tasks should be discussed more fully. The Committee of Historic Landscapes will perhaps find a formula for a more specific designation of its activity. The Committee of Historic Gardens and Landscapes (confirmed by UNESCO) decided, during its meeting in October 1978 in Paris, to replace the word 'landscape' by the word 'site' with a view to clarification and appeasement.

The task is immense in every way and common action is highly desirable so as to define the objectives and to get agreement on a list of priorities. But even common action is only possible with the help and very close attention of the authorities concerned.

Personally I hope that, as far as the Historic Sites are concerned, some action will be undertaken for Stonehenge, which should be fenced in and have seating accommodation around it – the fact that we have met in Great Britain is without doubt favourable to laying the basis for this.

HISTORIC LANDSCAPES IN BRITAIN
PROFESSOR BRIAN HACKETT

You will expect me to say something about historic landscapes and their conservation in Britain. There are, of course, three types of historic landscape and I will endeavour to summarise the most important measures and organisations concerned with their conservation. But the main emphasis in my paper will be on the problems of conserving the historic agricultural and forest landscapes.

The natural landscape in a completely wild state only remains in a few places in Britain, and even they inevitably change character, if ever so slowly, as climatic changes occur, and also new influences from man's changes to the landscape elsewhere are bound to have some effect. The Nature Reserves and Sites of Special Scientific Interest are the major defences for these areas, and the Nature Conservancy Council has legal powers, manpower to protect, and is able to advise organisations concerned with them. Some areas of natural landscape lie within National Parks and the Forestry Commission forests, and have the protection of these organisations. There is, also, the overriding duty placed on our national public bodies by the Countryside Act 1968 to have regard to the desirability of conserving the natural beauty and amenity of the countryside, but this is capable of wide interpretation and subject to much argument from both sides at public inquiries. In the Water Act 1973, the words 'have regard to' are changed to 'shall take into account', which is perhaps a little stronger. This duty applies to the natural landscape as well as the countryside generally.

There are many possibilities in the legislation for conserving the second type of historic landscape, namely those relating to archaeology, agriculture and forestry. It is with the former that the legislation and protective organisation is the most effective under the Ancient Monuments Secretariat of the Department of the Environment. It is also possible to prevent injury to ancient remains from agricultural and forestry operations, the occupier of the land being compensated for the loss to his work.

With historic landscapes of agricultural and forestry practices, there are many possibilities for conservation, but also a great many problems in practice. I have already mentioned the National Parks, which have a stronger pull in dealing with these examples than in the countryside generally. There is legislation for conservation areas, but although this was clearly meant to refer to built landscapes, the relevant legal wording leaves the door open for continual pressure to be put upon those at the top for allowing 'green landscape' conservation areas to be included – this is something the Landscape Institute might take up. We have the possibility of declaring Areas of Outstanding Natural Beauty within which stricter than normal planning control has a chance of being upheld at the national level, but you can argue about the word 'natural', because so much of our landscape is of the humanised variety. Tree preservation is possible under planning legislation, and there is the requirement to obtain a licence from the Forestry Commission for felling trees above a certain limit, but as everyone knows, preserving something with an eventual death certainty at some future date, and subject to the dangers besetting all living things, is not a certainty; this statement indeed applies very much to all types of landscape which has the birth and death cycle, and is affected by both changes in man's social and economic patterns, and by the changes to the climate. Perhaps our greatest hope for the conservation of historic agricultural and forest landscapes lies in what might be called 'voluntary conservation', which is certainly entering the portals of power as a result of public pressure, and I shall refer to this in the last part of my paper.

The third type of historic landscape comprises the historic gardens and parklands, and I refer you to Bodfan Gruffydd's book 'Protecting Historic Landscapes' for an authoritative account of the problems, possibilities and legislation. But briefly, the latter is a little more definite with regard to these historic landscapes, and when buildings are associated with them, the Conservation Area procedure is possible. Grants of money can be made for the upkeep of a garden or other land of outstanding historic interest, both whether or not associated with buildings of architectural or historic interest. There is the general power of the control of land use by planning authorities, but this is always subject to objections and the public inquiry procedure and probably compensation, which often reduce its likelihood of success.

I must now turn, after this brief and necessarily incomplete review of the official position to the possibilities for achieving the conservation of historic landscapes in the three types, and say something about the conservation of the historic landscapes of agriculture and forestry. At the outset it would surely be our hope that first priority must be the conservation of one example of each historical period and technique, although only one of each would be a long way short of satisfying all those concerned with landscape.

The major difficulty, apart from the birth and death cycle of landscape, is the pressure of a changing economy and technology, coupled with various kinds of tax burdens upon landowners. For this audience, there is no need for me to enlarge upon these problems.

The Council for the Protection of Rural England, failing the likelihood of strict conservation legislation for rural areas, suggested an early warning system in which farmers and others would have to notify an appropriate authority of their intention to change the landscape pattern, thus giving time for some action to be attempted. This useful suggestion was not accepted by the Advisory Council for Agriculture and Horticulture, but the Ministry of Agriculture now bears in mind the general directive to national bodies for the landscape when it gives grant aid on farm investments, and it is a matter for us to continually keep this commitment from being overlooked.

The establishment of the Countryside Commission has done, and is doing, a great deal for the landscape generally, not forgetting historic rural landscape. In addition to the Commission's special interest in National and Country Parks, Areas of Outstanding Natural Beauty, Areas of Mainly Open Country, Green Belts, and Urban Fringe Areas, and the coastline, its recent development of the idea of countryside management, with a management officer on the spot, has good prospects of achieving results on the voluntary goodwill basis.

The Forestry Commission has the difficult task of achieving profitability, when it has to change much open landscape to forests of a particular kind we know so well. But apart from its increasing efforts to ensure that new forests become acceptable landscapes, its historical New Forest policy is one to admire when you realise the many pressures upon the forest. Obviously, the Forestry Commission faces problems in conserving ancient woodlands, which need special selective felling practices and ecological care, and the historic coppiced woodlands really need to be linked to an economic use to ensure their future. This latter point raises the question that we need to find some way to cultivate historic agricultural landscapes, more or less as they were originally cultivated, in order to ensure their survival; this is difficult in an age of high wages and new technology. It is a matter for research.

We must not forget voluntary conservation which ranges from the landowner who manages to run his estate in a conservation manner so that ends meet, to those who repair and reclaim canals at weekends. I wish there was time to do full justice to the efforts of these volunteers, who also include the many local amenity societies throughout the land, and bodies like the Ramblers' Association. Co-operation between bodies involved in conservation can solve some problems too large for one organisation to accept; an example is the Cragside Estate in Northumberland, where the National Trust takes on the house and its immediate surroundings, while the County Council takes on the whole area as a Country Park. Mention of the National Trust, which has exemption from taxation and death duties, causes me to mention once again the need for more and more consideration at the national government level for the financial problems of estate owners who are trying to conserve their landscape. There is also the example of a voluntary agreement between an owner and the appropriate local authority, as at Upton Castle in Wales. And I was able to observe at first hand the evolution of a voluntary agreement on the future of afforestation areas in Northumberland which was made between the National Park authority and the Forestry Commission.

I have already mentioned the changing social and economic pattern in the countryside, and how this affects landscape conservation. I think a bigger financial contribution ought to come from those who earn their living in the towns, but seek to live or enjoy recreation in the countryside. And finally, we have to accept the facts of life over many areas of familiar landscape that there can be constructive conservation as well as static conservation. What changes that are inevitable need landscape skill as well as technological skill, and here we look to the day when planning with landscape conditions can influence land use change over all the landscape to a greater extent than it can today in the historic rural landscape.

THE REHABILITATION OF THE INNER CITY

REHABILITATION OF INNER AREAS DR WILFRED BURNS CB, CBE

STRATEGIES FOR ADAPTIVE RE-USE OF URBAN SPACE IN GEORGIA: THE CITY OF MACON AS A MODEL ASSOCIATE PROFESSOR VINCENT J. BELLAFIORE

REHABILITATION OF THE INNER CITY PROFESSOR WALTER BOR CBE

REHABILITATION OF INNER AREAS
DR W. BURNS CB CBE

The problems in inner areas of cities have now become matters of widespread political interest – internationally as well as nationally. They have not received this attention in recent years because the inner city was perceived as a new problem but because the solutions pursued over the last 30 years and more in these areas have either been inadequate or sometimes possibly misdirected. The problems have also been shown to be much more complex than was thought and our understanding of them has increased – though is still partial.

In this paper I use the term 'inner city' to mean the old 19th century settlement, ie, the central area and the surrounding residential and industrial areas developed at high density and now in part much decayed. The 'inner area' is the term used to distinguish this surrounding belt (at one time called the twilight zone) from the central area or CBD.

The Legacy of Past Urbanisation
The present conditions of Britain's inner cities can only be understood in the context of the changing form and function of urban areas and city regions.

The early 19th century witnessed a surge of economic activity which concentrated population in towns of increasing size. Britain was the first urbanised country in Western Europe: the census of 1851 showing for the first time that more than 50 per cent of this country's population lived in urban areas.

Even before the 19th century ended the density of population in the older tightly knit inner areas had begun to decline and peripheral suburbanisation as a growth process was in evidence. The last three decades of the century all recorded huge increases in the outer rings of London and by the 1890s the provincial conurbations began to reflect the same pattern.

Throughout the 20th century the twin processes of decentralisation and suburbanisation have quickened and come to represent the main forces of urban growth. These phases are causing fundamental shifts in the nature of the British city. Central areas have already undergone massive change[1]; inner areas are still in the process of change in rôle and function. The inner area problem is rooted in this process of evolution.

The Nature of the Problem
The shifts in population are clearly recorded: between 1961 and 1974, while the population of Great Britain increased by 13·4 per cent, the total population of the seven major conurbations declined by 6·8 per cent. Within the conurbations the largest population loss occurred in the urban cores. It has left a population which tends to have lower than average incomes and contains higher proportions of the relatively young and old.

Demographic change has been accompanied by complementary economic trends. During the 1950s the inner cores of the conurbations benefited by a marginal increase in the number of jobs, but during the late 1960s economic slowdown accompanied by extensive labour shedding made for an absolute and relative decline in employment in the urban cores.[2]

Substantial changes in economic structure have accompanied this spatial redistribution of job opportunity. Manufacturing employment has been badly hit and increases in office employment have not compensated for losses in manufacturing.

Bringing these demographic and economic trends together we see them both operating to the disadvantage of the inner area. Moreover, there is a developing mismatch. Jobs requiring higher education and professional qualifications have been accumulating in the central areas of cities, but the people who fill the jobs generally tend to live in the suburbs and metropolitan fringes.

The condition of the environment reflects these demographic and economic trends: a relatively deprived and poor population living in the oldest dwellings; obsolescent industrial stock; shortage of recreational open space but extensive areas of derelict/cleared land; evidence of alienation and vandalism; traffic noise and danger.

In England just over a quarter of existing houses were built before 1919. In the inner areas the proportion is much higher, three out of five houses in inner Liverpool and inner Birmingham were built before this date. Not only are the houses old but many are still without basic amenities. In the inner areas of Liverpool and Manchester/Salford 15 per cent of households lack an inside toilet.[3]

In England just over a quarter of existing houses were built before investment in these areas. In parts of inner Birmingham 40 per cent of industrial buildings were constructed before 1914 and in Manchester the proportion is estimated at upward of 60 per cent.

In many inner areas there is a shortage of usable public open space. Inner London Boroughs such as Lambeth, Southwark, Newham and Tower Hamlets have a total provision per thousand population of between one and two hectares. In Islington until recently, the public open space was around 0·5 hectare per thousand population – a figure that is less than 15 per cent of the average planned provision in the new towns.

In the face of these historic trends no one can be quite sure what, in changing economic and social conditions, the functions of a particular inner area will be; but we can at least make three points. First, they will not be the same as in the past; we cannot recreate the conditions which gave the inner area its earlier *raison d'être*. Second, since its functions cannot be precisely defined, it would be unwise to attempt to set out a detailed blue print. Third, if it is to prosper, it must develop an important functional relationship with the central business district and the surrounding suburban areas.

Against this background of uncertainty it is important that we should exploit, or create new, opportunities, even if that means changing some pre-conceived notions. Innovation at local level to suit local conditions is essential and policies and projects must allow maximum flexibility for accommodating future changes and capitalising on new opportunities.

New Policy for Inner Cities
A series of studies and policy developments during the late 1960s and early 1970s helped to develop a clearer appreciation of the extent and changed character of inner area problems. In June 1977 the Government set out in a White Paper[4] a new framework for giving inner areas an explicit priority in social and economic policy.

The key objectives of that White Paper were:
(a) strengthening the economies of the inner areas and the prospects of their residents;
(b) improving the physical fabric of the inner areas and making their environment more attractive;
(c) alleviating social problems;
(d) securing a new balance between the inner areas and the rest of the city region in terms of population and jobs.

To pursue these objectives it is important to create new confidence – a confidence in the people already living, working and doing business there, that conditions will change; a confidence in developers and investors that their interest and their money will not be wasted; a confidence in all those who are in any way connected with these areas that Government and local government are committed to the task of urban rejuvenation and that private enterprise has an important and innovating rôle to play in this endeavour. I believe that some progress has been made in this direction but I also believe that we need early improvements to the physical environment if interest is to be sustained and turned to practical account.

Improving and changing the environment of our inner areas will come partly through new developments, partly through refurbishment of buildings and partly through a new attention to the environment itself. We need to develop new and realistic planning proposals that will create the conditions for encouraging these changes and improvements. We need also to create or focus the demand for development. This means helping firms to survive or expand or improve. It means attracting new developers and working closely with institutions and organisations representing developers and financial interests. Understanding the demand for land and redirecting it or helping to create it is of prime importance in changing the environmental quality of our inner areas.

All these policies clearly demand on the one hand the injection of more resources and on the other better machinery for welding together the different sectors of central and local government involved in delivering and adapting particular services so that they all contribute to a greater good. It is only through the main expenditure programmes that real change can occur.

Central government decided therefore to ensure that as far as possible their policies and programmes were given an inner area dimension and priority and local government has been urged to adopt a similar approach. Supplementing this, however, there is the urban programme, a central government grant that can be used to aid a wide spectrum of projects benefiting the inner area. Additional resources are also available from special funds for tidying up operations and in loans and grants for industrial and commercial improvements and developments.

The central plank of this approach is that the main policies and expenditure programmes of central and local government should be fully co-ordinated in order to tackle the problems effectively. Central government therefore offered special partnerships to a limited number of local authorities. Central government ministries and agencies came together with the local authorities to develop programmes which would underline the government's commitment to the inner areas and instil confidence in their future. Simplified arrangements have been made in other cities where the problems are not so severe (our so-called Programme Authorities).

Rolling programmes for the inner areas will be prepared annually. These describe the nature and scale of urban problems in each area and show how far existing policies and spending will be redirected to the inner area as well as proposals for the use of resources from the urban programme.[5]

The first programmes came into effect at the beginning of April this year. They indicate the importance which the partnership authorities attach to the provision of a good environment not only in the interests of present inhabitants but also to enable the inner area to compete with other areas in attracting people and jobs. Approaches differ – in some cases environment being treated as a key issue whilst in others it is built into the policies relating to economic development or housing. Some programmes concentrate on limited parts of the inner area whilst others spread resources more evenly. Common to all programmes is work in industrial improvement areas, environmental traffic management schemes, public open space improvement, public health measures such as street cleaning and refuse collection, extending environmental improvements in Housing Action Areas and General Improvement Areas and environmental works in difficult-to-let council estates.

Improvement Areas

The Inner Urban Areas Act 1978 provides increased power to local authorities to help industry and commerce through loans and grants.[6] This should assist in the generation or redirection of demand for land and buildings. The Act also enables district councils designated by the Secretary of State to declare improvement areas that are industrial or commercial in character. Within such areas loans or grants for environmental improvements can be made and grants can be given for the conversion and improvement of industrial buildings. This means that in industrial and commercial areas within the designated districts it will be possible to improve conditions in a way that has for long been possible in housing areas. The approach was pioneered in Rochdale and though results cannot be expected overnight, one can now see what can be achieved if there is sustained effort and enthusiasm.

Powers and grants for improving housing areas have, of course, been available for a long time and most authorities have experience in this field.

Land

Powers and resources are available for the clearance of derelict land and a great deal has been achieved especially in the older coal mining areas. Many of the urban derelict land clearance schemes, however, are difficult and costly – heavily polluted land or land with awkward buildings or sub-structures for example. Nevertheless we expect to see the rate of clearance in inner areas considerably increased.

Vacant (but not derelict) land presents rather a different problem. Metropolitan counties seem to have about 5 per cent of their area vacant and urban areas with populations over 200,000 average about 6 per cent but with wide variations.[7] Much of the vacant land in the bigger inner areas is former slum housing land or has been cleared and reserved for uses which have now been abandoned or are unlikely to be achieved for many years; something like half the vacant land appears to be in local authority ownership. But there has also been a shift in some important land uses – public utilities, ports and railways for example – and perhaps another quarter of the vacant land appears to be owned by other public authorities.

It is important to do something with the eyesores created by vacant land as quickly as possible. Ideally, of course, it should be used for permanent development, and the first approach therefore is to create marketable sites and to take all possible steps to generate a demand for their use. There are, of course, many difficulties – not least the overall economic situation and the relatively low demand – but the creation of marketable sites and as necessary the erection of buildings (eg, advance factories) by the local authority is of the greatest importance.

Not all sites, however, can be developed early – or even at all. Some local authorities have therefore already taken steps to improve the conditions of their vacant sites. In September 1978 the Government announced a special programme for partnership and programme authorities under the title, 'Operation Clean Up'. This programme of £15 million expenditure over 3½ years is for a direct attack on the unsightliness of much vacant land so as to reduce the depressing impact it has on neighbourhoods and on the prospects for change.

Modest schemes will be appropriate for short life sites, but for longer term schemes the improvements will need to be designed in the knowledge of a continuing and realistic maintenance commitment. Drawing up programmes and carrying out the work may give opportunities for the involvement of community groups.

The inner areas policy involves everyone – not just DOE and the local authorities. An important contribution both to employment and to environmental improvements can be and has been made through the Job Creation Programme. By the end of March 1978, for example, about 4,200 projects which could be classified as environmental improvement work had been initiated under this programme.

Quality of the Environment

The quality of the environment to some extent determines the quality of life. Good husbandry, ie looking after things properly, therefore leads directly to improved living conditions – and you cannot sustain those improvements without a continuous programme of better maintenance. But not maintenance alone: you need a sharp-eyed awareness of what is wrong, what people want, and what can be done to put things right and keep them that way.

Research

In the research field much is happening. The Department of Environment has itself commissioned 22 projects in the recent past, quite apart from projects that are directly related to the work of the partnership authorities. The central government's rôle in research is to clarify what is happening, and why, in urban areas generally so that national urban policies can be guided by this increased understanding. It is therefore important to understand more clearly what is happening in the employment market, what problems arise in the large scale transition from manufacturing to service based industry, what factors contribute to the growth of employment, what conditions are required for more private house building, the refurbishment and renewal of older industrial buildings and the importance of underground services on land use changes. Work is in hand, too, on housing aspects of inner areas and on the scope and rôle of local authorities in the economic development of their areas.

These are all directly commissioned research but there is much more being done, through other funding arrangements, that is directly related to inner area problems or relevant, in a wider way, to our understanding of the functioning of urban areas generally.

Conclusions

The problems facing inner areas are not new but have been growing in severity as rapid changes in social and economic conditions have occurred. Much has been done in the past by local authorities on housing improvement and environmental work, derelict land clearance, face-lift schemes and pedestrianisation of shopping centres, and by community groups in such things as urban farms, in painting gable ends and laying out small open spaces and playgrounds.

The Government's rôle is threefold. First, and very importantly, it can generate confidence through its commitment to tackling the problems. Second, it is concerned with the distribution, or redistribution, of money through main programmes, new programmes, grants and loans. Third, it has to establish the necessary legislative base for action. But the Government went further by establishing new partnership arrangements with a small number of local authorities facing massive problems and by encouraging partnership between public and private enterprise. President Carter made Partnership a main theme of his urban policy. We are trying it out in rather a different way on the ground. The problem is vast and complex but it is not overwhelming.

References

[1] Quality in Urban Planning and Design. Editor Roy Cresswell. Newnes-Butterworths 1979.
[2] British Cities: Urban Population and Employment Trends 1951-1971, Research Report 10, DOE.
[3] National Dwelling and Housing Survey, HMSO 1978, unpublished tabulations.
[4] 'Policy for the Inner Cities', Cmnd 684, HMSO, 1979.
[5] See, for example, Inner City Partnership Programme Summary, Birmingham Inner City Partnership 1978.
[6] Inner Urban Areas Act 1978, HMSO (also explanatory Circular 67/78, HMSO 1978).
[7] See also Urban Wasteland, Civic Trust, Oct 1977.

STRATEGIES FOR ADAPTIVE RE-USE OF URBAN SPACE IN GEORGIA: THE CITY OF MACON AS A MODEL
ASSOCIATE PROFESSOR VINCENT J. BELLAFIORE

For complex and inter-related reasons, the intown portions of many cities in Georgia have been declining for the past 35 years. Congestion, housing shortages and run-down conditions are partially responsible for people leaving the inner city for the suburbs. The move to suburbia has been reinforced by the growing availability of the automobile, the rapid construction of super highways, cheap energy and abundant resources. In addition, Georgians, like most Americans, have an endemic need for independence – a pioneering attitude which rejects the co-operation that is necessary to create a liveable urban environment.

As the population has left the cities, so have many of the services. Commercial activities, normally found in the central business district, have migrated to shopping malls. People have opted to use these large climate controlled structures because they offer a pleasant and convenient pedestrian environment. But these shopping centres are now threatened by the ever-increasing costs of energy and building.

All indications are pointing to a gradual shift in emphasis from suburban sprawl to compact quality environments for people. There seems to be a growing and renewed interest in the Georgia central business district and many communities are attempting to re-establish a permanent intown population base through the adaptive re-use of buildings for condominium housing. Suggestions for the conversion of the unused space above shops into housing units and professional offices have been enthusiastically received. Furthermore, several communities are in the process of having plans prepared for the alteration of vacant downtown hotels into federally funded apartments for senior citizens. This has generated the need for the redesign of the central city, making it a more liveable environment.

Fortunately, expense has also tempered redesign efforts. Gone are the days of unnecessary and dramatic renewal of cities. No longer is it appropriate to tear down and rebuild large sections of the city. Planners and designers are forced to use their imagination in developing conservative solutions which work. Urbanists are searching out portions of the city which, due to the changes in function, have been left unused and derelict.

Many cities in Georgia have neglected spaces which are vestiges of initial planning. Of particular interest are communities that were planned with a system of alleys to provide service access to the rear of the property. In many cases these alleys were laid out for horse-drawn wagons and are now too small for modern service trucks. They stand vacant, filling with trash and only adding to the unattractiveness of downtown.

Macon, Georgia: A Model for Adaptive Re-use

Studies prepared for Macon, Georgia, a city of 123,000 people, located in the central portion of the state, clearly demonstrate the

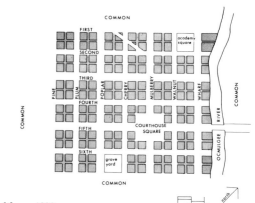

Fig 1. Macon 1823.

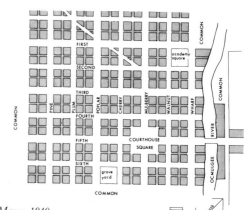

Fig 2. Macon 1840.

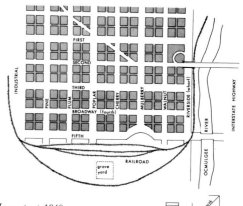

Fig 3. Macon post-1840.

potential for adaptive re-use of the alleys as a strategy for urban rehabilitation. Macon was originally planned in 1823 through the impetus of Oliver Hillhouse Prince, a prominent lawyer and member of the city commission (Figs 1 and 2). The actual street width is generally attributed to Simri Rose, a horticulturist and artist. Recognising the intense summer heat in this portion of Georgia, he insisted on the use of unusually wide streets to allow for a central island of shade trees.[1] The city was laid out in a grid pattern running parallel and perpendicular to the Ocmulgee River with alternating 180 feet and 120 feet wide streets.[2] This grid formed large square blocks of land approximately four acres in size. The blocks were divided by a unique network of crisscross alleys which formed four one-acre sections. Each section was sub-divided into two half-acre lots. The alleys served as public rights-of-way and provided service access to the rear of these lots. Over the years the half-acre lots were further sub-divided and buildings erected. Shops were constructed so that the front façades were flush with the property line, forming a contiguous line of buildings along the streets. The buildings did not occupy the entire lot and irregular spaces along the alleys remained to be used for stables, storage and other yard activities. In addition to the tree-lined streets and the network of service alleys, the city was surrounded by large green commons to be used for parks and gardens by the people.

Over the years the plan for Macon changed. The introduction of the railroad (circa 1838) put tremendous development pressure on the city.[3] The land platted east of 5th Street and the land along the river was taken over for railroad uses (Fig 3). Because of rail access, the common land south and west of the city was used for industrial development. Central City Park and Rose Hill Cemetery are the only vestiges of the original Macon greenbelt.

The green spaces within the city also felt the pressure of development. The courthouse square, a large secanted space located at the intersection of 5th and Mulberry Streets, is gone.[4] The only evidence of the square is an abrupt semi-circular bend in 5th Street at the intersection of Mulberry Street which marks the west boundary of the original space.[5] Recently the tree-lined island down the centre of Poplar Street was converted into a parking lot. These eliminations of precious green space are violations of the original city plan which have helped destroy the quality of downtown Macon.

The planned use of the alleys has also changed. Because the spaces in the alleys are limited and difficult to negotiate, much of the service has been shifted to the street entrances of the shops. Over time some of the buildings have been destroyed by fire and others torn down, rather than restored, to allow space for small parking lots. However, major portions of the original intricate pattern of the alleys still exist today.

These alleys, presently liabilities, could easily be converted to assets. They could be designed as a unique system of interconnecting pedestrian spaces that would re-establish much of the amenity of Macon's original plan.

Studies have been conducted for the core of the city – a four-block area delimited by 2nd Street, Broadway, Mulberry Street, and Poplar Street (Fig 4). According to pedestrian and vehicular traffic counts, this is the most heavily used section of the town. An indepth study was also conducted of the spatial quality, circulation, and climate for this area.

The spatial quality of the alleys is dynamic. Although the alley rights-of-way are a consistent width (15 feet in a north-south direction and 10 feet in an east-west direction), the fact that many of the buildings do not occupy 100 per cent of the lot causes the rear walls of the structures to form an interesting sequence of modulated spaces (Figs 5 and 6). The largest spaces generally occur at the intersection of the alleys. There is a wonderful contrast between the very rational, ordered and consistent spatial pattern created along the street and the very organic and dramatic pattern which exists in the alleys. The alleys have a charm, character and human scale which would be difficult to create on the streets.

Presently, the vehicular and pedestrian circulation is very inefficient and dangerous. People shopping downtown will park their cars on the street as close as possible to the desired shop. They will walk between shops along the street a maximum distance of two blocks (approximately 800 feet) and many times they will cross the street between parked cars and moving vehicles to shop along the opposite side of the street. People's desire to move their cars to a different location when they wish to shop outside the two-block area or on another street adds to the conflict. A lack of separation between cars and people, combined with the long distances people must walk, make this a very undesirable shopping environment.

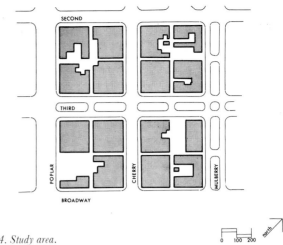

Fig 4. Study area.

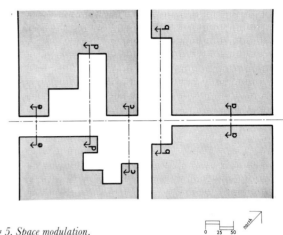

Fig 5. Space modulation.

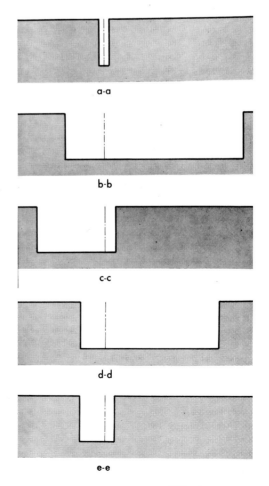

Fig 6. Sections.

The solution to this problem would be to turn the functional relationship of the city inside out. The wide streets could be used principally for service, vehicular circulation and parking with the alleys converted into attractive and convenient pedestrian shopping zones (Fig 7). This conversion would involve building additional entrances to the shops from the alleys. It would also require areas on the street side of the shops to be restricted for delivering and unloading goods.

This reorganisation would do much to create in downtown Macon the environmental quality available in the suburban shopping mall. The separation of pedestrian and vehicular circulation would offer a safe and attractive environment which would greatly complement efforts to attract people to intown housing. The alley system would also make shopping more efficient, providing access to the same number of shops in half the walking distance.

The only place where there would be a potential conflict of pedestrian and vehicular circulation is at the points where people would be crossing streets in order to shop in the next block. This problem is still minor by comparison with the existing confusion of people crossing anywhere along the street, as well as at corners where traffic is most intense. The alley entrances are at the centre of each block. This limits the crossing point to one location, making it feasible to design a well-controlled pedestrian crosswalk.

An alternative plan, which would eliminate the need for crosswalks, is to combine the area into a super block. This would involve the conversion of the streets, from the intersection of Third and Cherry Streets to the alley entrances, into pedestrian zones (Fig 8). The remaining portion of the street would be used for small parking lots. Since Third and Cherry Streets are not essential for vehicular circulation, eliminating through traffic would not be a liability.

In addition to the spatial quality and circulation benefits, these alleys can be climate-controlled naturally. Trees, arbors and awnings will do much to shade these spaces from the hot sun. Because these spaces are small, vegetation can quickly form a dense canopy.

Proposals have been made to cover the space with glass for artificial climate control. This proposal should be rejected because it requires heavy consumption of energy, one of the very problems planners are trying to solve. Every effort should be made to make the alleys comfortable by natural means because the cost of energy may be responsible for putting enclosed shopping malls out of business.

Based upon this investigation, it is clear that the alleys of Macon are a neglected resource. The design of these spaces through the use of proper paving, vegetation, fountains, lighting and other street furnishings could go a long way toward reviving the central business district of the community (Fig 9). All that needs to be done is simply to use the existing spatial pattern of the city. Many of the amenities which Simri Rose planned for in Macon could be re-established with the re-use of the alleyways.

Restoration Versus Adaptive Re-use

Savannah, Georgia, is a prime example of a quality urban environment which was achieved through rehabilitation of derelict space. It serves as an inspiration for what the people of Macon could achieve. However, it is important to understand that there are basic differences between the schemes for the rehabilitation of Savannah and Macon. Savannah simply involved restoration – revitalisation of spaces which have maintained their function over centuries. The task before the people of Macon will be more difficult because it will require the adaptive re-use of space.

The people of Savannah began revitalising their city in 1955. Savannah, with its park-like squares, was planned by Oglethorpe 90 years before Macon in 1733. Originally the plan was composed of four wards of which each had a square (Fig 10). On the north and south side of each square were two free-standing lots (total of four lots) reserved for public buildings. To the east and west of the square were two blocks of residential land with 10 lots per block (total of four blocks with 40 lots).

These squares were the centre of life in each ward and were originally conceived to enhance the quality of the urban environment. Even when the squares became run-down and disrespected, they remained as important green spaces in the community. The restoration tasks for Savannah were very obvious by comparison to the problems of adaptive re-use proposed for Macon. Savannah maintained its population base – it has always been a residential city. Macon's population for the most part has left for the suburbs. The Savannah squares are open and central: structures face onto them and people travelling through the city walk through or

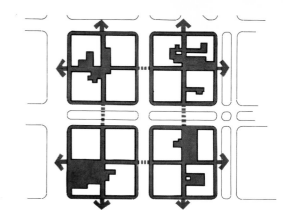

Fig 7. Pedestrian zones.

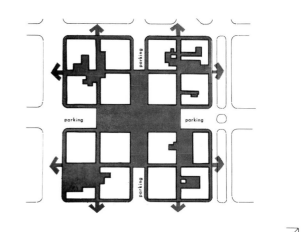

Fig 8. Pedestrian zones.

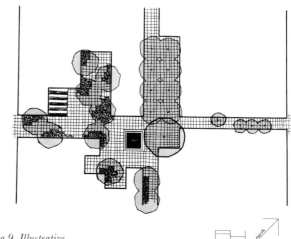

Fig 9. Illustrative.

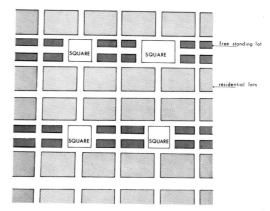

Fig 10. Savannah 1733.

drive around them. The alleys of Macon are hidden away and the average person walking by them cannot realise their potential.

It will take considerable effort to convince Macon residents that these spaces can be adapted to exciting pedestrian spaces. In addition, the problem of private ownership exists. Although the alleys are public rights-of-way, land adjacent to them, which contributes to the character of the area by modulating the space, is privately owned and a co-operative effort by all land owners will be necessary in order to achieve rehabilitation.

Other Cities with Adaptive Re-use Potential

This study of the adaptive re-use of urban space in Macon has led to the investigation of other cities with similar potential. Research into the planning of communities, along with review of air photographs and Sanborn Fire Insurance Maps has revealed three prototypical layouts. All of these cities were located in the coastal plain region of the state with the exception of two communities which are situated above the fall line in the Piedmont (Fig 11). The three types of plans were named after the spatial pattern formed by the alleys: the Crisscross Plan, the Centreline Plan and the 'T' Plan.

The Crisscross Plan, the Macon type plan, has been found in Fort Gaines, Fitzgerald and Jesup. Of all the plans, it is the most interesting and affords the greatest potential for pedestrian use: the alley network is oriented in two directions and all blocks are easily linked together (Fig 12). The design strategies prepared for Macon will serve as a prototype for these sister plans.

The Centreline Plan is composed of a system of rectangular blocks of land with alleys located down the middle. This plan is the least interesting spatially and the most common in the state. Communities with this plan are Albany, Cordele, Richland, Manchester, Arlington, Pelham, Moultrie, Adel, Quitman, Ocilla, Douglas, Claxton, Reynolds, Monroe and Rochelle.

The linear quality of this plan requires pedestrians to walk longer distances than does the crisscross system. Furthermore, the axial quality of the space channelises pedestrians in one direction, making access to adjacent blocks very difficult (Fig 13). For example, if the alleys run east-west, pedestrians would be restricted to this direction, with movement in a north-south direction inhibited. This problem could be solved by the removal of deteriorating buildings or by the conversion of selected shops into arcades for through circulation.

The 'T' Plan appears to be unique to Metter, Georgia. Metter is a railroad town with tracks located down the centre of the main street. There are 12 blocks of land platted – six on each side of the main street. The railroad must have been extremely important because the whole community is oriented toward the tracks. This is reinforced by the fact that there is no access to the alleys from the main street. Access to the alley system is restricted to the side and back streets.

From a design point of view, the railroad-main street of Metter will remain an irrevocable barrier for pedestrians. However, there exists excellent potential for the adaptive re-use of the alley system on either, or both, sides of the main street with good pedestrian circulation in all directions (Fig 14).

The alley systems in Georgia cities were concealed from everyday life because they were traditionally planned for unsightly service activities. However, today they can be viewed as a resource. American cities are often criticised for their lack of space – the 'voids' which make European cities liveable. Cities in Georgia have the potential, through adaptive re-use of their alleys, for the creation of a system of people spaces which would make the cities more habitable.

References

[1] Munroe D'Antignac, 'Simri Rose: Macon Pioneer', Macon News and Telegraph (Macon, Georgia, Sunday Morning, 31st January 1943).

[2] Historically, communities in Georgia were planned and laid out by a local surveyor. Although unsubstantiated, James Webb, Macon's surveyor, was probably responsible for the city's grid street pattern and system of alleys. Comparing the efforts of the early planners of Macon is interesting; Webb planned for service and efficiency while Rose emphasised aesthetics and comfort.

In the new plan for Macon, service and aesthetics are quintessential for a quality environment. However, the location of these functions have been changed. Service activities have been relegated to the streets while the alleys are planned to provide aesthetic and comfortable spaces for people.

[3] Since the map dated 1840 does not show rail lines it is assumed that the railroad did not impact the plan of Macon until after this date.

[4] The present county courthouse is located on a corner of Mulberry Street and 2nd Street and was completed in 1926. It is not known if a courthouse was ever constructed in the square.

Fig 11. Georgia.

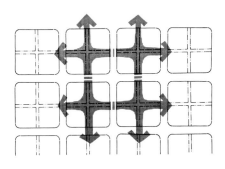

Fig 12. Crisscross Plan.

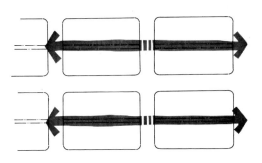

Fig 13. Centreline Plan.

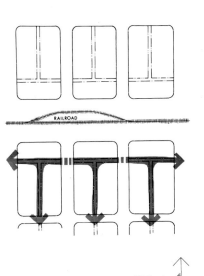

Fig 14. 'T' Plan.

[5]Early Sanborn Maps indicate that this space was used as a ball field. Presently, it is being considered for the location of a large parking lot.

Bibliography
American Institute of Architects Regional/Urban Design Assistance Team, *RUDAT MACON*, Macon, Georgia: American Institute of Architects, 1975.
D'Antignac, Munroe, 'Simri Rose: Macon Pioneer', *Macon News and Telegraph*, Macon, Georgia, Sunday Morning, 31st January 1943.
Historic Savannah Foundation, Inc., *Historic Savannah*, 1968.
McKay, John J., ed, *A Guide to Macon's Architectural and Historical Heritage*, Macon, Georgia: The Middle Georgia Historical Society, 1972.
Moore, 'Prince, Oliver Hillhouse', *Fact Book*, Georgia Room, University of Georgia Library, Macon File, P.1433.
Sears, Joanna, 'Planning Yesterday', Urban Georgia, Vol XXI, No 9, Atlanta: September 1971.
University of Georgia School of Environmental Design, *Intown: Macon, Georgia*, Macon, Georgia: Macon-Bibb County Planning and Zoning Commission, 1978.
Young, Ida, Julius Gholson and Clara Nell Hargrove, *History of Macon, Georgia*, Macon, Georgia: Macon Woman's Club, 1950.

REHABILITATION OF THE INNER CITY
PROFESSOR WALTER BOR CBE

Introduction
We in Britain have made considerable efforts over the past three decades to rebuild our war-damaged cities and improve living and working conditions in them. We have had quite a few successes such as some city centre reconstruction and public rehousing, the conservation of parts of our historic cities and our new towns development, as well as dismal failures such as the wholesale clearance of many old but socially cohesive neighbourhoods and their replacement, often with impersonal high density high rise housing. These and other errors together with the economic recession and the growing need to husband better existing resources, the widespread support for Schumacher's 'Small is Beautiful'[1] approach and the demand for increasing public involvement at the local level have created a whole set of new circumstances as we now embark upon the rehabilitation of the inner city.

The Decline of the Inner City
The decline of the inner city is due to its changing function over time, the obsolescence of old housing, the demise of factories and the flight to the suburbs of skilled workers and the middle class in search of better living conditions, but it has also been aggravated by our lack of understanding of this process. During the past 30 years or so we failed to recognise fully the complex interrelationship between the deteriorating home environment, the declining industrial base and the urban poverty syndrome, and as a consequence we did not take the appropriate remedial action.

The problem was seen largely as one of substandard old housing, which had to be cleared wholesale to be replaced with new housing. Industries were seen as non-conforming users which had to be removed, with little thought to where the remaining residents would work. In all this massive reconstruction quantities of new housing and displaced factories were the main goal rather than the quality of the resulting changes and their full implications. In terms of the built environment, traditional streets and squares were largely obliterated in favour of 'open planning' resulting in abstract geometrical patterns often with unusable bleak spaces between stereotyped high blocks.

All this radical re-shaping of the urban environment was planned and carried out with hardly any consultation of the people affected, as planners and politicians conspired in a well-meaning but misguided effort to give people what the decision makers thought was good for them. Since practically no effort was made to monitor the performance of what had been provided in terms of the newly built environment, the same mistaken approach was perpetuated for a decade or two longer after it had become apparent that this approach was wrong in many ways and was having unforeseen adverse environmental and social consequences.

This is not to minimise the very creditable efforts we have made in essential slum clearance and in the rehousing in decent modern homes of a substantial part of our population. The sole purpose of recalling these past errors of how we went about this task is to learn from these mistakes so as not to repeat them in our now overdue efforts to revitalise the inner city.

The massive post-war reconstruction of the worst slum areas has still left most of our larger cities with extensive districts, mostly in their inner areas, where there is a concentration of individual deprivation of disadvantaged households and a collective deprivation attributable to the shared poor environment. Characteristically, these areas suffer from bad housing conditions as their mostly late 19th century houses lack modern amenities and are often in a poor state of repair. At the same time, scores of factories having gone out of business or been removed, there is now a dearth of local employment and unemployment is twice to three times as high as the national average. Since many skilled and better-off have left there is now a concentration of the poor and unskilled as well as of coloured immigrants. In many of these inner areas there is also much vacant land left after unfit dwellings or old factories had been demolished. The environment is run down and neglected as public and private investment had dried up. Thus there is a general sense that these areas were going downhill and there has been a loss of confidence in their future.

The Revitalisation of the Inner City
The three studies of deprived inner areas in Liverpool, Birmingham and London which the government had commissioned in 1972 and which were completed and published in 1977[2], highlighted these and other inner area problems and criticised our fragmented and at times misconceived efforts. All three studies made a large number of recommendations to central and local government. Central government accepted many of these and proposed action to that effect in its White Paper 'Policies for the Inner Cities'[3] which are being implemented in the way Dr Burns has outlined.[4] Having been involved in the Birmingham Inner Area Study I propose to focus on changes in the approach to inner city problems with special reference to local issues and I shall illustrate these with some examples from the Small Heath study area in Birmingham.

If we are to revitalise deprived inner city areas speedily and successfully we shall not only have to allocate substantial financial and staff resources to them but, even more importantly, adopt new approaches in terms of urban planning and environmental design as well as with regard to urban government and community development. The most important innovation in the revitalisation of the inner city is the long overdue recognition that housing, employment, education, social services and their linkages must be considered together rather than as separate and ill-co-ordinated investment consequences as has been largely the case hitherto.

We in Britain are now in the process of revising our urban strategies to meet the particular needs of the deprived inner city. In order to encourage residents to stay in the inner city and others to return to it if they wish, better job opportunities and a more attractive environment is being created there. Increasing efforts are being made to maintain existing work places and jobs and develop new employment opportunities with improved access to them. Educational and training programmes are being stepped up to equip school-leavers to fill these jobs. Particular emphasis is placed on helping small businesses and workshops quite a few of which have re-established themselves recently in the inner city. The substantial decline in the population makes it possible now for the remaining residents to live in improved homes at lower densities with more open space and thus in a potentially more attractive environment. All these measures combined help to create more favourable conditions for private investment which is so essential to the revitalisation of the inner city, but in this respect we have a long way to go still before this happens in any significant way.

The urban fabric of most inner city areas in Britain is made up largely of late 19th and early 20th century two-three storey houses formed into streets and occasionally squares. Much of this existing housing will now be retained and rehabilitated in the General Improvement Areas while single parcels of the worst housing will be selectively cleared and rebuilt in the Housing Action Areas. Thus the existing urban fabric as well as the social fabric of the neighbourhoods will substantially remain undisturbed.

Within this existing urban fabric much can and is being done to improve the environment. Apart from the rehabilitation of groups of houses, whole streets and indeed whole areas, vacant factories, workshops, warehouses and community buildings are also being repaired and brought into new use, particularly by small businesses, craftshops and voluntary organisations. The traditional corner shop is being revived, especially where ethnic minorities live. Traffic management schemes make it possible for some streets to be closed to vehicular traffic and reformed into pedestrian spaces and play streets. Vacant sites are being temporarily or permanently landscaped, thereby increasing the local open space provision and contributing substantially to the improvement of the environment. It is heartening to realise how a typical run-down inner city environment can be transformed into an attractive place by these relatively modest improvements. This can be shown by the many successful recent examples of such environmental upgrading of newer areas in this country and abroad in those cities where similar approaches prevail.

Although this small-scale incremental approach is to be greatly welcomed as more appropriate and sensitive to the needs of inner areas than previous renewal policies, it could still be marred by being imposed, however benevolently, from above in the hitherto prevailing patronising way. There has been far too much passive dependence in the past on government to provide, and thereafter to complain about what had been provided, and far too little encouragement of citizen participation, self-reliance and self-help. In this respect we can learn a great deal from the way poor shanty-town dwellers in many developing countries organise and carry out their own housing and community development and it was interesting to note that the Asian immigrants who lived in the Small Heath Study Area mostly owned their homes, run their own affairs, and had no wish to wait for or depend on public assistance.

That is not to say that central and local government do not have major rôles to play. Indeed, working together, they must provide the overall economic and physical planning framework at the national, regional and city levels within which capital investment programmes for inner city revitalisation are designed and allocated. But it is at the local level of implementation that residents could and should play a more active rôle in the revitalisation of their living and working environment, by new partnerships between local authorities and local communities. For example, improvement and reconstruction proposals could be developed by local authority professional teams working in the locality jointly with local residents – and this in fact has been done in our study area with considerable success and is becoming increasingly practice in other cities. Local communities could be more fully involved in the management of their own environment, their neighbourhood advice centres, nursery classes and social clubs. In short, there is a need to experiment with a variety of complementary innovations to discover what works best. I propose to illustrate these grassroots initiatives with a few examples from our Inner Area Study in Birmingham as follows:

Examples of Local Initiatives
Shape[5]
Amongst the older housing in the inner city are often groups of houses which are unfit for human habitation but unsuitable for full-scale rehabilitation; they will therefore be scheduled for eventual demolition as and when the local authority is ready to rebuild. In the meanwhile, these houses are voided and boarded up and remain as an eyesore which attracts vandalism and arson. At the same time, poor families are desperate for housing, even just a basic shelter for a few years until permanent accommodation can be found for them. There is, therefore, an urgent need for some basic repairs to these empty houses to make them temporarily liveable.

The main idea of Shape was to combine basic repairs of these short-life houses with the rehabilitation of young dropouts from society. Youngsters, mostly school-leavers who, for a variety of reasons, have had difficulties in integrating themselves into society, live in hostels run by Shape and work on the repair of these houses, thereby learning a trade, gaining self-respect and doing a useful job. Shape managed this way to repair scores of houses in the study area but the rehabilitation of the youngsters proved to be more problematic. However, as an idea, it is worth pursuing further. It seems absurd that with so many youngsters unemployed and so much work to be done in terms of environmental improvements, that not more is done to employ them in this kind of work.

Caretaker[6]
The older houses in the inner city, apart from full-scale rehabilitation, require regular repairs if they are not to deteriorate into write-offs. As a rule, where these houses are owner-occupied, the owner in his own interest carries out these repairs or has them done. Where, however, the houses belong to the municipality, tenants are either less inclined or even discouraged to carry out these repairs themselves and so they wait for the local authority to do them, often for a long time since many authorities cannot keep up with the running repairs of their properties. As an experiment, a local caretaker, who happened to be an old age pensioner all-round handyman, was appointed for a housing area in Small Heath to carry out such minor repairs as mending gutters or fences. His help was much appreciated by the local residents, some of whom, after being taught how to go about it, carried out these repairs themselves with materials supplied to them by the local authority. A rather modest initiative, you might say, but one which, if multiplied in many areas all over the country, could not only save millions but give tenants a greater interest in looking after their rented houses.

Home-School Liaison Office[7]
Poor educational attainment is part of the deprived inner area syndrome and the Government's initiation of Educational Priority Areas with positive discrimination in favour of educationally deprived areas has gone some way to remedy this particular deprivation. However, there is still a vast gap in the relationship between homes and schools and many parents living in deprived inner areas have little knowledge or understanding of their children's education and school activities. A specially appointed liaison officer was responsible for trying to interest parents in their children's school activities and enlisting their co-operation with the teachers. Although this is clearly a long educative process some positive tangible results were achieved by the liaison officer during the period of his appointment and many more such appointments would go a long way in improving the vital links between homes and schools.

The caretaker and home/school liaison officer are but two examples of the need in deprived inner areas for such special appointments which are likely to be very cost-effective provided the right person is appointed. At a time of economic stringency investment in people may prove better value for money than into new buildings.

Neighbourhood Advice Centre[8]
The repair and re-use of hitherto disused church halls, workshops, warehouses, etc, is a cheap and convenient way to accommodate very necessary community service centres. The most successful of these was the Family Service Unit advice centre which was housed in such a previously disused building and staffed by voluntary workers; it provided important information about renewal plans for the area, about improvement grants, supplementary benefits, etc, and became the local community focus. This example also pointed to the need, at official level, for local mini-town halls where residents could meet representatives from various local authority departments whose advice or services they required instead of having to travel to the city centre and be sent from one department to another.

Playvan[9]
Deprived inner areas are notoriously short of playgrounds and imaginatively designed play facilities as well as supervised play activities. At the same time, these areas often have higher than the average proportion of young children. These considerations gave rise to the idea of a travelling play van, staffed by volunteer play leaders and equipped with imaginative play facilities, film projection, etc, to tour various localities in the area and bring play to the children. This initiative proved highly popular with the children and acted as a catalyst for them to develop their own play facilities. Again, a wide-spread development of this initiative would be an important recreational and educational asset for deprived inner areas with high child densities.

Artists Placement Group[10]

One of the most interesting and controversial innovations was an attempt to employ artists in inner area community work. Contemporary artists are often accused of creating works of art which are incomprehensible and irrelevant to the ordinary people, yet they are seldom given an opportunity to work for and within a community. A script writer and a video-cameraman were appointed to the inner area study team and produced several films with and about the local community and acted as catalysts for local residents to write and perform their own play about local issues. In the course of this work, some latent local talents were discovered and people involved learned to be more articulate about themselves and their problems and became greatly more self-confident. The artists also produced a film about the decision-making process which included a lively confrontation meeting between the planner and local residents. However, when they tried to film an important council meeting, they met with official resistance which may go to show that we have some way to go yet in our efforts to develop a more open system of government.

Street Meetings and Housing Action Area[11]

Local interdisciplinary urban renewal teams were formed by the city administration to plan and progress General Improvement Areas and the rehabilitation of groups of houses and whole streets. One such team worked in the Small Heath Study Area and was very successful in enlisting the interest of local residents into the renewal proposals for the locality. Several street meetings were held at which local residents commented in detail on the proposals which were then amended in the light of these comments so that the final plans had the full support and co-operation of local residents.

In a similar way we, as consultants, invited residents within a Housing Action Area to put forward their ideas how best to spend a fixed sum of money for environmental improvements of a small housing estate. We had a constructive and good common sense response which led to the design and construction of a playground, parking spaces and landscaping which met with the enthusiastic reception by the residents since it responded to their wishes and incorporated their proposals; in fact it was 'theirs'.

Sara Park

My final example is a new public park which was to be created in one of the areas where wholesale clearance had taken place many years ago for a major new housing project. This park was proposed in the redevelopment scheme but would, as a rule, have been the last component to be built, after all the new housing blocks had been constructed. Because of the delay in the housing project start, there appeared to be little hope that this park would materialise for many years, so the site would remain a derelict eyesore for a long time to come. However, for once, the sequence was reversed and we got permission to develop the park in advance of the housing. Next we enlisted the active participation of the local residents in the design and construction of the new park which was christened by them Sara Park at the official opening ceremony. Because the local people played an active part in the creation of Sara Park, they are proud of it and vandalism has been minimal. Once again, effective response to clearly perceived local needs, coupled with genuine local involvement proved to be successful.

Conclusions

From these few examples we can see that, at the local level, a large variety of new initiatives over a whole range of human activities may be required to breathe new life into inner areas, in parallel with the redirection by central and local government of policies and funds to the revitalisation of the inner city. Perhaps the most important short-term objective of these combined efforts is to restore the confidence of residents and potential investors in the future of inner areas.

The urgent and massive task of rehabilitating the deprived inner city and alleviating urban poverty has become one of our main concerns. The Government has accepted this task as a major political commitment and has begun allocating substantial funds for this purpose. There is now a real possibility emerging to improve significantly over time the run-down living and working environment in the inner city and thus halt its decline and maybe even reverse it.

It could also be the beginning of an important change in urban government and community development: from a patronising bureaucratic approach by planners and decision-makers imposing their views and values, however well-intentioned, on the local community to an attitude whereby essentially people would be helped to help themselves and encouraged to play an increasingly active rôle in the shaping and management of their environment.

References

[1]Schumacher, E. F., *Small is Beautiful*. A study of economics as if people mattered.

[2]*Policy for the Inner Cities*. Cmnd 684, HMSO, 1979.

[3]Wilson and Womersey, *Change or Decay*. Final Report of the Liverpool Inner Area Study, HMSO, 1977.
Llewelyn-Davies, Weeks, Forestier-Walker and Bor, *Unequal City*. Final Report of the Birmingham Inner Area Study, HMSO, 1977.
Shankland Cox Partnership, *Inner London: Policies for Dispersal and Balance*. Final Report of the Lambeth Inner Area Study, HMSO, 1977.

[4]Burns, W., BB, CBE, OSc, MEng, PPRTPI, MICE, *The Rehabilitation of Inner Areas*. I.A. Golden Jubilee Conference.

[5]Shape Housing and Community Project, IAS/B/25.

[6]Environmental Action Projects, Vol 1, IAS/B/18.

[7]Educational Action Projects, Vol 1, IAS/B/13.

[8]Neighbourhood Advice Centre, Family Service Unit, 435, Neighbourhood Centre, IAS/B/16.

[9]Trinity Arts, Playvan, IAS/B/17

[10]Artists Placement Group Project, IAS/B/14.

[11]Little Green: A care study in Urban Renewal, LLD, WFWB, IAS/B/7, DOE.

[12]Environmental Action Projects, Vol 2, IAS/B/19.

PROBLEMS OF RURAL LANDSCAPES

THE EDGE OF THE CITY   REGINALD HOOKWAY

LANDSCAPE IN ESSEX   A. G. BOOTH

RURAL LANDSCAPES   DAME SYLVIA CROWE CBE

THE EDGE OF THE CITY
REGINALD HOOKWAY

The Plan for an Experiment by the Countryside Commission

Most people in Britain, as in other developed countries, live in towns and cities. For some of them the countryside is near at hand. For those who live in the inner areas of the larger cities a visit to the countryside, even that countryside on the very edge of the city, is a special occasion involving time, transport and costs.

With the outward growth of cities the length of the boundary between town and country has increased. It is often a very irregular boundary, with pockets of open land between or surrounded by development. Along the boundary lies a zone of transition from town to country. It is often a zone of neglect and dereliction, of dirty rivers, of choked canals, rubbish rips and litter, blocked and muddy footpaths, broken fences and barbed wire, and inefficient use of land. Sometimes the zone is narrow. Sometimes farmland several miles from the city may be affected. All these uncounted acres on the edges of the cities are areas of difficulty for the farmer. Yet often the natural quality of the soil is high and substantial areas of good land lie neglected or under-farmed. The edge of the city is a place of many conflicts.

The conflict between the use of land for development and for food production represents one plane of disharmony; much land remains neglected or under-farmed because it is held for speculative purposes. But the conflicts between the interests of those who wish to farm and those who use the countryside for a leisure activity, or trespass upon it for the want of some place to go, or despoil it with their litter, or bicycles or motorcycles, or fail to control their dogs, or set fire to it, are another, and more immediate disharmony. The areas where these conflicts are serious are self-evident. They are to be found round most towns. They are to be found too in popular areas of countryside resort, whether they be upland, river or canal bank, or areas of coastline.

Such conflicts of interest are detrimental to the quality of the environment and to wild life. They can be a serious constraint on the effective use of land to produce food, and on leisure use. They are the result of the actions of those who live in, and in particular on the edges of, the towns and either have no understanding of or little respect for rural values. If the owner of countryside is to be helped to alleviate the effects of these public actions it will involve the use of public resources of manpower and money; though the amounts of both labour and cost may be small since so much voluntary labour can be organised. Nevertheless it represents a demand on public funds if it is to be done. If our values in society are such that we abhor the waste of resources of land which such conflicts produce then we have a straightforward justification to spend those public funds. The improvement in the appearance of the environment and better arrangements for recreation can be an additional benefit.

In exploring ways of tackling such problems the Countryside Commission have undertaken a number of experimental projects in upland areas, in coastal areas of high conservation value and on the edges of towns, over the last twelve years. They have evolved an approach which is simple, very cheap and popular with local residents. The experimental projects are well documented and reports on them can be obtained from the Countryside Commission.[1] A number of countryside management exercises are under way and experimentation continues.

What is Countryside Management?

In essence Countryside Management[2] is getting things done to resolve or reduce the conflicts between the private interests in rural land and actions by the public which depreciate those interests. To make Countryside Management work it is necessary to gain the confidence of all those concerned with the particular stretch of countryside in which the work is being undertaken: farmers, landowners, villagers, recreationalists, conservationists and public authorities. To gain that confidence it is necessary to establish direct contact with the people directly affected: in the main the landowners. Their co-operation is gained by offering them a service. It may be to give them advice. It may be to obtain their agreement to do something from which the public will benefit; either by using direct labour, or volunteers, or by giving the owner money to do the work. It may be no more than to provide the owner with an opportunity to voice his complaints. The importance of this must not be discounted. It is by listening to the complaints that one can often identify the roots of conflict.

These aspects of the approach can easily be identified by remembering the letter 'c', and the words italicised in the following sentence. To resolve the *conflicts* it is necessary to gain the *confidence* of landowners. To do that requires direct *contact* and out of contact will come *co-operation*.

Experience has shown that once a decision has been taken to choose an area in which an exercise of countryside management might be mounted, the first action is to appoint a Project Officer. He needs the ability to gain the confidence of the people concerned by making direct contact with them, by stimulating them to co-operate with him and thereby to start resolving, or diminishing, the conflicts that affect the area. A great deal of care is needed in selecting the right person, who has to be practical, responsible, understanding of countryside and sensitive to people's needs, but at the same time ready to dig a ditch or erect a fence, to show volunteers what should be done, or manage a small work force. In complex or large areas a project officer may need one or two full-time assistants. He needs the capacity to be a team leader.

He will need a responsible body, a steering committee, to whom he reports. This will be made up of those representing the public interest in the area, those who can speak for the private interests involved, and the voluntary societies. Whilst the project officer will be given a substantial amount of delegated freedom the steering committee will be responsible for his recruitment, employment, budget and broad policy guidance. He will have a delegated financial authority to spend up to a fixed sum on any project without further reference to his steering committee. The Commission suggest up to £400, depending on the officer's experience. For larger sums agreement of the steering committee will be needed; always remembering that the whole approach is to deal with the undertaking of small scale actions. In consequence large sums of money are rarely involved. Where large scale action is necessary this will probably be organised through the normal procedures of arranging for public authority work to be undertaken. A desirable component of Countryside Management is the conveying of the image of an unbureaucratic service of help to the landowner. The justification for Countryside Management is to secure a public benefit on private land. It requires a different approach from that normally involved in undertaking work by public authorities on public land.

The project officer is likely to be on contract employment. Early within his contract he should agree with his steering committee the limits of the project area within which he should work. If the steering committee seek to define the boundaries they may choose an area more extensive than, or with more complex problems than, the project officer can cope with in the period of his contract. Alternatively they may choose an area which does not offer him a sufficient challenge. Either choice will discourage him. It is far better to let the project officer suggest the boundary of the area. If he finds that he can undertake more work his boundary can be extended.

Once the project officer is in post, making contacts, gaining confidence, obtaining co-operation and resolving conflicts, a process of public participation is under way. Again experience has shown that this has a remarkable 'snowball' effect. Once he has obtained goodwill and people see that what he is doing is not only of benefit to them but to the area generally they will frequently come forward with a variety of suggestions as to what might be done within the area for the public benefit. Often these are ideas which have not occurred to local government officials but may well contribute to the making of a good plan. The making of a management plan for the area is a responsibility that the project officer, in association with the steering committee, should be capable of undertaking. He will not only quickly gain a deep knowledge of the area but he can tap the vision of those who are even more knowledgeable about it. He should also be able to relate his understanding of the possibilities and constraints in the area to the ideas the local government planners may have. The management plan for the area comes, in consequence, from a process of participation. In many respects this is almost exactly the opposite to the approach used in statutory planning for development, where the plan is made by an expert planner and then subjected to a process of participation through consultation.

It may again be useful to use a letter, in this case the letter 'p', to summarise that countryside management is undertaken by a *project officer* in a *project area* where, through a process of making contacts, gaining confidence and co-operation and resolving conflicts, he develops an exercise of *participation*, out of which it is possible to prepare a management *plan*.

In any area in which a project is being undertaken, there will be a voluntary body, or indeed several voluntary bodies such as wildlife conservation or recreation groups, keen to support the work of the project officer by voluntary action. The officer may be able to gain the support of schools and youth groups. He may be able to persuade the appropriate authorities to allow him to deploy community service offenders or indeed possibly prison labour. All sorts of possibilities are open; even to obtaining the co-operation of the armed forces to get things done.

What can be done?
The project officer can organise and carry out many different tasks, quickly and at low cost. Examples are:
 (i) the *clearance of eyesores* – derelict structures, areas of litter and rubbish, redundant structures (e.g. World War II fortifications);
 (ii) the promotion of *landscape improvements* – tree and shrub planting schemes, removing dead trees, treatment of areas eroded as a result of recreation use;
 (iii) the *maintenance of landscape features* – care of important trees and heathland, rehabilitation of small areas of woodland, repair of drystone walls and other small man-made features, cleaning up small water areas, improved protection of wildlife habitats;
 (iv) promoting *access for recreation* – improving or providing footpaths, bridleways and nature trails, repairing stiles and bridges, waymarking, securing agreement on alternative footpaths, securing access agreements, new picnic sites and viewpoints;
 (v) improving *traffic management* – providing informal car parks and turning areas; segregating vehicle, horse and pedestrian traffic; creating vehicle-free areas;
 (vi) *repairing damage by visitors* – to gates, stiles, fences and walls;
 (vii) providing *information and interpretation* – arranging guided walks, information boards, small interpretation centres or facilities, involving school children in area conservation, providing guidance to visitors and helping them to enjoy the area.

Of course there are things he cannot do because of cost or complexity, such as removing major industrial dereliction or remedying the effects of extensive gravel working and other mining. Nevertheless it is remarkable what can be achieved by attention to minor problems. The more we can remove blight and enhance the appearance of these zones, the more we can increase our self respect as a society. In two or three years the whole appearance of a stretch of countryside can be transformed, to the considerable benefit of those who use it for leisure. Many people fail to appreciate that the countryside on the edge of the town is the only countryside that a great many of their fellow citizens ever visit. The more that we can increase the capacity of the immediate countryside of the city to meet the countryside recreation needs of the city, the more we can protect the deeper countryside from visitor pressure. This can be of net benefit to society in reducing expenditure on leisure travel and on the provision of additional facilities and services in the countryside for leisure activities.

But there are other and perhaps more significant values involved. Where experiments have been conducted there has been a remarkable upsurge of interest, goodwill and support from the farming community. If farmers in these areas can be helped to farm with a greater degree of confidence not only will their care and work contribute to the quality of the scene they will also help the economy by providing more food nearer to the markets, to their own and to society's benefit. The concept of the countryside management project has been warmly endorsed by the Ministry of Agriculture's Advisory Committee on Agriculture and Horticulture in a recent report,[3] and has been welcomed in reports of the Countryside Review Committee.[4]

The Experiment
From this background of experience and knowledge the Countryside Commission, after consultation with the Department of the Environment and Ministry of Agriculture, suggested a major experiment to remove or reduce the conflicts of interest in the countryside round a major industrial city with a population of over a quarter of a million. The concept is to do more than to implement countryside management on a more comprehensive scale. It envisages the clearance, as comprehensibly as is possible, of the areas of major dereliction in the urban fringe. It will also explore the possibilities of helping the agricultural industry to adjust, and adapt to the situation of a 'protected' urban fringe through stimulating investment and more intensive production.

The Aims of the Experiment are to:
 (i) test whether, through a co-ordinated effort, the standards of land management, access, environmental quality and food and timber production, in the countryside round a city can be improved for the benefit of the city and surrounding settlements and the economy generally;
 (ii) stimulate an understanding of, and concern for, the countryside round the city, and of the opportunities it offers for recreation and education;
 (iii) provide liaison and information. By establishing and maintaining contacts with other cities in Britain and throughout Europe it is hoped that the practical lessons of the experiment can be deployed widely.

The Objectives of the Experiment are to:
 (i) enable the land round the city to be farmed better;
 (ii) reduce the conflict between visitors from the city and farming, forestry and water conservation interests;
 (iii) clear eyesores and dereliction and develop a programme of pollution control;
 (iv) improve the management of footpaths, bridleways, water areas, public open spaces and small-scale parking and picnicking facilities, and country parks, and provide new facilities where necessary;
 (v) improve the management and planting of small amenity woodlands, trees and shrubs and the maintenance of other key features in the landscape, such as attractive hedges, walls and minor buildings;
 (vi) increase care of wildlife habitats; and
 (vii) interpret the countryside to adults and school children.

The timescale envisaged for the experiment is five years. Whilst the cost cannot be assessed with any precision until the particular problems of tackling any major areas of dereliction are assessed, all the local government authorities interested in being chosen were asked to give an assurance that for each of the five years of the project they would be prepared to allocate to a special project fund £1 for each member of the population living within the outer boundary of the project area. The expectation is that Central Government funds of a slightly higher order will be available, as a minimum, to match that investment. Additionally special grant will be available to tackle the problems of major dereliction and to support the interests and actions of farmers in changing the systems of farming or improving production.

The Countryside Management aspects of the experiment will be implemented by a number of project teams located round the city, so that eventually the areas they cover will overlap to provide for a complete coverage of the urban fringe. These outstationed teams will be co-ordinated and supported by a central project team under a team leader.

Local authorities in England and Wales with populations larger than a quarter of a million, but excluding the really large cities, were invited to consider whether they would wish to involve themselves in such a project. To the surprise of all concerned no less than 23 submissions were made. After meetings and discussion, and the specification of more precise assurances from the participating authorities, 13 of the applications were withdrawn. The choice, nevertheless, from the remaining 10 was complex.

On June 7 the Countryside Commission, in consultation with the Department of the Environment and the Ministry of Agriculture chose the project area. This has yet to be announced.

The new government will wish to consider whether it will endorse the concept of the experiment by assuring that Treasury finance will be available for the project period. The policies of the new government may also influence the enthusiasms of the local government authorities concerned. It was felt prudent to defer the announcement of the chosen area and the date for a start of the experiment until firm assurances can be secured. In anticipation that they will be, the experiment could still start early in 1980.

It is believed that it is the first time that any such project has been envisaged, anywhere in the world, and in consequence plans are being made carefully to monitor the project both by film and analytical study. To members of the professions concerned with the land it is likely to be of great interest. For the landscape architect it can be seen as a major project of landscape enhancement. The land use planner will doubtless learn much about the relationships between farming and development. The wildlife conservationists will be interested to see what can be achieved in safeguarding and enriching the wildlife of such areas. The agriculturalist may learn about the development of new techniques of farming near to the city, and it may even be of interest to the forester for the small woodlands in and around our cities to contribute to the total forest project, as well as providing much amenity. The potentialities for improving access will interest the recreational planners and the sociologists.

It is anticipated that networks of communication will be established with cities throughout Europe so that the progress of the experiment can be reviewed by those concerned in the context of their own problems and experience. There are a great many cities of such size throughout the developed world. The implications of the experiment could be of considerable interest.

References
[1] *The Lake District Upland Management Experiment*. Countryside Commission publication No 93, £1·60.
The Bollin Valley – A Study of Land Management in the Urban Fringe. Countryside Commission publication No 97, £3·00.
Glamorgan Heritage Coast – Plan Statement. South Glamorgan County Council, et al., 1976.
Purbeck Heritage Coast – Report and Proposals. Dorset County Council, 1977.
Suffolk Heritage Coast Plan. Suffolk County Council, 1979. £2·00.
[2] Countryside Management is described in *Local Authority Countryside Management Projects*. Countryside Commission Advisory Series No 10.
[3] *Agriculture and the Countryside*. Report of the Advisory Council for Agriculture and Horticulture in England and Wales, 1978. HMSO.
[4] *The Countryside – Problems and Policies*. Countryside Review Committee Discussion Paper, 1976. HMSO.
Food Production in the Countryside. Countryside Review Committee Topic Paper No 3, 1978. HMSO.

LANDSCAPE IN ESSEX
A. G. BOOTH

I hope this paper will not seem parochial if I appear to dwell on the problems and occasional achievements of Essex, the county where I earn my daily bread. To some extent the problems are familiar throughout Southern England and also to similar areas in Europe; one or another occur in most other counties – the difference with Essex is that we seem to have them all. Our land is rich and most of it suited to intensive arable cropping, consequently we have moved rapidly away from the old landscape of mixed husbandry with the concomitant loss of hedgerows, groves, pasture and wetland – often inevitable, but sometimes unnecessary and afterwards regretted. Proximity to London has brought intense pressure for development for housing and industry; in 1951 the population of the county stood at 851,000, in 1976 it had reached 1,426,000, and this development has meant the loss of good productive land and the creation of a new problem: the conflict between an essentially urban population and those who produce food – a situation fraught with ignorance and damage, the familiar urban fringe problem that surrounds London and other conurbations. We have a considerable legacy of derelict land caused by mineral extraction, particularly in the extreme south of the county, and another problem where such land has been 'restored to agriculture', without the care and necessary assets – such as substantial overburden – to make it productive farmland. Instead we have another legacy of low-grade farming, often what my friends in Hertfordshire have dubbed 'horsiculture' – a landscape of poor pasture, ponies, tatty fences and shacks – perpetuating an air of dereliction and wasted land.

Nature herself has been unkind to us; hit early by the Dutch Elm disease, we have been robbed of the hedgerow trees of the heavy clays where elm was dominant. These were areas less suited to pressures for intensive arable farming and their landscape was verdant, with elms arching over country roads; now they are bleak and treeless. As amenity has declined, the use of the countryside for leisure and recreation has steadily grown. Epping Forest was acquired 100 years ago by the Corporation of the City of London, for the enjoyment of Londoners, who flocked there on Bank Holidays and summer weekends by tram, bus and train. With widespread car ownership we have had the 'leisure explosion', with the pressure concentrated on the home counties by the rise in price of petrol.

In short, Essex seems to have more than its fair share of the problems facing the countryside in Southern England, and I have omitted those of communities – the loss of village schools and industries, and invasion by commuters – for these are social problems rather than those of the landscape, and in any case I have only a limited time at my disposal. In landscape terms, the major calamity has been the loss of tree cover, for in a countryside of low relief and gentle topography, trees and shrubs form its basic material. The loss of these elements was the main theme of a report written for the County Planning Committee in 1972: 'The Essex Countryside – A Landscape in Decline?' from which I quote:

'In the mid-'sixties it was recognised that the national heritage of historic towns and villages was in considerable peril and a constructive framework of legislation, planning intervention, grant-aid, and the arousal of public awareness followed. There are many indications that the countryside, particularly in the South East, is in a similar situation. The purpose of this Report is to consider what is happening to the inland Essex landscape, the pressures that are affecting it and how it may well look at the end of this century – the conclusion is a bleak one, but not inevitable if planning policies for the countryside are re-thought.'

The countryside seemed to be returning to an open-field form of agriculture without the benefit of the woodlands and wastes between settlements:

'Protected woodlands would remain, but the principal features of the new open landscape would be poles, wires, pylons, crude prefabricated farm buildings, and the harsh edges of new buildings on the periphery of towns and villages.'

On balance, the Report was constructive and suggested many lines of action which we have been following subsequently and which I will refer to. It is well to remember the climate then in 1972 which was still that of the '60's – narrow professionalism held rein and environmental factors and consequences were rarely considered. New roads and road improvements were designed with scant regard for amenity and landscaping provision was pitiful; rivers and brooks were converted into treeless troughs; public utilities littered the countryside with 'things in fields'; drainage engineers improved the land and destroyed its hedgerows, spinneys and wetlands with the aid of government grant. Everyone had a job to do and did it without regard for anything else. Writers on landscape tended to condone this situation as inevitable and foretold the coming of the 1,000-acre field. There were similarities with architects' enthusiasm for Le Corbusier's 'La Ville Radieuse', until it began to arrive and there were second thoughts. The rural equivalent had begun to be seen by 1972 and few liked it – a farmer who had converted his land into a treeless tract told one of my staff 'I used to enjoy walking over my land on a Sunday morning, but now there is nothing to see'.

The immediate result of 'Landscape in Decline' was funds made available for farmland planting, backed by Countryside Commission grant. Many farmers responded and our planting programme has steadily grown ever since. In 1972 the only other county similarly embarking was Gloucestershire and neither of us had anyone to turn to for advice on a form of planting which was not forestry. We had often heard or read of the possibility of planting field corners, wetland, steep slopes and so forth, but nobody seemed to have done it. So we were on our own, and the schemes planted in the winter of 1972/73 were the prototypes for hundreds, indeed thousands, planted in subsequent years. We learnt as we went by failures as well as successes; to begin with, the farmer gave the land and County Council workmen planted and maintained the schemes; rapidly we moved to reliance on the private sectors and now all schemes are planted by private firms subject to a strict specification and surveillance. The drought years taught us that the local species survived (native provenance was not sufficient), careful preparation and planting will give takes of over 90% and our contractors have supported every step towards what is now a very strict specification. We have learnt as we went along, and as other counties in the South East have begun similar schemes, they have sent their specialist officers to see our work as a preliminary to their own.

Initially we saw the creation of a new landscape and used the analogy of the landscapes resulting from the parliamentary enclosure of commons and heaths in the 18th and 19th Centuries. We soon learnt that this was bad history as well as bad analogy. The parliamentary enclosures swept away a diverse landscape, socially rich, and while they may have created a more efficient countryside in terms of food production, their new landscapes smacked of hasty decisions and the dull hand of the surveyor; social costs were heavy; a whole class of cottagers and small-holders were deprived of their land and driven away to work in 'dark Satanic mills' or to remain as landless labourers. Fortunately, Essex was little affected as enclosure had already taken place over much of the county at a slow pace over several centuries; this had been done by agreement between tenants and manor and not, it seems, by imposition. The result was a rich landscape in terms of ancient, botanically mixed, hedgerows and a legacy of scattered relict woodlands – survivors of the post-glacial forest cover, modified by medieval and subsequent management. A detailed analysis of an 800 hectare estate at Bovingdon Hall (chosen by the Countryside Commission as a Demonstration Farm) revealed that one-third of the hedgerows were in existence before the Black Death (c.1350) and another third dated from the late Middle Ages or Tudor period. In spite of widespread agricultural improvement a surprising number of ancient features survived.

This awareness of the historic dimension taught us humility in our approach to the landscape and we found that farmers were often fascinated to learn that some of their hedgerows were at least as old as their 14th-16th Century farmsteads. A visit to a farm to discuss new planting frequently becomes a discussion on the value of existing woodlands, hedgerows and ponds, and the best way to manage them. The treatment of existing features is often more important than the establishment of new ones; they must always be respected for often they are non-renewable resources. We seek to work *with* the landscape, regarding our own 20th Century contributions as part of a long process of adaptation and change that has continued over more than five millennia. We try not to fake and seek to respect the Spirit of the Place.

The farming community itself is fascinating, usually hostile to planners who are seen as interfering bureaucrats, but favourable to my countryside staff who come to give advice, recommend grants, and are there by invitation. The diversity of farming practice, farm size, and the methods and predilections of farmers themselves is extraordinary and adds to the diversity of the landscape. The notion of stewardship runs deeply with many, particularly in farming families, and I fear results of fiscal legislation which could fragment family holdings. Remote control is a threat, with investment companies and foreigners buying land and farming through managers – fortunately managers are often sympathetic to conservation issues, usually coming from farming stock themselves. Land agents, similarly, tend to have farming or landowning backgrounds, which is just as well since the prospectus of a leading college makes no provision for training in conservation matters, let alone examinations, and I believe this to be typical of others.

When problems occur, discussion usually resolves them – often with mediation by the Farmers' Union or Country Landowners'

Association and the ultimate sanction of the Tree Preservation Order is consequently exceptional. The pendulum seems to be swinging strongly towards conservation and we often hear a comment on the following lines – 'in the '60's we were modernising our farms, now we are looking at other issues and welcome the advice and help that you offer'.

Most farmers and their advisors in MAFF agree that the pace of farm improvement has stabilised. Fields of 12-16 hectares represent a day's work, and I have observed that larger fields tend to be broken down into such smaller units for cropping. On flat fenlands, with giant machines, the 100 hectare field may be viable, but on our clays, dissected by watercourses, roads, rights of way and changes in soil, a more human division of fields seems to be accepted as convenient and sensible.

As things stand today, I am optimistic that most farmland in the year 2000 will reflect conservation rather than desolation, but there are areas, particularly on the urban fringe, where the trend is still towards desolation. The Countryside Commission has established several pioneer projects for landscape management employing rangers to enlist the support of both owners and volunteers. Their success is encouraging and we hope to establish two projects in Essex in which we hope to learn from the experience of our neighbours in Herts and Suffolk in this important field.

I mentioned earlier the ill-effects of professional sectionalism – doing one's job with one aim in mind – and looking back over the last seven years, matters seem to have improved tremendously. Much credit here is due to two national bodies: first the Farming and Wildlife Advisory Group (FWAG) who seek to reconcile farming and conservation interests and since their auspicious Silsoe Conference in 1968 have held exercises in most parts of the country. They guided us in an exercise at Widdington in 1975 which involved a great deal of preparatory work which has proved of lasting value; the working party consisted of the farmers themselves, the Ministry of Agriculture's professional advisors (ADAS), the Nature Conservancy Council's Officer for the County, and two of my landscape staff. This was not a cosmetic exercise – the fur certainly flew in the preliminary meetings as the different interests moved slowly towards an understanding of each other's positions and aims. By the day of the exercise the group had reached a strong *corps d'esprit*, which has led to the founding of an Essex branch of the FWAG, and subsequently provided a nucleus for the study team for the Countryside Commission's Demonstration Farm in Essex. The Countryside Commission is the second national body I wished to mention; I cannot speak too highly of their rôle as catalyst and their rapid evolution (in ten years) from a body mainly concerned with informal recreation in the countryside and with the establishment of country parks and picnic sites, to become the principal force for the conservation and renewal of the landscape. Those of us working in the counties would feel very lonely without their support. Their Demonstration Farm project involves 12 farms across the country in which every aspect is studied and evaluated – agriculture, forestry, sporting interests, public access, nature conservation and landscape quality. Farmers will be able to visit these farms and see efficient agriculture practised with respect for conservation measures – and, most important, see the costs involved.

The removal, at least in our experience, of professional blinkers in recent years is also reflected in the attitudes of statutory authorities such as the Electricity Boards and Water Authorities, British Rail, and our colleagues in Highways. The fragile nature of our landscape is recognised and the parameters imposed by a regard for the environment are now generally accepted.

I have referred earlier to the growing use of the countryside for leisure. In Essex we are fortunate in a legacy of land purchased to preserve London's Green Belt before and after the last war – purchased at prices which now seem incredibly low. Consequently we have a necklace of country parks where they are needed most. More still are needed, but the price of land and the restrictions on expenditure, make it unlikely that purchases remotely comparable with the past, will occur again. Further provision seems to lie in the use of land that is now derelict following former mineral extraction and through the planned after-use of land which will be worked in the future. Otherwise, there is the possibility of access agreements (which are not as popular in lowland Britain as in the uplands) and a better use of the existing network of rights of way. The latter would seem essentially a local matter – in arable Essex, villages and small towns have less accessible open space than most cities – a curious paradox.

Collaboration with farmers, landowners and the statutory authorities is slowly bringing long term benefits over most of our county. The bleak predictions of *Landscape in Decline* seem less and less likely. But we have our problem area – the south and south-west of the Borough of Thurrock, where thousands of acres have been ravaged by the extraction of chalk, sand and gravel and London clay. Restorations have led too often to the sub-agricultural uses I have referred to earlier. A dreadful air of dereliction and wasted land clings to our 'Mezzogiorno', if I may so call it, for it is the area where no-one seems to care and the problems seem too great to handle at a local level. We do of course care, but the problems have seemed too big and intractable for a county and borough to handle on their own, and government has made it clear that they are not able to help very much and we are left to our own devices.

Faced with the problems of Thurrock, we have proposed afforestation as the answer – indeed we have advocated the creation of a 'Forest of Thurrock' as the only solution to the environmental decline of the borough and a source of hope for the future. Poor grade land can grow good trees and with the likelihood of declining resources for import as this century draws to its close, all wood-producing land could be a valuable investment. The mineral operators support the concept and already sites are being fenced and planted, in twenty years they will start to yield crops and can be opened to the public – in the very long term, our great-great-grandchildren may examine the results of accumulation of broad-leafed litter and decide whether the land is once again productive to farm; that will be their decision – in the meantime the county and

borough, together with the Forestry and Countryside Commissions, are working with the owners of the land to effect what could be an environmental revolution.

Let me stress that the Forest of Thurrock will be no great gesture of landscape planning in the grand manner; there are no massive funds from the State to back it. Every step will be *ad hoc*, relying on negotiation and the best use of the meagre financial resources open to us. Above all, it depends on the support and co-operation of owners – the 'Greening of Thurrock' will be essentially a test of democratic processes and local desire to improve the environment.

So what of the landscape of AD 2000? If good sense prevails and it remains in the custody of our present farming families, it will be verdant as well as productive and efficient. There will be many young trees to enhance it, creating a balanced landscape compared with the elderly one of today. Trees in spinneys and hedgerows will be recognised as a resource worth managing – for all fixed chlorophyl will be of value. Straw will be harvested and processed and the present annual ordeal by fire will be a distant memory.

In South Essex, the Forest of Thurrock will be starting to take shape and the young coppices of chestnut coming up for their second cut. People will come to this landscape for pleasure and recreation, and at the same time it will be productive. So, in conclusion, if things continue in the manner of the present, I am confident that lowland Britain will show a greater care for conservation and less desolation than we see today.

RURAL LANDSCAPES
DAME SYLVIA CROWE CBE

The problems of the countryside are inherent in what I suggest is the definition of 'rural'. For when we term an area rural as opposed to urban, surely we mean that in that area organic nature is dominant over man and his cerebral emanations, or at least that she is the senior partner in a working partnership.

If this is so, then any increase in the numbers, wants and activities of men must cause problems in maintaining nature's supremacy.

It is because of our increased numbers and, even more, our ever-increasing demands, that we are now worrying over issues which never occurred to our forefathers.

Because of this new tension, one of the many categories into which landscapes may be divided, is the degree of influence or dominance of the human over other species and over natural features, in any particular area.

At one extreme is the wild, where man is absent or insignificant. From this primal condition, there are gradual stages of human influence, from the minor impact of small areas of cultivation, through the full partnership of agriculture on a basis of sustained fertility within a background of natural biosystems, to the final submergence of nature under man's domination.

Each of these stages poses its own problem to us today.

The greatest risk to the true wild is, of course, commercial exploitation. This has occurred in the past in all parts of the world, and is today threatening the Amazonian forests and the oceans.

A more recent problem, and one with which we, as a profession, are particularly concerned, is the impact of too many people, with an over-sophisticated life-style seeking the solace of the wild and thereby destroying it. Eroded footpaths on Fuji and the Pennine Way are examples of this, and they are indeed hard problems to solve.

The policy of honeypot areas to relieve pressure elsewhere is sound, but it must be realised that a visitor centre equipped with video tapes and a car-park is more at variance with the spirit of the wild than a shepherd and his dog. One is an alien, the other a working ingredient of the landscape.

This distinction is at the root of many of the difficulties encountered in the use of the countryside for recreation.

The cultivator is a part of the biosystem, the visitor is not, and therefore his impact as an outsider must either be minimised so that he does no more harm than a passing migrant bird, or he must become identified with the landscape through sympathy and understanding. It is in promoting this understanding that interpretation centres have their justification.

Countryside where nature is still a senior partner, although men live and cultivate within it, presents two problems: one is the impact of visitors and the other is the changing pattern of the landscape as men intensify and extend their cultivation.

In the Hartsop Valley, in the Lake District, the Countryside Commission has studied some of the problems of public access over farmland and has opened up a useful dialogue between farmers and visitors, which could be extended to other holiday regions of the countryside.

Another problem involving the impact of the urban population on the countryside is the prevalence of second homes, and the tendency for men who work on the land, to live in adjacent towns, while those working in towns wish to live in the country. The effect of this on villages is to divorce them from the rural landscape and social structure of which they were once a part. The worst visual effects result when urban ideas are introduced into the architecture and village landscape, such as the substitution of urban fences for country hedges. The social impoverishment is particularly evident when many of the houses are second homes and the population seasonal. Although basically a social problem, it also affects the landscape by changing the whole character of a village, in robbing it of life. Some mitigation could come from three directions. An increase in suitable local employment (a matter to be considered when applying planning restrictions), the retention of primary schools and local transport services and the active participation in rural life by the urban householders.

The problem of changing agricultural methods has been recognised for many years.

In the past, full and equal partnership between man and nature has produced some of the most beautiful landscapes in the world. The rice fields of Kashmir and Japan, set within a background of forested hills; the terraced Tuscan vineyards, combined with olive groves, beneath which grow the wild flowers of the region and the 19th century English countryside, are examples of perfectly balanced relationships between men and nature. The basis of the beauty of these landscapes lies in the close relationship between cultivated land and topography; the sense of maturity given by sustained fertility and the balance maintained between cultivation, dwellings and natural habitats.

The problems besetting this type of countryside are very evident here in Britain. They are caused by growing populations and increased demands which have to be met by more extensive agriculture and the use of machinery which increases the scale of the units of cultivation and removes the natural barriers to its extension onto terrain formerly left undisturbed. This change of scale and removal of restraints make vital impacts on both conservation and the visual quality of the landscape.

The size and shape of the old fields responded to change of soil and topography. The dividing network of hedges gave a scale comprehended by the human eye and a patchwork of habitats suited to a great wealth of natural species. Infinite variation of scale gave an infinite variety of visual experience and range of habitats. The monoculture inherent in crop production was limited to individual areas and broken by a change of conditions and vegetation.

The studies being carried out by the Countryside Commission explore the means by which visual and conservation values can be restored without impairing the productivity of the land. The retention of ponds and small areas of wasteland, often rich in species; the establishment of trees along boundaries, near buildings, on steep slopes and on poorer ground, can together bring back life, interest and variety to the agricultural landscape. Such measures are dependent on a seeing eye, and on a farmer who looks at every aspect of his land and sees the potential for wild life and for beauty as well as for crop production.

There is now hope that this outlook is becoming widespread among those owning and working the land. A paper entitled 'Caring for the Countryside', published jointly by the National Farmers' Union and the Country Landowners' Association, has now been followed by the 'Countryside Conservation Handbook', produced by the Country-side Commission, the Forestry Commission, the Ministry of Agriculture, Fisheries and Food and the Nature Conservancy Council, in consultation with the Country Landowners' Association and the National Farmers' Union. The subjects dealt with include tree-planting, conserving old grassland, farm ponds and ditches and the maintenance of hedge-rows. This shows a remarkable and very welcome advance in the understanding and co-operation which alone can save our countryside.

The same principles of considering conservation and landscape throughout all types of cultivation has already been adopted in forestry, where their application is perhaps easier than in purely agricultural countryside. Extensive monoculture timber production which ignores local changes in soil and topography is to the detriment of good landscape and conservation, whereas planting in sympathy with the terrain and continuous thought for conservation and landscape can produce scenes of great beauty and habitats for a wide variety of wildlife, at a negligible cost to crop production.

One problem of the countryside which we are beginning to tackle is the incursion of public works unrelated to agriculture. Notable examples are roads and reservoirs and mineral workings. Much has been done to make roads an acceptable element in the landscape and to use the opportunity to create linear nature reserves along their verges. Reservoirs can usually be converted from a problem to an asset. They always provide a potential for landscape beauty and for wildlife habitats and they may on occasion serve to absorb some of the pressure of visitors to the countryside. These two land-uses exemplify

a guiding principle – that every activity and construction in the countryside should contribute in some way to conservation and landscape values, whatever the prime object of the development may be.

This injection of landscape quality into every land-use, I believe, holds the key to solving many of the problems of the countryside. There is great danger in defining too rigidly, zones for separate types of development and degrees of care. There must, of course, be strict nature reserves, some areas free from traffic, some where new development is excluded, but the designation of these special zones should not mean that they are islands of beauty and conservation within a background where these values go by default. For conservation they should rather be nodes linked by a network of ecologically rich corridors. For countryside recreation they are rooms served by the passages of pleasant ways.

This close intermeshing of land-use and habitats, common to many long settled and densely populated countries, is perhaps more evident in Britain than anywhere else, with its geological and climatic diversity, added to a long history of settlement. The pattern which we must recognise and perpetuate is quite different from that, for instance, of the USA, whose large tracts of one type of countryside make zoning a more feasible solution. There is great danger in importing solutions from other lands without realising the basic differences of terrain and population.

As for landscape beauty, it should certainly not be confined to zones. It can be present in different forms everywhere – as much in the areas of high cultivation as in National Parks. A silo can be beautiful, so can farm buildings grouped with trees, within the wide, fertile landscape of the fens.

It is specifically for the landscape architect to see the potential beauty of every land-use, and to use his specialised skill to help the conservationists and the farmers to create a landscape of fertility, natual habitats and beauty.

If the countryside is to retain its definition as the area where organic nature is dominant over mechanics, then men who visit it, use it, or dwell in it must understand the workings of nature and become a thinking, if not necessarily a working, partner in the countryside. This attitude, which was instinctive with the good husbandman, must now be the conscious attitude of us all. The concerned participant must replace the detached observer.

The participation may be the active work of the conservation corps, building stone walls, laying hedges and maintaining ponds and water-ways, carrying out for love all those desirable country activities which are no longer economically viable for the farmer to undertake. Or it may be the more passive participation of understanding the working of the countryside, identifying with nature and with the farmer, and respecting their needs.

THREAT TO WORLD COASTLINES

THREATS TO WORLD COASTLINES
BOYD WARREN

World coastlines cover vast areas of the globe and by their nature as an interface between land and sea coastlines are very rich in both aesthetic and economic resources.

Landscape architects are concerned with landscape as a whole but because of the richness and diversity of coastlines with the accompanying population pressure there is a need for increased participation by the landscape architect in dealing with coastlines.

The greatest threat to world coastlines is the lack of awareness of the systems operating in the coastal zone. These systems include those operating on the sea, the interfaces of the sea and the land and those systems operating on the land. Only by understanding all three of these individual systems and their relationship to each other can the integrity or inherent identity of any particular stretch of coastline be understood. With this information available the potential or possibilities for maintenance and care for coastlines can be set out and achieved.

The following are examples of areas of concern in the balance of the various systems in the sea, at the interface of sea and land and on the land. These represent potential threats to coastlines.

In the sea the careless exploitation of fish and mineral resources (including drilling for oil) can have effects on the breeding, feeding and natural migration patterns of fish and other sea creatures.

At the interface of land and sea natural buffer zones are needed for the maintenance of seashore and dural stability.

On the land, regard is needed for the integrity of areas by the retention of natural greensward strips between development.

Estuaries tie land and sea together in an extended interface situation. The maintenance of estuaries and their supporting organic material banks such as swamp lands are most important for the well-being and continued richness of coastlines.

An approach to the object of reducing the effect to coastlines and the stability of systems involved need to be surveyed to understand the integrity, potential and threats of coastlines. Priorities need to be established to understand which threats to coastlines should be tackled first. Publicity of the results and new understanding gained in the surveys should be published to maximise the effectiveness of these studies.

In conclusion the effectiveness of understanding and dealing with the threats to world coastlines depends on the ability to involve as many people as possible from local, state, national and international bodies through the various stages of survey to publicity and implementation.

At this stage of the congress, members may wish to begin the discussion by introducing the various threats that exist to coastlines in their part of the world so that ideas and approaches can be worked out for the many and varied situations of individual members. By this means a sense of oneness of purpose can be achieved on lessening threats to world coastlines.

THE COASTLINE AND ITS IMPORTANCE TO AN ISLAND COUNTRY IN THE SOUTH PACIFIC
R. D. GAY

One may well ask what a small and isolated country like New Zealand has to contribute to a discussion on world coastlines. With a land area similar to that of the United Kingdom, a population of just over three million and approximately 16,000 km (10,000 miles) of coastline New Zealand would appear to be well off when compared with other countries where industry, urban expansion, recreation and detrimental uses have greatly modified, and still threaten many coastlines. When looked at in this way, New Zealand should not have to worry about its coastlines at all, but it does, for it is just as threatened as other young countries where attitudes are still changing from a pioneering rôle to a realisation that the coastal resource must be carefully managed if benefits are to accrue in the long term.

In preparing this document I am reminded of the XV World Congress in Istanbul and the many fine papers which were presented there. What more is there to say? For as J. B. Perrin and Professor Brunn so adequately stated in their synthesis report 'All over the world, coastal areas undergo deep deterioration at an accelerated pace, and although such phenomena may vary in intensity and extent it appears to follow similar patterns everywhere'. This applies equally well to New Zealand and I can offer no new solutions although I believe that we are in the fortunate position of being able to learn by the problems experienced in larger and more densely populated countries. This paper then is an overview, a general statement of the history of this country and the situation we have reached in managing our coastal resources.

The small land mass of New Zealand lies in a remote position by world standards and is surrounded by vast areas of ocean. Over 1,200 nautical miles to the west the Tasman Sea extends to Australia the nearest major land area. Over 300 million years ago it was linked with New Zealand as part of 'Gondwanaland' the great southern continent. Due to continental drift over the following 130 million years New Zealand became a separate archipelago. As time progressed it became further separated and evolved in almost complete isolation for a further 60 million years. As a consequence it has birds, reptiles and vegetation that are unique. Much of this uniqueness is still present particularly in the coastal areas of the three main islands and more than 500 offshore islands that extend from the warmer northern areas to Stewart Island in the south. In the Sub-Antarctic there are a further five groups totalling over 85,000 hectares, all of which are reserved for the protection of flora and fauna. New Zealand and the island system are but the surface areas of an undersea bathymetry made up of deep trenches, plateaus, troughs, and ridges. Between this marine environment and the land surface the coastline intervenes with its very form dictated by the geology of sedimentary, volcanic and metamorphic origins that are the basis of this country's diverse relief.

When Captain James Cook first approached New Zealand shores in 1769 Lancelot Brown was no doubt busily involved with the reconstruction of Blenheim Palace with its great park, formal gardens and man-created landscape. At this time it was a totally different scene in New Zealand. The Maoris who had migrated from Polynesia and who had occupied the country for perhaps a thousand years before went about their tasks using simple tools of wood and stone. Apart from the occasional large fires they touched lightly on the natural landscape. The Maori settled mainly in coastal areas or inland lakes where water made for easy transport and the rivers, estuaries, and open sea were an important food source. Coastal hills, headlands and bluffs were frequently selected for fortified pas because of the security offered in being able to sight and fend off opposing tribes. Instead of great castles and extensive fortifications which typify other civilisations the impact on the landscape was limited to ditches, terraces and hutments made predominantly from plant materials and of which little evidence now remains. By the late 18th Century sealers and whalers were beginning to frequent the coast and as they established shore bases the pattern of coastal habitation began to change.

Understandably it was the accessible coastal areas that first felt the axe, fire and ploughshare, as thousands of acres of forest were cleared for farming. Settlements sprung up wherever it was possible to handle shipping and establish trading centres. Although settlers from many countries have left their mark and many examples remain today, it was those from an English background who have had the greatest influence in their desire to recreate the character of the countryside they had left behind. Today this influence is present throughout New Zealand where the topography, climate and social attitude is sympathetic. Stately English trees vie with sombre greens of native forest while hedgerows and traditional English architecture are reminders of this nation's European ancestry. It is the coastal areas that provide some of the greatest diversity however, as different land uses of the coastal zone lie adjacent to the beaches, bays, sand-dunes, headlands, wetlands, estuaries, islands, rivers and bluffs. The coastline is still in a state of rapid change and as can be expected in a country young in terms of world geology and settlement this is the area where natural processes coupled with the impact of man are most obvious.

Coastal Legislation

While it is beyond the scope of this paper to provide a detailed explanation of all the legislation which has been enacted to control the coastal land and water of New Zealand, it is important to understand the motivation that has brought us up to the present day. There appears to have been three main phases influenced by politics and the attitude of the population as the country has developed. Although there were exceptions, the emphasis in the 1800's to early 1900's was on the allocation and vesting of the land resource itself. The attitude was in most instances one of 'taming the land' by draining swamps, controlling sand drift, making rivers navigable and clearing the land. From the 1930's to the 1950's the legislation was wide-ranging and typifies a young country attempting to both maximise its resources as well as becoming aware of the deeper values of a country richly endowed with natural beauty. Some of the most significant legislation protecting National Parks, Reserves, Wildlife, Water and Soil Conservation and Planning were firmly established during this period.

Legislation of the 1970's has brought a period of updating and review. I believe that it is fair to say that a new conservation ethic is emerging which will help avoid many of the previous pitfalls associated with the divergent views of preservation and development. While the extensive system of National Parks, Reserves and other protected areas will remain, and will in many cases be reinforced by other Acts, it is now realised that conservation of the total resource means much more than the protection of scientific areas and scenery alone. This then is a new hope for the coastline. In spite of increasing pressures the formation of new laws developed by the people and the politicians will give us a better chance of protecting this important environment than we have had in the past.

Compared with many countries New Zealand has been more than amply catered for by way of legislation. Today at least 30 Acts of Parliament are involved with the control of the coastal lands and waters. At first impression one could be excused for considering that the greatest threat to the coastline is over-legislation and administrative mismanagement. Or that conversely in the face of such legislative power any likely threat would not have a chance to become a problem before being dealt with by one or more of the nine Government departments or the many local authorities involved. In order to see the situation in better perspective I refer briefly to several of the more important and recent pieces of legislation concerned with landscape protection.

National Parks Act 1952. National Parks cover one-thirteenth of the country's land, with legislation protecting them under a strong preservation ethic. While the 10 National Parks include mountains, lakes, forests, glaciers and other types of unique landscape, some coastland is also included in Fiordland National Park and Abel Tasman National Park. It is anticipated that future areas for new National Park will include a wider representation of coastal landscapes.

Reserves Act 1977. Based on a 24-year-old Act the Reserves legislation was recently revised to cater for a changing public attitude in the protection of natural, recreational, cultural and historic values. It provides a wide range of options that will enable landscape features to

be protected as Reserves either in public ownership or under a registered covenant if privately owned. Seven categories of reserves have been classified:

Scenic (of which there are 1,076 reserves at the present time indicating the importance of scenic landscape)
Scientific
Historic
Nature
Recreation
Government purpose
Local purpose

Emphasis is given to:

The preservation of open spaces for public use and enjoyment, and to the protection of historic, cultural, archaeological, biological, geological and other scientific values in reserves, in addition to their natural landscape and scenic values.

The provision of access for the public to and along the sea coast, its bays, inlets, and offshore islands and to and along lakeshores and river banks.

The promotion and preservation of the natural character of the coastal environment and of the margins of lakes and rivers and the protection of them from unnecessary subdivision and development.

As will be seen there is considerable emphasis on the coastal environment and it is expected that this will contribute significantly to a conservation philosophy for the protection of this important area.

The three Maritime Parks located in the Bay of Islands, Hauraki Gulf and Marlborough Sounds are composed of many previously reserved areas which have been enlarged to form independent systems of protected coastline and islands. Although operating under their own Acts they are deemed to form part of the Reserves Act for the purposes of administrative and legal control.

The Town and Country Planning Act 1977 provides the main mechanism for planning at national, regional and local levels. Aimed at maintaining a balance between the pattern of land use and economic growth the recently revised Act places a stronger emphasis on regional planning and the coastal environment. New provisions cover aspects of maritime planning to enable a greater integration of land and water use. Not the least of these provisions are the following extracts from the general policy.

Provision of as wide a variety of active and passive recreation opportunity and experience as the coast is able to offer now and in the future including a wide range of types of recreational reserves and holiday accommodation.

Retention in sufficient quantity of the native coastal flora and fauna in its natural state as well as the unique and typical in coastal scenery.

Ensuring that any development of coastal land for urban and holiday purposes is in sympathy with the landscape and makes the most of each site's natural characteristics.

Recognition that the stability of a large proportion of coastal land depends on the efficiency of sand-dune fixation and that unstable dune areas should not be subjected to a high level of recreational use.

Harbours Act 1950 covers the administrative and management needs of harbours, also foreshores, seabed, navigable rivers and lakes. One of the most significant provisions in this Act is the control exercised over reclamations for agriculture or harbour extension purposes. Also included are controls over structures, removal of materials, rubbish dumping and noise. In terms of reclamations the Act must be considered in relation to the Soil and Water Conservation Act and the Town and Country Planning Act.

Water and Soil Conservation Act 1967 deals with the allocation of water rights, the establishment and control of a water classification system and control of water pollution. It is important as far as the coastal environment is concerned for it covers recreational needs, scenic and natural features, fisheries, and wildlife habitats from a water quality point of view.

Marine Reserves Act 1971 provides for the establishment of marine reserves in the sea and on the foreshore to protect the habitat of the marine environment. Although only a limited number of marine reserves have been declared provision is made for the preservation of:

'. . . *areas of New Zealand that contain underwater scenery, natural features, or marine life of such distinctive quality, or so typical, or beautiful, or unique, that their continued preservation is in the national interest.*'

Marine Farming Act 1971. The farming of sea-fish, shellfish, oysters, and marine vegetation is controlled by the granting of leases and licences after reference to the controlling authority adjacent to or having jurisdiction over the seabed concerned. The public may object to interference with:

any existing right of navigation
commercial fishing
existing or proposed usage for recreational or scientific purposes of the foreshore or the sea in the vicinity; or
otherwise be contrary to the public interest.

The Queen Elizabeth the Second National Trust Act 1977. An Act to commemorate the Silver Jubilee of Her Majesty Queen Elizabeth the Second. The Trust was established to encourage and promote the concept of open space for the benefit and enjoyment of the people of New Zealand. In its interpretation open space is defined as being:

'any area of land or body of water that serves to preserve or facilitate the preservation of any landscape of aesthetic, cultural, recreational, scenic, scientific, or social interest or value.'

It is intended that the Trust will act as a co-ordinating body in an endeavour to encourage the protection of landscape by the application of covenants for land in private ownership or to accept gifts of land to be placed under protection provisions. The concept, new to this country, is expected to fill an important gap in the conservation and protection field.

Each of the Acts outlined is administered by a different Government Agency and as can be expected problems of co-ordination and responsibility do arise. This is a most unfortunate situation when dealing with the land and sea with its dramatically different requirements from a management point of view; yet, with such a close ecological and recreational relationship. Over the years recommendations have frequently been made concerning the establishment of a Coastal Commission or some other such body modelled on the English system, that would assume a general oversight of the coastline. Although this has not eventuated both revised and new legislation now provides a better scope for unified management than occurred in the past. National policies with a greater emphasis on regional planning, the protection of land not under public ownership, involvement and participation by the people in decision-making, the Walkway system and other examples will go a long way towards achieving a greater awareness of coastal needs.

Planning Dimensions

While I do not think it necessary to delve into a deep discussion on the state of coastal planning as such, there are two dimensions which are of interest and which I see as being important. Firstly, the preliminary stage of data and resource gathering by way of a coastal survey and, secondly, the state of management planning in New Zealand.

Early legislators concerned at the rate at which more important parts of coastal land was being inappropriately used for urban expansion and other uses brought down legislation which at the time was far sighted by world standards. It provided for a strip of land one chain in width to be established along the mean high water mark of the sea, its bays, inlets and creeks. As a result most of the coastline was protected, but there were areas where this was not achieved or where local authorities under local development pressure reduced the width to an unacceptable degree. By the mid-1960's it had become obvious that this approach was not going to meet the country's needs in the long term. Steps were then taken to initiate a more comprehensive coastal survey so as to review all coastal land in both public and private ownership and to provide a better basis upon which planning could commence.

The first stage of the survey incorporating sea coast, islands and lakeshores has been 60 per cent completed. The second phase including rivers and streams is due to be commenced by 1980. The work is undertaken on a district by district basis by the Department of Lands and Survey whose responsibilities include Crown lands and reserves, and the Ministry of Works and Development who administer the Town and Country Planning Act. Criteria to be covered includes natural features, historic and archaeological sites, recreation, land use, existing development and urban areas. A priority system of action for protection purposes is established to ensure that important areas receive early attention.

The question is frequently asked if the survey provides sufficient in depth information on which to base planning and decision making? There is no easy answer to this for although the methods have become more embracing and the data more useful in a scientific sense it is only when a demand has been made on a particular area of the coast that the need for a more sophisticated and quantitative approach has

become obvious. Generally speaking the lack of team-work by a comprehensive range of specialists including landscape architects means that this approach cannot be regarded as the ideal although it is at least providing a reference point and data source. Already the arbitrary approach of the one chain strip has changed in many areas as the coastal zone has been extended to incorporate landscape and other features of importance. Some excellent work is being done at smaller and more detailed scales in harbour systems and important regional coastlines close to larger areas of population.

Management planning is now a basic requirement in National Parks and Reserves following early attempts with the more static and inflexible approach with design oriented master plans. The aim is to stimulate action by the development of objectives and policies based on the available resource information and planning data. In this way administering bodies have an immediate reference to the overriding legislation covering the particular reserve, plus management policies to help guide decision making. This continuing and flexible approach has now been made mandatory in the new Reserves legislation with administering authorities having to prepare and submit management plans for approval within five years.

Basic requirements of the plans are that: they shall provide for and ensure the use, enjoyment, maintenance, protection and preservation and development as the Act allows and the administering bodies' resources permit.

An important aspect of the management plan system is the provision made for public participation in the management of reserves. The intention to prepare a management plan must first be advised publicly, with comment and suggestion invited from the public or interested parties. Once the draft plan has been prepared it is open for inspection and further comment. If necessary submissions are then heard before the administering body in order that full consideration is given to all factors before final approval is sought from the Minister of Lands.

Some Typical Case Histories

It seems to be human nature that we allow ourselves to get into a crisis situation before action is taken to remedy the problem. I know full well that landscape architects, planners and others in the environmental game attempt to do just the opposite, but history has shown that the social and political climate must be right for the reception and effective action of environmental philosophies. New Zealand seems to have reached that stage where it is aware of the special attributes it has in a physical – biological – visual sense and is now developing legislation accordingly. One of the difficulties now faced is being able to put these principles into practice. To do so means breaking new ground in terms of effective long term landscape planning and the application of landscape proposals and management systems. Demands made on the coastline to date are typical of those in other parts of the world, although generally speaking at a much reduced scale to those experienced in larger and more developed countries. In order to see the situation in better perspective the following sections briefly describe three broad categories of existing and likely future threats.

Extractive Industries and Energy Production

Reference is made to the use of non-renewable resources for both industry and energy production. Impacts and demands on the coast affect both the marine and land environment. Frequently the land-sea interface is also concerned.

As with other parts of the world New Zealand is currently undergoing a deep questioning in respect of energy production and use. Prospecting licences for oil and gas cover extensive areas of the surrounding ocean but so far oil has not been discovered in commercial quantities. While the actual wells of both oil and gas create little coastal impact in themselves the need for onshore installations poses some problems and should oil be discovered in the southern ocean the unique flora and fauna reserves of the sub-antarctic islands could be affected.

Natural gas located off the Taranaki coast has become an important commodity. This is brought ashore by submarine pipeline before being processed at an extensive plant located in rich dairying country on the slopes below Egmont National Park. The landscape is comprised of low lahars of volcanic origin now softened by weathering and agricultural use. In this case the offshore well dictated the location of the processing installation which is close to the coast and in a visually prominent position. The pipeline carrying the processed gas to main centres has created considerable disturbance to delicate coastal areas and special restoration techniques have had to be implemented.

Coal as an energy source is mined at the rate of 2-3 million tonnes per annum from deep mines and open-cast operations. At the present time it is undergoing a resurgence as a heating fuel because of the increasing cost of electricity and imported refined fuels. Mines are located throughout the coastal area of Westland, a region rich in scenery. The formation of transportation routes, loading installations, sub-standard housing, rail yards and port facilities while necessary, greatly detract from the scenic resources of the region but are not as devastating as open-cast workings in other parts of the country.

Minerals cannot be discussed without reference to gold mining which, historically speaking, has been responsible for some of this country's most desecrated landscape. In 1873 it earned 75 per cent of this country's export earnings but production is today restricted to small scale and one large dredging operation. It appears that the increasing demand for steel has assumed importance over gold. The largest resources of black sands are located on the western beaches of both islands and are estimated at 1,000 million tonnes. Bulk loading from North Island sources is made direct to Japanese freighters moored offshore. At the present time conservation practices appear to be adequate in this situation although many beaches near Auckland City have been severely modified by the mining of sand for the building industry in the past.

Limestone for agricultural use is exploited wherever the quality and quantity occurs. Frequently this is in the coastal zone as is the basic material for cement manufacture. One such deposit is located in the Nelson Region on a particularly scenic and vulnerable part of the coast. An artificial harbour is being built which could well influence the already rapidly changing coastline. The long term effect has not yet been determined but could well prove disastrous to a highly used recreation reserve and beach area.

Throughout the country the mining of sand, gravels, clay, pumice, serpentine and other materials follows world-wide patterns affecting aesthetic, ecological and recreation values. While the offshore islands have so far been relatively unaffected the presence of large quantities of peat wax on the Chatham Islands will, if harvested, threaten an extensive ecosystem of vegetation and bird life found nowhere else in the world.

While some valuable landscapes should never be mined, there are locations where I believe this can be carried out without significant loss to the coastal environment. In some situations the change has been for the better especially where the creative aspect of conservation has provided a new and varied pattern of land use for agriculture, forestry and recreation. The Mining Act 1971 requires that: mining privileges over the foreshore and seabed cannot be issued unless the consent of the Minister of Transport has been obtained and with the concurrence of the Minister of Agriculture and Fisheries. In National Parks and Reserves and State Forests conditions relative to the protection of natural features, flora and fauna may be imposed. Conditions are also required for the restoration of the land surface and prevention of damage to natural features. There is no mandatory requirement however to submit and have approved landscape evaluation, design, or restoration plans. This to me is a great weakness in the Act for at the present time the interpretation of what constitutes 'adequate restoration' is open to wide abuse.

Agriculture, Forestry, Marine Farming

By using the resources of the land or the sea for commercial harvest agriculture, forestry and marine farming influence the coast to varying degrees.

Agriculture assumes many forms: dairy, sheep, cattle, cropping, and a wide variety of intermixes. The importance of agriculture to New Zealand needs little explanation occupying as it does over 20 million of the 26 million hectares of land in the country. As the coastal zone varies in its topography soil and climate so does the type and extent of agriculture. It contributes much to the coastal character but unfortunately poor land use practices adopted by early settlers are still evident as raw scars caused by the removal of vegetation cover on skeletal soils, fires and overstocking. Some carefully managed coastal farms reflect a stable situation where both natural and cultural elements complement each other and provide a landscape of balance and interest. Today the agricultural management of coastal land is better understood with an increasing awareness of the social and scientific needs. Even so, problems in the use of toxic pesticides, herbicides, other chemicals, and nutrients in the form of fertiliser are contributing to eutrophication and accumulation in streams, wetlands and estuaries. While the aerial application of fertiliser and spraying of noxious weeds has revolutionised farming in many areas it is often non-selective, difficult to control and frequently spells doom to remnant indigenous forest and other ecological systems. The draining of swamps and wetlands, once common practice, is now questioned and a Government subsidy is available to reinstate wetland for wildfowl habitat in many areas.

Partly because the public in New Zealand do not have free access to privately held rural land, a privilege enjoyed in some countries, the Department of Lands and Survey has, wherever appropriate, been establishing a system of farm parks. These are located in selected coastal areas from the far north of the country to the Marlborough Sounds where pressure for public recreation exists and where the farming operation has special management requirements. They fill an increasingly important opportunity for the public to experience camping and other recreation pursuits in the coastal/rural environment.

In the early 19th Century indigenous forests covered two-thirds of New Zealand. Today it is but a minute portion of this amount with the main protected areas in National Parks and Reserves.

At a late stage the country has realised the importance of indigenous forest cover and has taken steps to protect it wherever possible. Even so the exploitation of native timbers continues in some areas to the detriment of the scenery, soil-water regimes and long-term management of sensitive coastal areas. Exotic forestry comprising mainly of fast-growing North American species has expanded rapidly and now totals 740 thousand hectares. Considerable concern is expressed where exotic forestry is expanding into natural areas of coastal landscape. Although *Pinus radiata* and other species are used effectively to stabilise dune country there are many areas where their use as a commercial crop is questionable. One such situation is in the Marlborough Sounds, the location of one of the Maritime Parks. A geomorphologist would describe the landscape as an embayed coastline of submergence, while the layman sees it as water, hills, valleys, headlands, remote beaches, sheep farming, native forest and tussock grassland, holiday homes, fishing and other aquatic recreation. The landscape architect sees it as a landscape in a state of flux far apart from the protected areas. The landscape is being scarred with access roads, power pylons, inappropriate buildings and structures in delicate foreshore situations and a wide variation in management approaches between the reserves, sheep farming, marine farming and now forestry. The area has recently been the subject of an intensive land-use study to help guide the multiple resource uses proposed. The public are concerned that *Pinus radiata* as the main timber tree will take over the landscape, visually, economically and ecologically. It is a landscape planning problem the scale of which deserves more attention than has been possible to date. For although a systematic landscape evaluation exercise has been carried out with attended recommendations neither the authorities nor entrepreneurs have yet seen fit to apply the principles to the degree required to provide a balanced approach.

Marine farming is a comparatively recent phenomena to the shorelines in sheltered harbours, sounds and estuaries. It poses particular problems and operates under the Marine Farming Act 1971. Applications to establish farms must go through the process of application, advertisement and hearing of objections, if any. Interference with navigation, fishing, recreation, scientific use or adjacent land use is not permitted. The visual intrusion of large areas of moored rafts in previously uncluttered natural settings is a threat which concerns adjacent landowners and recreation users.

Tourism and Recreation

Tourism and recreation are two functions which require a quality landscape for a satisfactory user experience. If the coast is mismanaged the resource upon which they depend is easily destroyed.

As it becomes better known New Zealand is 'being discovered' by an increasing number of overseas tourists. Not surprisingly it is sold on the basis of its scenery, it being claimed as being a pocket miniature of the world. It is one of the fastest growing industries with the average tourist staying 20 days and spending $215 million annually. Such expansion is placing an increasing pressure on transport, accommodation and other services in coastal and alpine scenic areas. Although there is an acceptance that environmental controls must be exercised in the development of facilities the demand is in some instances placing sensitive ecological areas at risk. For instance in Fiordland National Park, at Milford Sound, conflict has developed between the pressures of the hotel tourist, the day visitor and the commercial fishermen who all require facilities on the limited area of shoreline available. The one access road which traverses a particularly scenic route through high mountains, lakes and forest and is an attractant in itself. This generation of visitor traffic is placing still more pressure on the Fiord terminus than can be sustained.

Collectively these pressures have been responsible for a detailed study of future planning needs.

The Bay of Islands in the far north, has been described as the cradle of New Zealand's history. Here special efforts are being made to protect much of the early culture of Russell, an historic settlement. The development of a plan for urban conservation has had to be balanced with its main function as a tourist attraction and base for big game fishing in the region. A new Bay of Islands Maritime Park was recently created to protect more of the distinctive landscape of islands, mangroves, rivers, inlets, estuaries, rolling hill country and history. Even so, pressures of transport, accommodation, forestry, agriculture, minerals and fishing, tourism and recreation are having to be seriously questioned in terms of their likely impact.

In a recreation sense the New Zealanders regard themselves as 'belonging' in the coastal environment. With most of the main cities and urban areas being located close to harbours or beaches it is not surprising that the recreation preferences based on research are: swimming, fishing, picnicking, walking, driving for pleasure, boating and sporting events, in that order. The most readily available outdoor recreation resource available to 90 per cent of the population are the coastal areas. With the majority of the population living within 10-15 miles of the coast and the furthest distance of travel being approximately 70 miles the importance of the coastline is obvious. While enjoying the coastline the recreationist has, even in New Zealand with its low population, exploited parts of it to a critical degree. Some of the earliest pressures developed with the desire to own a second home at the beach; frequently these were squatter situations where shanty settlements grew without title to the land, blocking access and disturbing sensitive foreshore ecology. Then came the speculator who, while formalising the land title, added insult to injury by poorly designed sub-divisions creating pseudo urban landscape. These days are not yet over, but fortunately there is now a greater public and developer awareness of what constitutes sensitive and appropriate design in a coastal setting. The advent of the trail bike and off-road vehicle has recently added a new dimension to problems in this country and there are many examples where the physical impact on sensitive coastal terrain has already broken down whole ecosystems. Efforts are being made to co-ordinate and encourage user groups, carry out research and determine the location of landscape types which will support this activity.

As the effort to secure land for coastal recreation increases, as facilities are developed for camping, picnicking, boating and other aquatic pursuits the professional is becoming increasingly involved. It must be remembered that recreation is a personal choice and that collectively it involves the community who must be part of the decision making.

Summation

In the wake of the Istanbul Conference when extensive thought and discussion centred on the coastline it would be superfluous to repeat many of the principles upon which we would all agree. I am sure that the opportunity to air the subject again at this Congress will be constructive and provide reinforcement in many areas. With this in mind and having provided a general statement on New Zealand it leaves me to sum up from a landscape architect's point of view.

As this country is young and receptive, so is its attitude towards accepting the need for sound planning and design. As a colleague once put it: 'we usually associate education with classrooms, lecture theatres, seminars or conventions. Farm management is associated with field days, personal advisors, wool sales and hard talk'. We are a rurally oriented country from the mountains to the sea and my own feeling is that a lot of hard talk is still necessary. We have the assets, we must now perfect the strategies.

There is no doubt that New Zealand has a great opportunity to plan for the wise use of the coastal resource compared with many countries where the population/coastal area ratio is much greater. Although this country's population growth is expected to be zero by 1980 there is no room for complacency. Pressures based on technical requirements will continue to increase as resources are exploited to 'improve' the standard of living. More leisure time and a longer life expectancy typical of other countries can also be anticipated.

Recent legislation reflects contemporary attitudes towards a conservation ethic, this in turn places a greater emphasis on landscape protection and management. While this is an encouraging sign from the point of view of the landscape profession, its application has yet to be tested. For instance, the determination of what constitutes a particular landscape value is open to wide interpretation. There is unlikely to be argument about the unique, dramatic or spectacular

Milford Sound, Fiordland National Park, South Island.
Tourist Hotel, this and other facilities minimise the limited area of land available.

Boating activities are popular in areas close to urban populations. Parematta, Wellington.

Some residential housing areas have been located too close to the coast. Wainui Beach, Gisborne.

coastal landscapes but those which fall into a less definable class will require more debate. This does not say that they are any less important. They will, however, require a greater degree of evaluation and judgement before their ultimate use can be decided. Only after such a consideration will a balanced coastal landscape result. I believe that we are on the fringe of this problem in New Zealand. Similar comment can be made with respect to the coastal survey. As regional planning becomes more widely accepted the need for a landscape planning approach will become more obvious and applicable. At present landscape planning methodologies are not well understood in spite of the use of inter-disciplinary teams that in most cases include landscape architects.

Although it is encouraging to see landscape architects involved in the application of planning, design and ecological management techniques there is still a tendency to involve them late in the process. This is a source of professional frustration but is expected to improve as the product is accepted and the numbers increase. It is pertinent to comment here that as a profession in New Zealand it is not yet a decade old, and that the total number of landscape architects in both private consultancies and government departments is approximately 40. This is still far too few to achieve fully effective results in a country still developing its coastal land use pattern and own design image.

With the year 2000 a little more than 20 years away the Congress theme 'Conservation or Desolation' begs to be answered. As far as New Zealand is concerned I can do no better than to quote from a publication on the Future of New Zealand's Shoreline.

'Men came to these islands more than a thousand years ago. In another thousand years the long swell of the Tasman will still be crashing along the West Coast beaches. We need to lift our sights a little, to give some credence to cause and effect, to allow some responsibility for the effect of our actions on the long term future. In short, we need an ethic of land use, the cornerstone of which can be the use of the coast.'

References

Cotton 1974. Edited by B. W. Collins. Bold Coasts. Reed, A. H. and A. W.
Commission for the Environment 1976. A Guide to Environmental Law in New Zealand. Government Printer.
Department of Lands and Survey and Department of Recreation and Sport. 1978. NZ Outdoor Recreation Proceedings.
Department of Lands and Survey 1977. The Seas must Live. The Land-Sea Interface. Government Printer.
Department of Statistics 1978. NZ Official Year Book. Government Printer.
Peel, J. F. University of California. Coastal Zone Management Multiple Use with Conservation.
Ketchum, B. Editor. The Waters Edge 1972. Critical Problems of the Coastal Zone. M.I.T. Press.
Morton, J., Thom, D., Locker, R. 1973. Seacoasts in the Seventies. The Future of the New Zealand Shoreline. Hodder-Stoughton.
New Zealand Institute of Engineers, 1974. Regional Management of Sea Coasts and Lakeshores. Proceedings of Symposium NZIE Annual Conference.

Cape Maria van Diemen in the far north of New Zealand. This area is now a Coastal Farm Park.

LANDSCAPE DESIGN

THEN AND NOW BRENDA COLVIN

Great strides have certainly been taken in these 50 years, from the stage when that little group standing in the garden design tent at a Chelsea Show decided that it was time to found a national organisation, to the situation today when the LI membership is 1,650 and when landscape consultants are seen as essential members of the team in almost every major work undertaken in this country.

Nevertheless progress has not gone nearly far enough. There is still a large majority of the community who are totally ignorant about the profession – who have never even heard of it and seem to assume that good landscape occurs inevitably without human effort or who are not interested in having pleasing visual surroundings. Few of those who do appreciate the need for fine landscape recognise its ecological basis or its potential social rôle. In this matter of public understanding, the profession has not caught up with those of architecture, medicine, law or any of the longer-established professions. Perhaps, however, it has an inbuilt evolutionary capacity to outdistance some of them in the long term. Personally I believe that its inherent 'program' has a capacity for further development beyond anything hitherto foreseen.

We are celebrating the 50th year of the ILA. But for reasons on which I propose to enlarge further, I feel sure that it was wise to give the profession a wider base and to adopt the new title 'Landscape Institute'. Our problems differ from those of architecture both in time and in space. Most landscape design projects take far more time to reach maturity than architectural features, but are also highly vulnerable to destruction before maturity, either by neglect or by mistake. The time needed for successful establishment of major landscapes is related to (and must influence) the initial design from its outset. Long term management in harmony with the intention of the design is the best hope towards the objective, but the high likelihood of changes must be foreseen and flexibility has to be built into the design so far as possible.

In terms of space, landscape covers larger areas than architecture. Agriculture, forestry, lakes or reservoirs and other land uses form the greater elements of many major landscape projects: in many cases architectural features may be absent or of secondary importance, though where they exist and are important in themselves, man-made artefacts form the focus of attention.

The basis of landscape design is biological rather than geometrical: the laws of nature remain dominant over human fashion and convention.

The growth of the Institute to include land management and land sciences recognises these facts and is a normal evolutionary development of this young art. Unless land managers and land scientists appreciate the rôle of design, landscape change would probably produce a different and duller or uglier setting for human enjoyment and social health. Unless designers work closely with managers and scientists who understand this, mistakes and failures are likely to wreck their work before maturity. Unless all three work together their political influence will be insignificant, and clients will fail to appreciate the need for team work. This need has been too seldom understood hitherto and that is perhaps one reason why the profession has not gained wider recognition up to the present time.

The status of the Institute should also rise when the public (and our clients) realise that a strict professional Code of Practice is mandatory on all members of the three branches alike. The code, calling for a sense of responsibility to the future of the land, emphasises recognition of the dominance of long-term interests over short-term needs. In landscape changes there is often conflict between long-term and short-term objectives: holding the balance in the interests of landscape calls for integrity and restraint (and sometimes for denial of self-interest) on the part of professional consultants.

I would like to end by quoting Geoffrey Jellicoe's comment in 'The Landscape of Man'.

'The world is moving into a phase when landscape design may well be recognised as the most comprehensive of the arts . . . It is only in the present century that the collective landscape has emerged as a social necessity. We are promoting a landscape art on a scale never conceived of in history.'

LIST OF CONTRIBUTORS

Patron: HRH The Duke of Edinburgh, KG, KT

ADAMS, Robert, BSc(Hort), ALI
Principal in private practice *(GB)*
ARONSON, Shlomo, MLA
Director of Shlomo Aronson Ltd, Jerusalem *(Israel)*
BARTMAN, Dr Edward
Director of Landscape Institute, Agricultural Academy, Warsaw *(Poland)*
BELLAFIORE, Vincent J.
Associate Professor of Landscape Architecture, University of Georgia. Delegate-Elect to IFLA *(USA)*
BOOTE, Robert, CVO, BSc, FCIS, DPA, HonMRTPI, HonALI, FRSA
Director General, Nature Conservancy Council *(GB)*
BOOTH, A. Geoffrey, DipEng, DipTP, FRTPI
County Planner, Essex County Council *(GB)*
BOR, Professor Walter, CBE, FRIBA, PPRTPI, RIBA Dist TP
Consultant, Llewelyn-Davies Weeks *(GB)*
BOTHA, Professor R.
Member of IFLA *(S Africa)*
BUCHWALD, Professor Konrad
Former Director of Institut für Landschaftspflege und Naturschutz der Universität Hannover *(W Germany)*
BURNS, Dr Wilfred, CB, CBE, DSc, MEng, PPRTPI, MICE
Deputy Secretary and Chief Planner, Department of the Environment *(GB)*
CABRAL, Professor F. C.
Past President of IFLA *(Portugal)*
CLOUSTON, Brian, DipLD, NDH, DHEdin, FLI, FInstPRA(Dip)
Senior Partner, Brian Clouston and Partners *(GB)*
COLLINS, Norman, FRTPI, SPDip, ARIBA, MITDip
County Planning Officer, Gloucestershire County Council *(GB)*
COLVIN, Brenda, CBE, PPILA
Founder Member of ILA and IFLA. Past President of Landscape Institute, Senior Partner of Colvin and Moggridge *(GB)*
CONTRERAS, Arq Carlos
President of Mexican Society of Landscape Architects *(Mexico)*
CROWE, Dame Sylvia, DBE, PPILA, HonFRIBA, HonMRTPI, HonDocLitt, HonDocLaw, HonFAustralianILA, Cons Member IUCN, Correspond Member ASLA
Landscape consultant *(GB)*
DANIEL, Peter, MCD, BArch, FRIAS, MRTPI, AILA
Consultant landscape architect *(GB)*
DENMAN, Professor Donald, DSc, PhD, MSc, MA, FRICS
Professor Emeritus of Land Economy, University of Cambridge *(GB)*
DOWER, Michael, MA, ARICS, DipTP, MRTPI
Director, Dartington Amenity Research Trust *(GB)*
GAY, Robin, DipHort, DipLA, AILA, NZILA
Chief Landscape Architect, Department of Lands and Survey; President, New Zealand Institute of Landscape Architects *(New Zealand)*
GILLESPIE, William, DipLA, PPILA
Principal, William Gillespie & Partners *(GB)*
HACKETT, Professor Brian, MA, PPILA, RIBA, MRTPI
Emeritus Professor of Landscape Architecture, University of Newcastle upon Tyne *(GB)*
HANDLEY, Dr John, PhD, MSc
Natural Resources Officer, Merseyside County Council *(GB)*
HARDIE, Heather
Third-year student at Ball State University, Indiana *(USA)*
HENKE, Hanno, Dipl.-Ing
Member of IUCN Commission on National Parks and Protected Areas; Member BDLA. Research scientist, Institute for Landscape Planning and Landscape Ecology, Federal Research Centre for Nature Conservation and Landscape Ecology, Bonn *(W Germany)*
HOOKWAY, Reginald, BSc, FRTPI
Director, Countryside Commission *(GB)*
JACOBS, Professor Peter, OAQ
President of Canadian Society of Landscape Architects; Professor of Landscape Architecture, Associate Dean of Faculté d'Aménagement, University of Montréal. Chairman of Environmental Planning Commission of IUCN *(Canada)*
JELLICOE, Geoffrey, CBE, PPILA, RIBA(DisTP), AADipl, MRTPI
Principal in private practice *(GB)*
de JONGE, Nico
Associate Professor of Landscape Architecture, University of Wageningen *(Netherlands)*
KAHN-ACKERMANN, Georg
Secretary-General of Council of Europe, Strasbourg *(W Germany)*
KEMP, Edward, MBE, VMH, NDH, DHEdin
Curator, University Botanic Garden, Dundee *(GB)*
KIEMSTEDT, Professor H.
Chairman of IFLA Working Party on Education *(W Germany)*
KLINGE, Dr Hans, DrScAgr
Senior Research Associate, Department of Tropical Ecology, Max Planck Institute for Limnology *(W Germany)*
KLIASS, R. Grena
President of Brazilian Association of Landscape Architects *(Brazil)*
KUENEN, Professor Dr Donald
Doctor of Sciences, University of Leiden; Hon Doctor, University of Dundee; Professor of Environmental Biology, University of Leiden. Past President of IUCN; Adviser to Council of Europe on environmental matters *(Netherlands)*
LOVEJOY, Derek, MA, PPILA, DipTP, FRIBA, FRTPI, FRSA
Former Secretary-General and former Vice-President of IFLA; Senior Partner, Derek Lovejoy & Partners *(GB)*
MILLER, Zvi
Vice-President, IFLA *(Israel)*
MOGGRIDGE, Hal, FLI, AADipl, RIBA
President, Landscape Institute. Partner, Colvin and Moggridge *(GB)*
MORZER BRUIJNS, Professor Dr M.
Former Professor of Conservation at University of Wageningen *(Netherlands)*
OGRIN, Professor Dusan
Professor of Landscape Architecture, University of Ljubljana. Chairman of IFLA Editorial Committee *(Yugoslavia)*
OWENS, Dean Hubert, PPASLA, PPIFLA, Draper Prof
Landscape Architecture Emeritus, University of Georgia; Dean Emeritus, School of Environmental Design, University of Georgia *(USA)*
ÖZTAN, Professor Dr Yüksel
Head of Department of Landscape Architecture, University of Ankara; President of the Association of Turkish Landscape Architects *(Turkey)*
PARRY, Dr M., BA, MSc, PhD
Lecturer in Geography, University of Birmingham *(GB)*
PECHERE, Professor René
Past President of IFLA; Chairman of International Committee on Historic Gardens and Landscapes, ICOMOS/IFLA *(Belgium)*
PICKERING, Maurice, DipArch, FRIBA, FLI
Senior Partner, Maurice Pickering Associates *(GB)*
POLAKOWSKI, Professor Kenneth
Chairman and Professor, Landscape Architecture and Regional Planning, University of Michigan *(USA)*
PURDY, Ian, RIBA, DipTP, MRTPI
County Planning Officer, Cambridgeshire *(GB)*

ROSENBRÖIJER, Maj-Lis
Principal in private practice *(Finland)*
St BODFAN GRUFFYDD, J., PPILA
Past President of Landscape Institute *(GB)*
SANDFORD, The Rev Lord, DSC
President of the Council on Environmental Education *(GB)*
SCHAUMAN, Sally, BA, BLA, MS
Chief Landscape Architect, Soil Conservation Service, US Department of Agriculture *(USA)*
SHEPHEARD, Peter, CBE, BArch, HonDLitt, PPRIBA, FRTPI, PPILA
Partner, Shepheard, Epstein & Hunter *(GB)*
SMITH, Alan, BSc(Hort), FLI
Course director, Landscape Architecture, at Leeds Polytechnic *(GB)*
SMITH, Douglas H., DipArch, FRIBA, FLI
Senior Partner, Douglas Smith Stimson Partnership *(GB)*
SÖZEN, Dr Nur
Assistant Professor, Department of Landscape Architecture. University of Ankara *(Turkey)*
STORTENBEKER, Professor Dr C.
Professor of Conservation at Agricultural University of Wageningen *(Netherlands)*
TABORA, Fernando
Associate Professor, Environment Department of Faculty of Architecture and Urban Planning, Central University of Venezuela. Founder member of Venezuelan Society of Landscape Architects *(Venezuela)*
TANDY, Cliff, OBE, PPILA, RIBA
Principal of Land Use Consultants, and landscape consultant to Forestry Commission *(GB)*
TASHIRO, Dr Yoritaka, MLA, PhD
Planner and architect; lecturer at Tokyo University *(Japan)*
TOCHTERMANN, W.
Division of Human Settlements Social Cultural Environment, UNESCO
VAN GENDEREN, Dr John, BA, MSc, PhD
Co-ordinator, Environment and Resources Consultancy Fairey Surveys Ltd *(GB)*
VISICK, Sally, MA, DipLD
Graduate Member of Landscape Institute; Landscape architect with Department of Environment, Northern Ireland *(GB)*
WALTERS, Dr Stuart Max
Fellow of King's College, Cambridge, and Director of University Botanic Garden, Cambridge *(GB)*
WARREN, Boyd, BLA, AAILA
Assistant Town Planner, Ballina Shire Council *(Australia)*
WEDDLE, Professor A., BArch, DipTP, PPLI
Immediate Past President of Landscape Institute; Granada Professor of Landscape Architecture, University of Sheffield *(GB)*
WERKMEISTER, Dr Hans F.
President of IFLA *(W Germany)*
WOERNER, Robert
President-elect, American Society of Landscape Architects *(USA)*
YOUNGMAN, Professor Peter, MA, PPILA, FRTPI
Landscape consultant *(GB)*

WigginsTeape Limited

GATEWAY HOUSE, BASINGSTOKE

ARCHITECTS: ARUP ASSOCIATES
PLANT CONSULTANT: JIM RUSSELL
LANDSCAPE CONTRACTOR: CHARLES FUNKE

Wiggins Teape Limited supplied the paper for this book.
Manufacturers of fine papers, tracing papers and other specialities.

A unique building and landscape has created a fascinating complex at Basingstoke.

Technical details. The concrete roof covered with 38 mm of insulation and three coats of asphalt.

Three layers of Leca and fibreglass for insulation, filtration and drainage. The water from the garden is collected and sprinklered back in dry weather.

A 150 mm depth of soil for grass areas, 450 to 600 mm for shrub area and 900 mm for trees.

Very close planting has been provided to make wind-proof blocks.

Ground level: Large trees and shrubs with under-planting.

The sheltered area, particularly on Level 2, includes more sensitive plants with azaleas. The exposed sections and levels have a number of wind-resistant trees to form screens. On Level 6 there are three small gardens – herb garden, full of thyme, sage and rue with a few apple trees.

Care has been taken to produce a garden that is interesting throughout the year.

All the plants including the larger trees were in tubs or pots for a year before planting.

RANSOMES

Giant step forward

Ransomes, who have been responsible for most of the World's significant grasscutting machinery designs, now take an even greater step ahead with the revolutionary 138″ cut Motor 5/3 gang mower.

New hydraulic foot control gives variable machine speeds resulting in very fine cutting, while the high performance 4-cylinder water-cooled engine has power in plenty for today's high-speed, heavy-duty mowing.

Even the cutting units are of a totally new design incorporating hydraulic drive, through gears to the impact-resistant blades.

Naturally, we'd like you to try it – a test drive arranged by your local Ransomes distributor is worth far more than any words written by us. But in the end you must agree with us – it's a giant step forward in grass care machinery!

Outstanding features

Supplied in a 5 unit or a 3 unit form (138″ or 86″).

Completely hydraulic transmission with variable delivery pump and wheel motors.

Designed to cut 6 acres/hour at 6.9 mph (5 units).

Height of cut $\frac{3}{4}$″ to $2\frac{3}{4}$″

Inside turning circle 24″ (5 units).

Cutting speed, up to 6.9 mph.

Transport speed up to 13.8 mph.

See your Ransomes Distributor or write direct to: Ransomes Sims & Jefferies Ltd., Ipswich

Motor 5/3

Buy or ask for Leasing details